"Where there's music, there can be no evil."

—Cervantes, *Don Quixote*

TABLE OF CONTENTS

CHAPTER 7: RELEASE AND DISTRIBUTION,
or "How do I know if and when they will release the CD?"

CHAPTER 8: AUDITING, or "How can I catch the label in a lie?"

CHAPTER 9:   INDEMNIFICATION AND WARRANTIES,
or "What happens if I get in trouble with the law?"

CHAPTER 10: TERMS AND "EXCLUSIVITY,"
or "How long do I have to put up with this shit?"

INTRODUCTION:
BUT I DON'T WANT A RECORD DEAL,
SO I DON'T NEED THIS BOOK

It is a mathematical fact that 50 percent of all lawyers graduate in the bottom half of their class. In stressful economic times, the "better" lawyers tend to follow the money in exchange for their legal talent. In other words, the bonuses and benefits by major labels. Therefore, as an artist your chances are at best two to one that the lawyer helping you to the top … was in the bottom half of his class.

To make matters more challenging, in the past you knew who to look out for, because all the best sneaky lawyers worked in the same big skyscrapers on Sixth Avenue or 30 Rock in New York, or on Sunset Blvd. in Los Angeles. But today, "record deals" are not just offered by major labels anymore. They come in all shapes and sizes from various types of companies, and go by many different names.

But regardless of what names these deals go by, if you want to support yourself with music and nothing else, get ready to sign some type of contract with a "record company" of some kind.

Signing anything means lawyers. And lawyers means you need someone to help you translate their mumbo-jumbo into terms you can understand. There is no school, no class, no lecture that will teach you this skill. When it comes to helping you best the system you are facing, this book is probably your only friend.

In this book, I will attempt to make the complex simple. I'm going to take a 100-page recording/licensing contract with obnoxious phrases like "Notwithstanding anything herein contained to the contrary," and "without limiting the generality of the foregoing" and break it down so that it can be understood by a five-year-old. These pages are filled with hundreds of secrets from me and top attorneys, dissecting the weak points in music contracts and describing how to outmaneuver The Man's lawyers. You will learn all the nasty secrets, and in so doing, you will gain an intimate understanding of how large companies "think."

Think you don't need to understand this boring stuff? Whatever. Do you like listening to naysayers about the "dying music biz" or how "labels will be extinct"? Be my guest. It might be entertaining to read such drivel, but actually taking their advice is a surefire losing formula. Hopefully, the day a rich corporation makes you an offer will come. What a pity it would be if you were not prepared with the knowledge this inexpensive little book provides, or worse yet, if you blew them off out of some rebellious allegiance to "staying indie."

And what if you do sign that tome of a contract they put in front of you? Then what? In the old days, if you signed a bad deal and your album didn't do well, you still had hope of making money. Artists still had touring, publishing, merchandise, and other revenue streams. But these days, big music deals (sometimes called "multiple rights" or "360 Deals") involve the label in *every* aspect of an artist's career. Now more than ever, you cannot afford to be stuck in a bad contract.

"But Moses," I hear you screaming, "I read your first book and you seem to hate majors. This seems like a contradiction."

No. I don't hate majors. I just hate the way majors suck money from artists. But I don't kid myself. There is no better, more proven way to make millions with music, than with a *good deal* on a large company dole. There isn't. Not yet. Maybe someday, but until then...

> *I don't say, "Screw the labels."*
> *I say, "Screw the labels... **but use protection**."*

Know the game, be in it to win, get the best deal you can, and take no prisoners. That is what this book will help you do.

Who the Hell Am I?

I started out as an assistant in an 8-track studio in the 1980s. At that time, there were no "tell all" books on how things were done behind closed doors in the music business. There were only rumors and disjointed stories of how *this* artist got ripped off by *that* company.

Between then and now I've produced probably close to a thousand hours of music and earned several platinum record awards. I watched many artists with multimillion-dollar deals grow poor from listening to "expert advice." I grew tired of it. I retired from the producing business in 1995 and became an artist's rights activist and music business consultant. I wrote my first book, *Confessions of a Record Producer*, with the hope of empowering artists, annoying a few people at the top, and inspiring the incumbents in this business to practice their trade with dignity and honesty. In a few short years, *Confessions* went from underground manifesto to required reading for over 50 music business programs at schools including Harvard, UCLA, NYU, Full Sail, and Loyola Law School.

From the publishing of *Confessions* evolved a consultation business for new artists, small labels, and attorneys that has grown very quickly. The company advocates for artist's rights and has clients spanning half the globe. Over the past 10 years, I've received e-mail after e-mail on how people are now making a steady and solid living both outside and inside the major label system. They used *Confessions* and *Secrets* to take some of the crapshoot aspect out of this game and taught me something in the process—that it is possible to do.

I am, however, sensitive to the fact that many of you have mixed feelings about pursuing a label deal. That's natural. I am not against labels. I don't think they're evil, just *very* determined in their goal to squeeze every little nickel and dime out of your pocket. But don't you feel the same way at the end of the day? Don't you also want to make the most money you can from *them*? Of course you do. The record business is not a game for the weak. And the hardest thing that you might have to admit to yourself is that, in spirit, there is little difference between you and the big bad corporation.

Unfortunately, they have an unfair advantage. Labels set the rules years ago while you, the newcomer, have to learn by making mistakes. But all that changes for you today, right this minute, with the book you are holding.

Turn the page and enter their world.

Moses Avalon

A Quick Note to Lawyers

I know that many of you reading this book are likely to be attorneys or other professionals in the music business. This book will be very useful to you. It will teach you things that are deliberately left out of symposiums, lectures, and certainly law school. You are welcome to all this knowledge, but remember that you are a guest here. This book is written from the artist's point of view. It is designed to empower them. Attorneys and label execs receive a healthy dose of criticism. As advocates, you should understand why this is necessary for this book to be effective. I mean no offense to you or your trade. (Well, maybe a little.) But, if you want a book designed to empower attorneys and record companies, there are already many, probably on the shelf in front of you or the webpage where you found this. Go buy one.

"Few things are harder to put up with than a good example."
—Mark Twain

WARRANTY & WARNING

Every clause in this book and every interpretation has been scrutinized for accuracy by music industry attorneys and litigators, as well as by a veteran major label accountant. Together they represent a total of over 75 years of experience in the recording business. The situations described here, in order to communicate their lessons, are deliberately designed as worst-case scenarios, and will likely undergo some changes as record companies adjust their practices over time. Every contract is different. Therefore, use this information, but do not worship it. Nothing in this book should be construed as legal advice.

The Key to It All: How to Best Use This Book

The concept of this book is simple: that the key to success in the record business game lies in learning a new language that I call *LabelSpeak*. Many words in *LabelSpeak* sound like common words you already know. But they are not the same at all. Words like "distribute," "promote," "delivery," "master quality," and most important, "sales," all have meanings unique to the rituals of the Recording Contract and its mystical alchemists—the lawyers.

You may skip around and read the chapters of this book out of order as they interest you. Each one is relatively self-contained. But I have gone to a lot of trouble to organize this information in a way that will teach you exactly how these deals work, so that with each chapter you learn more and more how to talk and "think" like *them*. **This means that I will be defining new words in each chapter, and from that point forward, the new word will appear in quotes.** If you see these words, you'll know that that subject was covered somewhere earlier in the book. In case you get lost, there is a complete Glossary of LabelSpeak in the Appendix. So before you go any further, take a minute to notice it. I know, I know—glossaries are for geeks. But just take a quick look at it, 'cause you never know.

This book will also work best for you if you become so familiar with the formatting that it becomes second nature to understand. The origin of this book comes from a chapter in my first book, *Confessions of a Record Producer,* called: "Decoding of an Actual Warner Bros. Record Contract." In that chapter, three opening paragraphs to a major-label deal are translated into plain English. The result is an eye-opening look at how crafty lawyers, working for the major labels, can stealthily transform a five-year, five-album contract into a seven-year, 14-album contract. A typical recording artist would be lost trying to figure it out. Even experienced lawyers are fooled. For those of you not familiar with that chapter, this quick guide will be very useful.

Below is a sample.

On the left in this "old type-writer" font is the actual contract, verbatim. Nothing has been changed except reference numbers and the name of the label. In this book, we always use a fictitious label called Pacific Records. (My lawyer says I have to say that this does not represent any real label, living or dead, in particular. And that any similarity to any label living or dead is just a coincidence.)

In this column, in this font, we have my translation, word for word. [*When you see italicized words in a bracket, it's my personal editorial, based on experience from the experts. It is not* directly *part of the clause being translated at the left.*]

Sometimes there are spaces between paragraphs. This is to align my translation with the clause being translated and make it easy for you to find things. See the footnote.[3]

I also used the worst, most poorly worded, most confusing versions of each clause that I could find, after reviewing all the major label's recording contracts.[1] Now go read the other column, right now.

The examples used are "worst-case scenarios" designed to teach you the ropes. They are taken from the recording contracts of the five biggest record labels in the world. Now go back to the left column and pick up at this point.

Sometimes entire lines will be in bold. These are important key points to identify in the clause, and, if one is a Loophole Creator,[2] I underline it and translate it directly to the right. Go ahead and look in the right-hand column now.

See, I told you. The exact translation of Key Points to the right will be over here in bold, and, **if it is a legal phrase that creates a snag, it will be underlined and in bold.** (A complete list of these phrases is listed in the Appendix, under "Legonics 101.")

Occasionally you will see things like this: (5)

Numbers in a circle like the one above are quick references to the master "road map" of deal points on pages 352–353. They will be very helpful as references.

[1] There are one or two exceptions in which the issue was confusing on its face. There I used the least confusing version.

[2] Loophole Creator: My term for any phrase of legalese that, in a sneaky way, contradicts the spirit of what was verbally promised to the artist.

[3] In this book, footnotes can save you a lot of time. They will refer to other areas of this book, and *Confessions*, so that you can compare information. Sometimes they contain historically relevant facts or personal comments and snide remarks.

REALITY: In "REALITY" I interrupt the preceding text to demonstrate how this clause will work in practice, not theory. Reality follows all important clauses, and includes my personal experiences as well as those of my colleagues, built up over many years.

NEGOTIATE

Tips and strategies for each point from the experts.

SIDEBARS

These contain real-life examples and other anecdotes that I couldn't fit elsewhere.

Okay. Enough instruction. Let's get to it.

Contract Basics:
Basic Rip-Offs and the First Things You Need to Know About Them

From Deal Memo to "The Thick"

Without question, the most aggravating part of doing business in the world of music is the stress of negotiating a deal. The contract itself comes to metaphorically represent our own self-worth. We slave to make good music, and then it's qualified by a team of suits into a series of terms on an unreadable piece of paper. It's enough to make you physically ill. So much so that very few artists ever actually read their 70-plus-page recording contract, called in legal circles "The Thick." Normally one is presented with a five-page paper outlining the basic terms, called a "deal memo." It seems innocent enough; artists routinely sign them as a "working contract" to demonstrate good faith while their managers and the label's business affairs people diddle and fudge The Thick into shape. Deal memos read something like this[4]:

[4] To see what a real deal memo looks like, see the Appendix, page 327.

Pursuant to a completed recording contract, Pacific Records hereby agrees to the following:

1. An initial period consisting of two albums, with five options for one album each.

2. An initial advance of $250,000 for the first album, with increments for the next six albums up to $1,000,000.

3. A sliding scale royalty starting at 14% and going up half a point after 250,000 units sold; 15% for album three, 16% for album four, 17% for album five, all subject to the same 1/2-point bonus at specified sales markers.

4. At least one video produced for each album released hereunder.

5. Guaranteed distribution.

6. Up to $75,000 in tour support and promotion for each album distributed.

7. Territory: The WORLD.

The day an artist sees this offer from a major label will surely be one of the most riveting in his or her professional life. But all is not rosy. Read the above very carefully. It seems to promise a great deal, but in fact it promises very little. After finishing this book, go back and read this deal memo with your new eyes. That will be the true benchmark of what you have learned.

For most recording artists, the memo above will be the last thing they see until the day comes to sign their finished recording contract. During the several months it can take to finalize the deal, the artist gets courted by the label with limousines, parties at modeling agencies, and lots of recording time in class-A studios. What goes on in between the deal memo and The Thick is a mystery. The artist knows only that a machine will be set into action. It's a hungry beast that costs thousands of dollars to feed, and when it's done feeding, it sits on its marble throne and squeezes out a 70-plus-page document that you will be asked to sign. It will become your new Gospel, your professional Torah, your career Koran.

When signing day comes, you only see the last page of The Thick, where your signature is required. You have relied on your professionals to tell you that the deal is a good one, and now you take pen in hand and, with all due enthusiasm, hold your breath and sign on the dotted line.

About two years later, the honeymoon with the label will have worn off. Then come demand letters, disappointments, and a bill from the label for $175,000. And for the first time, you will sit down and actually *read* your new bible and, with all due indigestion, reach for a Tums.

It has become a cliché, this concept of the musician's relentless mantra: "I don't have a head for business, I just write the tunes." It's an attitude that is often encouraged by lawyers, managers, and A&R persons—that artists are not expected to be good at "the paperwork." This is the same as telling a mental patient that it's okay if he bangs his head against a wall, because he's insane.

Contracts are complex, true, but they are complex because if they were written in plan English, you wouldn't need a lawyer to interpret them for you. That's going to change, right now. Behold…

A Contract and the Torah

Have you ever seen an ancient Hebrew bible (called a Torah)? It's nothing like the English translations that you can find in most hotels. The first five books were written in a special form of ancient Hebrew where all the words were strung together, like URLs. Kindoflikereadingthissentence. This goes on for pages and pages. How do you know where paragraphs end—or the sentences, for that matter? Each scroll has a "key" or "primer code" that reveals how it was indexed against other portions of the Torah.

Many years later, when the Scriptures were translated, chapters were created and each line was broken down into numbers to make it easier to understand. Without this technology, the great religions of the world might never have made it past small, local cults.

What does this have to do with recording contracts?

Recording contract authors took a tip from the ancient Torah. A recording contract is also one continuous phrase that only seems to have separate parts. The authors of the contracts instilled a codex, however. The main one is buried deep in the back of the Thick under MISCELLANEOUS. The clause reads something like this:

> "The captions preceding the text of the provisions in this agreement are inserted solely for convenience only and shall not constitute a part of this agreement nor affect its meaning, construction or effect."

In English this means that subheadings in the contract, such as ROYALTIES and ADVANCES, are meaningless. All the terms and provisions for Royalties do not necessarily reside under the subheading ROYALTIES, and all the terms for Advances do not necessarily reside under the subheading ADVANCES.

The 100-page document is, in fact, one continuous paragraph wherein each sentence is interactive with every other sentence. This makes it possible to take a singular point and, instead of covering the entire point in one paragraph, spread it out over all 100 pages, sprinkling bits and pieces of the issue here and there. Unless you know the primers to decode this, you are forced to scour through the contract like a hunter, looking for relevant information. Often the key point is buried in the back or the middle, concealed within several other points. Eventually you grow exhausted, and this is a victory for the contract drafter.

One example of this will be enough to demonstrate its power: Under ADVANCES, you will see this:

"Pacific Records will pay to artist an advance of $1,000,000 per year."

[5] "Negative Covenants" means "things you must not do while under contract with the label." See pages 310 and 345.

Then many pages later, under a clause labeled NEGATIVE COVENANTS,[5] you might get this:

"Notwithstanding anything herein to the contrary, Pacific Records will only pay advances if the artist has performed nude in a national TV show."

[6] Phrases such as these and many others are covered in "Legonics 101," page 333.

The use of the common loophole creator "notwithstanding anything to the contrary ..." overrides the clause many pages earlier.[6]

Okay, it's an extreme example. But I'm trying to make a point and get you to start thinking a certain way about the contract. That point being that you cannot rely on the subheadings of the contract to be your navigator. **It's for this reason that, in this book, I've scavenged through the entire agreement and regrouped the clauses for a single issue, together under one chapter.**

Definitions

A second technique creates confusion with *definitions*.

In any learning situation, the first thing you do is define the terms and words to be used. Once those are agreed to, you forge ahead to construct sentences and rules. But in a typical Thick, the definitions of its terms and words are usually buried in the back. Lawyers say this is for convenience. *Whose* convenience is a good question.

One of the biggest reasons that contracts seem complex to us is that we have been taught to read left to right, front to back, and to accept definitions of words at face value. We were schooled in this until we applied it by rote. In decoding contracts, however, this instinct can be a handicap, because the lawyers will use it against the artist. In many situations, a recording contract *should* be read last section to first section (ironically, much like a Torah, which is read right to left) in order to extract its keys and primers.

Farther down the page from the last example, probably in the same paragraph, NEGATIVE COVENANTS will be another bit of legal trickery. The primer will read something like this:

```
"Every word or phrase defined herein shall, unless
herein specified to the contrary, have the same meaning
throughout."
```

This means that words you already knew now can have new meanings, based on whatever definitions the labels decide to use. Drafters of music contracts use this technique to introduce new words and then slip in clauses that contradict the new meaning, thus creating loopholes.

Your lawyer, if he or she is any good, does not suffer from this *induced dyslexia* to the same extent that you do. He or she (hopefully) has seen many similar agreements and knows where to look for the hidden loopholes and primers. But, as any decent attorney will have to admit, some contracts are contorted, either deliberately or by negligence, and can make for a six-bottle-of-aspirin read.

This brings us to our first axiom for this book:

A confusing contract is nothing more than one that takes common words
and assigns new, covert meanings to them,
to the benefit of the contract writer.

The Loophole and the Double-Dip

As stated earlier, loopholes are places where, through the use of both techniques above—misdirecting subheadings and redefined words—the contract's author constructs a contradiction that favors his client. Here is where we see attorneys trying to outfox each other with a clever enfilade of legal mumbo-gumbo. Observe a common Double-Dip rooted in this clause found under the ROYALTIES subheading in a contract from Universal Music Group (UMG):

```
"You (the artist) shall be paid on all sales, 17% of
the Suggested Retail List Price (SRLP) of the record. If
records are discounted, then the artist's royalty will be
reduced by the amount of the discount."
```

On the surface, this sounds reasonable. The deal was that you are to get a royalty for each record sold. Your royalty is 17% of the retail sales price. If the label discounts the CD by, say, 10% to encourage the store to take a shot on a new artist, then your royalty will be reduced by the same amount—10%. So you will be paid only 15.3% for each album "sold." But buried deep somewhere else in the subheading called DEFINITIONS is the real meaning of the word "sold."

"Sold" as defined previously, means 100% of those records shipped by us for which we get paid, and which are not returned, or exchanged. But if records are shipped subject to a 10% discount, the number of records shipped shall be determined as 10% less."

In case you missed it, the record company just sunk in a second deduction. They defined "sold" as the number of units that are actually shipped and sold, minus a discount. In this case, 10%. Translation: if they shipped and sold 1,000 CD albums to the store and gave it a 10% discount on the price, then you only get paid on 900 units.

The record company says that this is okay because they are only being paid on 900 units, but that's not true. They are being paid on 1,000 units at a 10% discount.

What they claim is happening ($10 − 10% = $9) × 900 units = **$8,100**	vs.	What is actually happening ($10 × 1,000 units) ÷ 10% = **$9,000**

Using simple math to illustrate the point, the record company has made $9,000, but claims they only made $8,100, and that's the number of dollars that the artist's royalty or profit share will be calculated against. Add to this the fact that the second part of the definition of "royalties" allows an artist's royalty to be reduced by the amount of the discount, and you get a classic Double-Dip, meaning that the company is establishing the same deduction twice. It's created by the combination of these two phrases:

From "Royalties" clause above		From "Definitions" of "Sales" clause above		The Double-Dip
"If records are discounted, then the artist's royalty will be reduced by the amount of the discount."	+	"But if records are shipped subject to a 10% discount, the number of records shipped shall be determined as 10% less."	=	

See how it adds up: A record sells for $10 and is discounted by 10% (or $1 per record). If the label ships the store 1,000 CD albums, and all of them sell, then:

The way it sounds
As advertised in the deal memo, the sneaky lawyer has made the artist think he should earn 90% of his royalty on 100% of sales.

Price of CD	= $10
–10%	= $9
× 1,000 CD albums shipped and sold	= $9,000
@ 17% royalty	= $1,530

The way it actually reads above
But in fact, in this contract, the artist only earns 90% of his royalty on 90% of sales.

Price of CD	= $10
–10%	= $9
× 1,000 CD albums shipped and sold, but royalty only calculated on 900 units	= $8,100
@ 90% royalty or 17%, or 15.3%	= $1,239

I know that CDs don't always cost $10. The numbers above are simplified to illustrate the point that this Double-Dip costs the artist $291 for every 1,000 units that the label makes money on. Not much, I know, but multiply those numbers times 1,000,000, and it starts to add up.

Double-Dips are laid in everywhere in major-label contracts like land mines. It's your lawyer's job to sweep the perimeter, find, and defuse them. But to know whether or not he's doing his job, you should know where the most common ones are.

If I've made you a bit paranoid, if I've made you want to question the essence of every comma, dash, and word in your contract, then I've done my job. Throughout this book, we will take a close look at what many words mean, and what you thought they meant. We'll look at the enigmatic definition of "sold," and reveal some audacious and laughable Double-Dips. Now, flip back for a second and *really* look at the deal memo on pages 9–10. Its entire premise is based on the definition of several key words: "release," "Advance," "distribute," and "sold." It's best to know what those words mean to the label—agreed?

CHAPTER 1

Advances,
or How much will they give me up front?

Some good news about the Advances section: you'll find all the pertinent information under one heading, called ADVANCES. This makes it a good idea for you to learn how to decode LabelSpeak for two reasons: 1) It's the one subject that is usually and basically self-contained; and 2) Advances are the most important part of your contract, since they represent the only tangible money that you can rely on getting from the label.

Most people read the numbers without ever really looking at the definition of "Advance." It's worth a moment of your time.

"Advance" – A prepayment of royalties. **Mechanical Royalties** will not be chargeable in recoupment[1] of any Advances except those which are expressly recoupable from all monies payable under this Agreement.

"Advance" – A special type of loan that you pay back out of the money Pacific Records makes off the music you will record under this contract. Except you will not have to pay it back from the **money you specifically earn from writing the songs that appear on the record** (called "Mechanical Royalties").

[1] Recoupment– legalese for paying back money out of future income.

As I have said time and time again in many ways, in many articles, and in *Confessions*, record companies do not *give* money to artists, they assign *loans* to artists in the hope that the artists will make enough money on the sale of records to pay the money back. When you read about big stars signing a $1,000,000 recording contract, what that means is that the label has agreed to "lend" the artist up to $1,000,000, and that the artist is indebted to the label to pay back that money out of their royalties. If an artist doesn't sell enough records to pay it back, the debt is then forgiven. That is, unless he is signed to a 360 Deal, in which case there will be several Advances, each with their own formulas for recoupment and separate revenue streams.

One thing worth noting here is that within the definition of "Advance," any money you earn from songwriting royalties (called "Mechanicals") is *excluded*. Or so they say. Watch in coming chapters how the label's sneaky lawyer gets around this, and re-includes the recoupment of songwriting money in your Advance.

Why This Clause Exists

The foundation of any contract is something called "consideration." It's a legal word which means, "nuttin' fer nuttin'," or "I have to give you something so I can get something from you."

Without an exchange of money, contracts can and have been completely voided by a court of law.

Labels have to offer what seem to be large sums of money to persuade artists to accept a seven- to 10-year commitment. (And since most careers are likely to last only that long anyway, this is, in essence, a life contract.) The usual amount for an Advance is between $200,000 and $500,000 for a first album, with the promise of a substantial increase for future Advances—usually up to $1,000,000—if an Album goes platinum in the US (1,000,000 copies). Labels write these checks while simultaneously sticking turkey thermometers in their eyes to distract them from the pain. They know that without this bait, artists would shop for a career elsewhere. Thus we can create the following axiom for decoding Advance clauses:

The art of writing the "Advance" clauses lies in creating the perception (or illusion) that the label will pay large sums of money for each Album and each year on your contract. In fact, they are creating restrictions for the amount of money they're required to pay for each record under the deal.

The reason that the money paid to an artist is called an *Advance*, rather than a *fee*, is because it comes in the form of a prepayment of royalties that the artist will earn from the sale of sound recordings. The label is "advancing" money to the artist, usually on an "Album basis," meaning that each Advance is tied to the delivery of an Album. Why an Album, in a world where singles are gaining as a preferred sales platform? Well, for several reasons. One is because the label can contract for your work on a wholesale level, obligating you to deliver at least 12 songs for one Advance. (If they really dig you, that's what they'll want.) Second, almost every contract and royalty accounting model still works off of the Album structure. All royalties are figured off of "Album sales," even though many royalty statements have as many singles download sales as CDs or other types of Album sales. The third reason is a bit speculative on my part, but I do seem to know what I'm talking about from time to time: Labels have a plan to bring back the Album as a popular format. It will take years, but they have hope.

So, the bottom line is money for music. It sounds simple, right? But, as we'll see, the label is quite clever about taking this money back. Why are they so mean?

HOW A LOLLYPOP BLEEDS A PINEAPPLE DRY WITH A GENTLE SUCK

In the Dark Ages of the recording industry (the '60s), Advances clauses were relatively short. Everyone expected to make money off royalties. But these days, managers of artists have learned that waiting for royalties can be like waiting for an engineer to finish miking the drum kit. The school of thought has usually been, "It's better to owe the label than for the label to owe you." This means getting bigger Advances for artists that include not only record budgets, but also royalties owed.

Witness the case of a band called Lollypop, an all-girl group from the early 1970s. When they were signed, Molly, their lead singer and songwriter, was the centerpiece. Pineapple Records, rich from success with a Moptop group from the '60s, was one of the first labels to offer staggering Advances (but a low back end), and gave Lollypop $200,000 for each Album, with a seven-Album deal, totaling almost $1.5 million in guaranteed Advance money. Molly was so excited she could barely bake her smack.

The first Album did well. So well, in fact, that Molly got over her shaking hands syndrome and increased her monthly drug quota. Soon she was not showing up for gigs, and missing TV interviews, even Yoga classes.

It was clear to all concerned that this act would not last. Eventually the band asked Molly to take a hike, and replaced her with a more low-maintenance lead singer. But without Molly's songs and personality, the group was missing its edge.

Pineapple wanted to drop them, but because their deal guaranteed $200,000 over the next five to seven years, they were stuck.

Pineapple allowed Lollypop to make two more records, for $200,000 each, under the deal and then cut them loose. The manager of Lollypop sued for breach of contract. The group settled for a "get lost" fee of an additional $250,000.

Molly tried to launch a solo career on another label, but her first solo album—a quintessential hard rock masterpiece—was released just in time for the disco craze of 1977. She now works as dental hygienist. The other three girls took their money and invested in a fledgling software company called Microsoft. All major labels learned a lesson from the Lollypop case. *Don't guarantee anything. Make Advances conditional.*

Over the years, labels have been burned by artists, so they've learned to construct some clever restrictions in the Advances clauses. They come in three forms:

1. The amounts
2. When they will be paid (where they get ya), and…
3. Special deductions (where they *really* get ya)

❯ The Standard

NOTE: Because these clauses are taken from different contracts, various terms that mean more or less the same thing are often combined. An example of this is the term "Product LP," or just "LP" itself ("LP" is short for "Long-Playing Record," and is more common to older, starchy contracts on Sony). Any of these terms usually mean eight songs or 35 minutes of recorded music. This is, more or less, interchangeable with the term "Commitment Album," which means 10 songs or about 45 minutes, and is used by most other labels.

In my translation to the right, I combine these two terms and only use the term "Album" for clarity.

Also, "Contract Period" and "Option Period" are interchangeable. Both mean an amount of time it takes for the recording and promotion of an Album or—in the event that it's a singles deal—a release. In the translations I only use "Option Period."

The Signing Bonus and the Advance for Your First Seven Records

1. (a)(i) Pacific shall pay to you an advance of Fifty Thousand Dollars ($50,000) within five (5) business days following your and Artist's execution of this Agreement and Pacific's receipt thereof.

ii) Pacific shall also pay to you an Advance set forth below corresponding to the respective Product LP. You agree that such advances include the prepayment of session union scale to you, as provided in the applicable union codes, and you agree to complete any documentation required by the applicable union to implement this sentence. It is understood and agreed that Pacific shall not be responsible for paying any charges or fees for arrangements or orchestrations supplied by you.

1. (a) (i) Because we're buddies now, here's fifty grand so you can quit your day job and get props from the 'hood. We'll give it to you five business days after you sign this contract.[2]

ii) We'll also loan you a lump sum of money with each Album you make for us. This money also has to cover your "session fees" for performing on the record, as per our desire to cooperate with the American Federation of Musicians (the Musician's Union). You're going to have to fill out their forms 'n' stuff. But this "session fee" money is only for your performance as a musician. We're not paying you for doing any arrangements of the songs. [*Arranging is generally the producer's gig. You can still do it, but they won't pay extra for it.*]

[2] It is worth noting that very few bands or groups decide ahead of time how the money will be split up: equally, or with "key members" getting the lion's share. This more than anything else is what splits up successful pop acts.

REALITY: The Musician's Union *requires* that arrangers be paid a minimum fee for their work, yet the label is refusing to pay this to you if you are both the artist *and* the arranger. The label maintains that any contributions you make to the arrangements of the songs—even if you fully arrange them yourself—are part of your participation as an *artist,* and *not* as an *arranger*. Plus, they assume that the 50K or so that they gave you as an Advance is sufficient compensation for this work.

But beware: As shown in this and other chapters, you will be forced to use that money in several ways you might not like. So you'd better wait before placing a down payment on that Dodge Challenger you've been ogling.

(iii) With respect to the First LP, the advance shall be Two Hundred Fifty Thousand Dollars ($250,000). With respect to each of the Second LP through the Seventh LP,

the advance shall be an amount equal to sixty-six and two-thirds (66-2/3%) percent of **the aggregate royalties accrued hereunder** on the average aggregate Top Line sales through Normal Trade Channels in the United States of the two (2) Prior LPs released immediately prior to the Current LP;

but in no event shall any such advance be less than the "Floor Amount" or more than the "Ceiling Amount" set forth in the schedule below.

For the first Album you record for us, we're going to loan/Advance you $250,000.

For the second, third, fourth, fifth, sixth, and seventh Albums, the loan/Advance is going to be calculated this way:

We're going to take the last two Albums of yours that we released, add up all **of the money you earned** from sales in major US record stores at the highest list price of your record (for CDs that's usually $17.95, unless it's been marked down) and then give you two-thirds of that.

But if your record sales are pathetic, and the two-thirds calculation falls under the lowest amount of money in the table below (the "Floor Amount"), we'll just give you that lowest amount. And the reverse is also true: if the two-thirds calculation comes out to an amount higher than the highest amount below (the "Ceiling Amount"), you'll never get more than that.

	Lowest amount of money you could get	Highest amout of money you could get
Current LP	**Floor Amount**	**Ceiling Amount**
First LP	$250,000	$500,000
Second LP	$250,000	$500,000
Third LP	$300,000	$600,000
Fourth LP	$325,000	$650,000
Fifth LP	$350,000	$700,000
Sixth LP	$375,000	$750,000
Seventh LP	$400,000	$800,000

Ⓘ

REALITY: One problem here: I don't see anything in the clause above that provides any **adjustments for inflation**. While $800,000 for your seventh Album might seem reasonable to you *today*, you may not make that Album for about 10 years (See *Terms and Exclusivity* for the reason why). By then, 800 large may seem like diddly.

NEGOTIATE

Ask for and compute a sliding scale based on the US Consumer Price Index rating for inflation *at the time that the Advance is being given.*

But aside from the snag above, all this sounds very reasonable. What this says is that the label will guarantee a minimum amount for your next Advance, called "the Floor." But they hold out the larger number—"the Ceiling"—as an incentive for you to sell more albums. The special loan/Advance is an amount that fits into a range, and will be based on the performance of the previous releases. If you sell in abundance, they promise, you will then be awarded a larger loan/Advance on your next album. It *sounds* fair: big sales deserve a big Advance. But is that what they're actually promising? Observe …

For purposes of calculating advances pursuant to this subparagraph only, reserves[3] with respect to each applicable Product LP **shall be limited to fifteen percent (15%) of units of the Prior LP(s) shipped prior to the Deadline Date.**

But here's a catch: when we calculate the amount of the next Advance, **we're not going to use all the records you sold in the calculations—no sir. Only on 85% of the units we shipped.**[4]

[3] Reserves: A percentage of records that the label deducts from the amount of records "sold" before they calculate your royalty. See page 238.

(2)

Each such calculation shall be made as of the earlier of the last day of the month prior to the month in which the Current LP is delivered or the last day of the month prior to the last day for timely delivery hereunder of the Current LP (the earlier of such dates being herein called the "Deadline Date").

And we completely cut off the amount of units that we count from whichever of these days comes first: 1) one month before the Album you're working on *presently* is finished [*how can they know that? Are they fortune tellers?*][5]; or 2) the last day of the month before you were supposed to finish it. (BTW, whichever of those dates comes first is referred to in your contract as the "Deadline Date." This is the date on which you are expected to have finished your next Album.)

[4] See "Royalties," page 39, for the definition of "Units Shipped."

[5] To find out how, see "Reserves" in Chapter 8: Auditing, page 244.

[6] Most CDs and physical product in the US are sold as a consignment item. Unsold units are returned for a credit. There are exceptions, like 7-Elevens and some other "discount stores."

REALITY: **This is the start of a special factor in recording contracts called a "Reserve."** We'll learn more about the reserve in other chapters. Essentially, it's a special bank account in which a percentage of the money you've earned is withheld in anticipation of records that were not sold, and which will most likely ship back to the label for a refund.[6] You will eventually get this money (as to *when* you will receive it, I've saved that for Auditing, in chapter 8). Of course, deducting money that *could* be owed on *shipped* records from money which is *definitely* owed from *sold* records doesn't make a lot of sense. It's about the same as your credit card company charging you interest on money you *might* borrow in the future. But, as we just discovered, the label will calculate the reserve from "Records shipped" and apply the calculation when figuring your next Advance.

"Ceiling Amount" or "net monies" payable on total units sold for last two Albums	×	.667 (2/3)	−	15% of total units "Shipped" (for reserve)	Or, if too low	The "Floor Amount"	=	**Amount of next Album Advance**

We'll get into the long eggheaded math later, but for now let's use an oversimplified example: Let's say you've accrued royalties for 1,000 records over the past two years, and that you're about to start recording your third record for Pacific. It means that only the money earned for 850 of those 1,000 records sold will be counted when calculating your next Advance. Considering that your royalty is about $1.00 per record, you would have to accrue <u>about</u> $900,000 in royalties for <u>LPs</u> One and Two in order to qualify for the Ceiling amount of <u>LP</u> Advance number three, $600,000. That's about 1,058,823 Albums you must sell between both LP One and LP Two. Think that's a snap? Here's an important piece of reality for you:

80% of all artists on major labels
never sell over 125,000 units per Album.

NEGOTIATE

By the time the next Advance is to be issued, the sales department should have a good idea of how many records actually sold and how many are coming back. This isn't the Dark Ages, after all, when a team of accountants had to ride for miles to the king's castle with a chest of receipts strapped to the back of an ass. This is the Digital Millennium. These days labels can monitor record sales with the speed of a microchip. The labels deny this, but if it wasn't so, how could *Billboard* publish sales figures less than a week after they happen?[7]

[7] They have the help of a company called SoundScan, but that will be covered on pages 239, 240-241, and 244.

The good news is that regardless of what it may say in the contract, labels generally liquidate your reserves long before your next Advance is due (six months to a year), so it is often not a real factor. But if you feel that this is important to get straight in the contract, Step One would be convincing the label to throw it out based on this logic I just stated. If that doesn't work, then try to get them to apply this reserve *only* to "records *sold*," not shipped.

A final point is to ask for something called **"pipeline income."** This refers to money that is in the pipeline of sales, but has not yet matured into a real payment due to a variety of factors: Confirmed sales that are overseas that take an extra pay period to reach the US; or income from licensing to TV and Motion Pictures or Commercials. Stuff like that. Though labels will resist it, this is income that *should* be counted at the time they are figuring your next Advance. If you don't ask for it, you won't get it. And I've rarely seen a label make this part of the initial offer.

The 10 Tune Out Clause

Even though the label agreed to a sliding scale of loans/Advances above, there's a little twist:

(⑩)

(iv) **Notwithstanding anything to the contrary contained herein,** if any Product LP contains any Side(s) that were not made in the course of the same Product LP recording project and were theretofore paid for by Pacific in connection with a prior Product LP and you have delivered less than ten (10) Sides with respect to the applicable Product LP, the advance hereunder for such Product LP shall be reduced by ten percent (10%) of said advance for each such Side.

Regardless of what it says elsewhere in this contract, the following is the rule:

We can use leftover recordings that we discarded from your last Album if we feel you haven't given us 10 quality cuts for this new Album. If we do that, we will subtract 10% from your next Advance for each sloppy-seconds tune we decide to use.

REALITY: So it was trash last year, but now we'll use it and charge you 10% off your Advance for each "bad" song we use. This is a scam. Everyone records more than 10 songs for their first record. Usually it's about 14, from which the best 12 are chosen. But this clause gives the label free tunes. As you'll see in future clauses, the label can tell you to go back and record more and more tunes until you record 10 that they like. Even if it means you have to record 20 tunes to get 10 acceptable ones. Then on the next Album, if inspiration is waning, or if the market has now caught up to your avant-garde recording and you want to include it in the new Album, you can—but only at a 10% per song reduction. Nice.

NEGOTIATE

Unfortunately, the label has a good argument here: They say this is to ensure that your new record has at least 10 current songs, and that you don't give them outdated junk. Okay, if that's their point of view, then put a clause in that says that any tunes they reject from the last "Option Period"[8] will now be considered "new" tunes once the next Option Period begins. They won't like this, but they

[8] *Option Period*: See "Terms and Exclusivity," pages 281-288.

will probably do it if you push. If the deal is a singles deal and the total amount of the delivery commitment is only three or four songs, then this clause is completely without merit and should be removed in its entirety.

Tardy Smarty: Is It in Yet?

What if you're a little late finishing the record? Will the label understand? Does your credit card company? This clause is a killer. You'll lose serious coinage for the next Advance if you delay getting the Album in on time. And remember, "finished" is dictated by their standards, not yours.

Each such Advance will be reduced by the amount of any reasonably anticipated costs of mastering, remastering, remixing and/or "sweetening"; any such anticipated costs which are deducted but not incurred will be remitted promptly to you.

We will be deducting the cost of mastering, remastering, or remixing a single from your next Advance, unless we don't do any remixing, remastering, etc. [*unlikely*] and...

If any Commitment Album is not Delivered within ninety (90) days after the end of five (5) months after the beginning of the Contract Period,[9] (the "Deadline Date"), the Recording Fund for that Album will be reduced by five percent (5%) for each thirty (30) day period (or fraction thereof) occurring subsequent to the Determination Date and prior to the Delivery of such Album.

If your Album is not completed (to our standards) within eight months from the start of each Option Period[10] (the "Deadline Date"), the Advance for your next Album will be reduced by five percent (5%) for each month (or fraction of a month) that you are late.

[9] See "Terms and Exclusivity," pages 281–288, for the exact lengths of Option Periods.

[10] See "Terms and Exclusivity," pages 281–288, for the exact lengths of Option Periods.

REALITY: It's just like a credit card, but 50 times worse. Records always need to be remixed, at least a song or two, virtually without exception. So you should count on this deduction occurring.

Labels sit on finished Albums for months before releasing them anyway. This is nothing more than the label's way of having power over you and picking your pocket at the same time. Notice that there is nothing in the clause above that talks about you being late because the label screwed up. But what happens if they send you back to record more material and that puts you over the Deadline? This is something that happens more often than you could possibly imagine. Unless you insert a clause that covers this possibility, you could regret being so obliging. The good news is that if your first Album does well, this clause will be easily forgotten about when the time comes for your second Advance (see "Date of 'Delivery'," page 133, for more on this). But that doesn't mean that you shouldn't try to get it anyway.

Special Considerations for Producers and Band Leaders

When producers are selling an act signed to their production company (i.e., New Kids on the Block, TLC, Boyz II Men, Backstreet Boys, 'NSync), they will insert a special clause regarding Advances they, the producer, must flow through to the artist. The label, in those cases, does not actually sign a contract directly with the artist, they sign with the producer.[11] Therefore, the producer gets the entire Advance, but must guarantee that they will pay the artist a portion of the money (sometimes known as a "Special Advance"). (This goes for Royalties as well, and is covered in "Royalties," chapter 2). But if a producer convinces the label to give him $5,000,000 for this new pop or singing group, how much of that is he required to pay the artist? This clause, usually placed under the WARRANTIES AND REPRESENTATIONS subheading, deals with that.

It's the same situation as when a rock band has five players but only one member is considered to be the legal owner of the band/brand. The other musicians are considered hired hands—*employees* of the band's corporation. This happens with most bands that sign to majors.[12] In those cases the band owner is considered the "producer" for the purposes of this next clause.

[11] See "The Artist/ Producer Production Deal" in *Confessions* for complete details on these types of deals and how they pay out.

[12] See "The Band as a Corporate Entity" in *Confessions* for the ups and downs of this.

You warrant and represent that, under your agreement with the Artist, you guarantee to pay the Artist during each of the first seven (7) "Fiscal Years"[13] (as hereinafter defined), and you will pay aggregate annual compensation ("Annual Payments") as set forth in sections (1), (2) and (3) below.

You further warrant and represent that, under your agreement with the Artist, the Artist has agreed to accept all such Annual Payments.

(1) Nine Thousand Dollars ($9,000) for the first Fiscal Year of this agreement;

(2) Twelve Thousand Dollars ($12,000) for the second Fiscal Year of this agreement; and

(3) Fifteen Thousand Dollars ($15,000) for each of the third through seventh Fiscal Years of this agreement.

You swear on a stack of Jimi Hendrix records that, under your agreement with the Artist (or band members), you will pay the Artist (or band members) the amounts listed below. (Which we will call "Annual Payments." Whether or not you actually pay them every year is irrelevant.)

You also swear on Tupac Shakur's grave that, under your agreement with the Artist (or band members), the Artist (or band members) has agreed to this arrangement.

1) $9,000 to live on for the first year of this contract;

(2) $12,000 to live on for the second year of this contract; and

(3) $15,000 for each of the next four years of this contract [*or until we cancel your contract*].

[13] As used in this paragraph, "Fiscal Year" means each block of 12 months, starting with the date of this agreement; not January 1 to the next January 1.

REALITY: It seems as though the artist is assured of getting some upfront money from this. The numbers above are typical. But what happens if the producer doesn't make his "Annual Payments"? Well, not too far below the clause above will be the following, which outlines a "Deficiency Payment." This simply means that if there are any payments that the producer is supposed to make and doesn't, the label will step in themselves and peel off some Benjamins. It's an important clause because, as you might guess, any Deficiency Payments come out of your next Advance.

DEFICIENCY PAYMENTS:
TLC GETS ANYTHING BUT

I f you followed the TLC bankruptcy story, you may recall how they claimed that even though they sold over 2,000,000 records, they only received about $12,000 a year, which all three band members had to share. It seemed hard to believe for those unfamiliar with major-label deals, but now, with the information above, you know what they were talking about. As you'll see in "Terms and Exclusivity" (page 310), the artist is not allowed to work toward any other goals while under contract. And since this money is about all the artist will see for a long, long time (see "Royalties," page 104), it has to last. These numbers are typical for Artist/Producer deals; even though they seem low, the abundance of these types of deals scientifically proves that artists can pay their limo bills on $12,000 a year.

Deficiency Payments

[14] **Money accrued for songwriting is almost always paid to the songwriter's publisher. See "Controlled Compositions and Mechanical Licenses," page 153.**

Each Deficiency Payment and Additional Payment made by Pacific will constitute an Advance and will be applied in reduction of any and all monies due or becoming due to you, and any and all monies (other than Mechanical Royalties) due or becoming due the Artist, under this agreement.

Each time you wimp out and don't pay your band or artist, Pacific will step in, pay them, call it an Advance and collect it from any Royalties that you earn. The only exception to this will be money owed to the songwriters, assuming the songwriter is also the artist.[14]

<u>Notwithstanding anything to the contrary contained herein</u>, whenever in this agreement **Pacific has the right to deduct excess expenditures** (including, without limitation, excess Recording Costs, Mechanical Royalties and Special Packaging Costs) **from**

<u>Regardless of what it says elsewhere in this contract, the following is the rule:</u> **Anytime we feel you've gone over budget, we can deduct money from what we owe you, and we will.** For example, if we determine that we've accidentally overpaid you, or if keeping you on the label gets too expensive [*but we do it anyway because we're*

any and all monies otherwise due or becoming due under this agreement, Pacific's such right shall not extend to deducting such excess expenditures from any Deficiency Payments or Additional Payments made by Pacific.

such nice guys], **that additional money comes out of your next Advance.** The only exception to this is the Special Advances detailed above, which will remain sacred [*since this is the only money you will likely ever get*]. So, no matter what we decide we can rightfully deduct, the Special Advance will still be paid.

REALITY: If you are a producer and you owe your artist or band members cash, and you don't pay it, the label will pay it and call it an Advance. In fact, *anything* the label pays on your behalf—paternity suits, bail, fines, back taxes— is an Advance.

NEGOTIATE

Though this might sound comforting if you're the artist signed to a production deal, you should try to get rid of the first half of this clause. Why? Because you don't want the label deciding what is a "bullshit expense," paying it, and then having it chipped away from your monies.

(v) All sums paid to you or on your behalf, other than royalties paid hereunder, including without limitation all sums paid by Pacific in connection with tours by Artist, shall be charged against and recoupable at any time from any and all royalties (except mechanical royalties) accruing hereunder, unless otherwise expressly agreed in writing by Pacific to the contrary.

If any particular payment hereunder is to be made to multiple payees, such payment shall be deemed to be

(v) All the money we give you (other than royalties), including money we provide for your concert tour, will be repaid to us out of your royalties. The only exception to this is money we give you or your publisher if you are the writer of the songs on the record.[15] If for some odd reason we agree to waive this right, you will be relieved of repaying this money. [*Don't hold your breath.*]

If you have several people in your group and we have to pay them all, then it will be assumed that each

[15] See "Controlled Compositions and Mechanical Licenses," page 137.

equal individual payments to each person listed as a payee.

Notwithstanding the foregoing, costs for artwork, separations and publicity photographs shall not be recoupable from royalties hereunder, except any such costs which Pacific has agreed in its sole discretion to incur, at your request, in excess of Pacific's standard costs therefrom (which are currently (i) Fifteen Thousand ($15,000) Dollars for camera-ready artwork for each LP, inclusive of costs for publicity photographs and artwork for one (1) Singles Record therefrom, and (ii) Five Thousand ($5,000) Dollars for separations for each LP).

check will be divided up equally among all the people in the group. But all the checks together will be deducted from royalties.

Regardless of anything already said: You are not obligated to repay the label for the costs of promo material such as posters, flyers, and big life-size cutouts of you. The exception to this rule is if you ask us to do things we wouldn't do in the normal course of promotion. [*Which is what we will claim, even if you want so much as an extra staple in your lyric books.*] Our normal costs, by the way, never exceed $20,000 for all artwork created for the cover and liner notes of each record.

REALITY: This is a lame way for the label to get you to assume the costs for the artwork. $20,000 may sound like a lot, but remember that the contract is open-ended about how that money is used. When you figure in the costs of life-size cardboard cutouts of the band for display in record stores, 20 Gs goes pretty damn fast. Naturally, any overage here gets taken out of royalties or your next Advance, or "Net Profits" if it's a 360 Deal.

NEGOTIATE

The smart negotiator will do one of two things: get the label to specify precisely what this money is used for, or specify yourself that the money will only cover artwork expressly for the cover and liner notes. If you don't do this, expect charges down the line for every piece of paper that was ever used, or destroyed, to promote the artist. The following can be added to modify the clause a bit so you don't have to go into your own pocket to pay for the record.

In no event shall the Recording Fund for said Album be reduced to an amount less than the actual and approved Recording Costs for said Album.	We agree not to reduce the amount of money we give you for recording any more than what we agreed to in the budget.

360 Advances and "Recording Costs"

In the world of 360 Deals, Advances are a bit more complex, because the way they are recouped is a bit different (which will be covered in the next chapter on Royalties), and also because there are several different types of Advances: one for recordings; another for merchandise ($5,000–$35,000); one for touring ($25,000–$100,000); others for Fan Clubs and Web rights ($5,000–$50,000); and yet another for personal appearances, which includes acting jobs. Each is filtered through two magic words called "Net Profits." A detailed explanation of this concept is on page 83, but for now contemplate just this:

"Net profits shall be gross receipts less direct costs (including recording costs, manufacturing costs, marketing costs, distribution costs)."

This means that the only part of the Advance that will see the inside of your pocket is whatever does not get spent on Recording Costs. But what exactly is a "recording cost"?

"Recording Costs" as defined herein means: All amounts representing direct or indirect expenses paid or incurred in Pacific in connection with the production and distribution of finished Master Recordings under this Agreement.	"Recording Costs" means: any money that we spend to produce what we think is a quality recording of your music.[16]	[16] See "Master Quality and Delivery," page 107.

Recording Costs shall include, without limitation, union scale payment of musicians, travel, rehearsal, and equipment rental and cartage expenses, advances to Producers, transportation costs,

These could include: payment of all people who work on the recording and their personal expenses, rehearsal time and space,

mechanical licenses, hotel and living expenses approved by Pacific, studio and engineering charges in connection with Pacific's facilities and personnel or otherwise,

songwriting royalties ("mechanicals"),

[17] **See "Sampling Rights," page 163.**

all costs and expenses of obtaining rights to all samples of Master Recordings selections and other materials embodied in Master Recordings hereunder (including without limitation, all advances, licensee fees,

costs for getting the permission to use any samples that are in your songs,[17]

attorneys' fees and clearing house fees), **all costs of mastering,** remastering, remixing and /or "sweetening" and all costs necessary to prepare Master Recordings for release on digital media.

attorney's fees, **and mastering costs.**

REALITY: I hope you notice that they included "mechanical royalties" in the recording costs. If you missed it, go back and re-read, because this is very important. It means that the 90 or so cents that the label will pay the Artist, if the artist is also the songwriter, for each record sale will now first be deducted as an expense before your split is calculated. (See Chapter 4: Controlled Compositions if you do not know what a mechanical royalty is.)

So, basically anything that relates to the recording is a Recording Cost, and if it's a 360 Deal, then all Recording Costs are deducted as part of the calculation of "Net Profits." Depending on what they are, the amount of money you make on the sale of an Album could actually be *less* than under the traditional deal, even though you're getting higher percentages. (Again, this will be covered in more detail in the next chapter, on Royalties.)

> Conclusions

So here's a riddle: When is a ceiling lower than a floor? Answer: When referring to the Advance numbers for an Album.

Advances are loans, plain and simple. Lawyers love to disagree with me about this point. They love to go on and on about the legal definition of "loan," claiming that this is not technically a "loan," because you don't have to pay it back if you don't sell enough. But I say, *look*, if your partner gives you money to go into business, but he won't give you your cut until you pay him back everything, and if you can't go into business with anybody else until you pay back everything, and you can't even go into business for *yourself* until you pay back everything, then let's call it what it is—a *loan*! It's a loan that you will have to pay back out of your royalties or "Net Profits" before you get any more money from the label. Your only other choice is to go out of business.

How easy will earning royalties or "Net Profits" actually be? Let's see.

Turn the page.

CHAPTER 2

>Royalties

and/or Revenue Share

or "How much do they claim they will pay me later?"

or "How phat can I get if I only suck wind?"

"There are only two tragedies in life:
one is not getting what one wants, and the other is getting it."

—**Oscar Wilde**

Okay, so the big fat Advance is not what you thought it would be. So what? Who cares about Advances? *Royalties* are where you have the potential to live large. Isn't that why they call it a Royalty, because now you can live like a king? Let's see.[1]

This is, by far, the most difficult chapter in this book. Royalties are extremely complex, and as you'll see, they're kept that way for a reason. But I promise you, if you get through this chapter in one piece, the rest will be a breeze.

[1] The term *royalties* came from the right of kings to collect taxes from serfs. The "right of the royals," as it were.

Why This Clause Exists

This is obvious, right? This is the section where the label tells you how much they're going to compensate you for all your hard work. Well, you'd think, can't that be done in one sentence? For example: "We hereby agree to pay to you X% of all the money that your record makes." Simple enough, but it doesn't work that way—even in 360 Deals. Instead, the "Royalties" section of a major-label contract is rarely less than 10 pages. The reason for all the verbiage: records sell at many different price points, and under many different types of circumstances.

By way of example, let's say that I sell coffee made from your beans, and I promised to pay you 10% of the price of every cup of coffee made from your beans that I sell. I sell coffee for $1 a cup. That means I'm promising to give you 10 cents for every cup I sell. Right?

But wait a second. I sell lots of different types of coffee. $1 will be the "royalty base" I give you, but there are going to be a few variables for the different types of coffee. Coffee with milk, for example. Milk costs money, and I don't charge the customer for using the milk. That means that I make less money every time a customer uses milk; therefore *you* should make less money. So for every customer that uses milk, I'm going to deduct 10 cents from that particular sale, which means your royalty base will be reduced to 90 cents from $1. For sugar, I'm going to deduct 20 cents from the royalty base. Agreed?

Now, the coffee also has to sit in something, right? We can't have hot coffee burning the cupped hands of our customers, can we? Those fancy sip cups cost a bundle, so I'm going to deduct another 25 cents. Therefore, for black, unsweetened coffee in a sip cup, your royalty base will be 75 cents, not a dollar, and you'll get 10% of that. And, if someone orders a coffee with milk and sugar in a fancy sip cup, your royalty will be figured this way:

$1.00 = Retail price of coffee
−.25 for the container charge
−.10 for the milk charge
−.20 for the sugar charge
_____

TOTAL: 45 cents (Royalty Base) @ 10% = $.045 earned

Then there's espresso, decaf, decaf latte—each of these in different sizes and special holiday cups. The list goes on and on.

In a recording contract, each of these circumstances is often called a "configuration." (The word comes from a combination of "con," as in "confidence game," and "figure," as in "We *dare* you to try and figure this out"—kidding.)

But, instead of a decaf soy latte, in a recording deal we have things like:

- CDs sold at their highest price in big outlets (usually called "Top Line" records)

- Downloaded singles

- Streamed singles over subscription services

- CDs sold to discount stores and marked down

- 12-inch vinyl records (still selling well in many parts of the country)

- CD sold to the military for, at, or below manufacturing costs

- CDs sold to foreign distributors at premium prices

You get the idea.

Basically, any combination of the type of record, the packaging, the region where it's being sold, and the price it's being sold at comprises a new configuration. Your 12%–17% royalty (or 35%–50% revenue share, if it's a 360 Deal) will be affected according to these variables.

This explains why many clauses about royalties are required—we need a clause to define each configuration and what the label will pay for each. There are literally dozens of them, but the main ones will be examined in this chapter. Before we get into all that, though, we need to put this point on PAUSE and spend several pages defining one little word called "sales." Since, no mater what type of deal you have, one thing you can bank on is the fact that how much you're paid will be determined by how many "sales" of music you have. What a pity if, even after having over 100,000 albums distributed to the public, you don't have any "sales." How can that be? Read on.

The Definition of "Records Sold" and "Records Shipped"

All royalties are contingent upon selling records. But with so many words being redefined, should we trust the meaning of "sold" on its face? The label doesn't expect you to. As you will see, they spend 303 words defining the phrase "records sold." So I think it's worth our time to see exactly what they mean.

The following clause from DEFINITIONS will have you signing up for English as a second language:

"Records Sold", "Record sales" and "sales" mean one hundred (100%) percent of those Records shipped by Pacific hereunder for which Pacific is paid and which are neither returned to nor exchanged by Pacific nor (in the case of any record configuration as to which Pacific does not identify returns of Records according to selection number) treated as returned to Pacific under then current policy with respect to the percentage of shipped units so treated. In the case of any Record configuration as to which Pacific does not identify returns of Records according to selection number, returns hereunder shall be treated in the same manner as returns are treated with respect to Pacific artists of a similar stature to that of Artist.

"Records Sold," "Record sales" and "sales" mean *all* the records shipped by us for which we were paid, not counting any that were returned to us, or any that were exchanged by us, or considered unreturnable because they were special issues and don't really exist as a standard configuration, such as *promo compilation discs*. In all these cases, we'll give you the same consideration that we do other artists of your popularity that are also on Pacific, and we will treat the returns the same way we do for them.

REALITY: In short, you qualify to be paid for records that are shipped and not returned. *Sounds* fair. That's what it seems to say. But there's a catch…

For the purpose of this sub-paragraph:

For the purpose of defining "sales":

(i) If Records are shipped subject to a discount or merchandise plan, the number of such Records deemed to have been shipped shall be determined by reducing the number of Records shipped by the percentage of discount granted.

(i) If Records are shipped to stores with a "discount" or "merchandise plan" [*which almost all records are*], then the amount of records that we're going to count as "shipped" will be reduced by the percentage of the discount.

DOUBLE-DIP DETECTOR

EXPLANATION: The definition of "shipped" and "sold" should never include, as part of its matrix, a built-in discount, but they always try to do it.

REALITY: A "merchandise plan" is when the label bundles the music itself, whether it's a CD or a download, with T-shirts, posters, concert tickets, or even music by other artists that they are trying to sell as a "lot" to an entire chain of stores, like Best Buy, or as promotional packages to radio stations. (A hot artist who is *not* part of a "merchandise plan" cannot be all that hot.) When this happens, some records "disappear" because enthusiastic employees and radio station interns help themselves to them like free chicken wings at happy hour. So "records shipped" does not include those "giveaways." And if those helpful interns resell those promo records (or return them to the bin for a credit[2]), well, then that's too bad for the artist, because as far as their royalty calculations are concerned, that chicken wing doesn't exist. (Tell that to your love handles.)

[2] If a record is returned, not only will it not count as "sold," but the return may register against the artist's account and be deducted from their royalties.

Total units manufactured and shipped from warehouse to stores and subdistributors	−	Units given away as part of merchandising plan	=	Units "shipped"

And now here's the evil twist that keeps lawyers and auditors in business. It's called "Free Goods." The label calls it that because they are giving away free copies of your music to induce sales. But there is another reason they call it "free."

WILL TRADE "FREE"
RECORDS FOR FOOD

There is a misguided perception that labels rejected the idea of downloaded music sales because they want to hang on to the CD format. Here's the reason why that's utter bunk.

In 1998 a small record store I'll call CRD (Creative Record Distributions) in California was well known for having a standing "street offer" of three bucks per unit for any records that were received "free" from record companies. These were the ones with the little holes cut in the corner.

CRD was appealing to those who often get promotional records: DJs, music journalists, stockpersons, friends of the artists, and record company employees who get them routinely as "gifts." CRD was willing to accept CDs that flopped upon release, something people were happy to part with—getting cash in return for CDs that suck is something most people would consider to be a good trade.

Why would the company pay three bucks for a bad record that they could get for free? CRD had a team of illegal Korean textile artists in a back room, filling in the punch hole with matching paper. If the punch hole was over the barcode or the catalog number, the worker would use a Rapidograph[3] to "redraw" the numbers.

Think they were just putting them on the rack and selling them to the public? Think again. Selling a loser act to the public means only getting about $8 for the unit, if it sells at all. Why would they do that when they could return the record to the label for a full wholesale credit of $10.98 per unit? (Remember, records are a consignment item.)

One might think that the receivers at the label (who make about $10 an hour) would try and make sure that this doesn't happen. But they rarely do. They handle several thousand units a day on average, and look just closely enough to make sure that the numbers are right before tossing it on a pile.

CRD was only one of many such entities that took advantage of a system where tracking physical units is difficult. They moved over 500,000 units in this way until they filed for bankruptcy in 2001, owing over $6,000,000 to various major and indie labels. No one was ever charged or arrested. No artist or label ever received payment for these "sales." In the digital world, there are no manufacturing costs, every sale can be tracked, and there are almost never any "returns." As much as big companies like the status quo, they like getting paid even more.

(ii) If a discount is granted in the form of "free" or "bonus" Records, such "free" or "bonus" Records shall not be deemed included in the number of Records sold.

(ii) If we reduce the price of a box of your records by giving away some of them "free" [*If someone orders 10 cases and we throw in a box at no charge*], we're not going to include the "free" ones as part of records "sold."

REALITY: Okay, I admit math was not my best subject, but if a label ships 10 boxes, but only charges the store for eight boxes, that's the same as giving a 20% discount. This means that the two extra boxes will not count when figuring out how many records were "shipped" or "sold." The one example below in "Shipped and Sold," or 'Slipped and Doled?'" should be enough to convince you of the insanity of this.

"Shipped and Sold," or "Slipped and Doled"?

Defining "sold" as a percentage of units shipped, minus a discount, has a huge advantage for a company that manufactures and distributes tens of thousands of records. But how does it work out for the artist? The label says it's good for them too because they want to create incentives for stores to stock inventory on unknown artists.

Examine the case of Irish rock sensation Ewe Tu. Their brand of political pop had crossed over to mainstream America in the early 1980s. At that time, their label—Continental Records (a fictitious label)—normally sold a record wholesale for $10 per CD unit, and packaged 30 units in each box that they shipped to stores. This meant Continental would get $3,000 for every 10 boxes they shipped and sold, and Ewe Tu got paid on the sale of 300 units.

1 Box 30 CDs @ $10 each = $300 per box	×	10 boxes shipped	=	$3,000

But when Continental raised the price of CDs to $13 per unit, retail stores reacted harshly. Continental announced that they wanted $390 a box, and $3,900 for 10 boxes.

1 Box 30 CDs @ $13 each = $390 per box	×	10 boxes shipped	=	$3,900

[4] This happens all the time. Distributors issue new prices and retail responds with objections. The company usually responds with a discount like the one described above.

The stores bitched that they couldn't pay that much.[4] They said Continental (and all the labels) should give retail a break. So instead of lowering their price (and losing face), Continental and other labels simply gave retail stores two "free" boxes for every 10 boxes they ordered.

Continental started to accept $3,120 for 10 boxes ($120 more than when they "shipped" the record for $10). But because they claimed that they had to give a 20% discount, they only counted 240 CDs as being "shipped and sold." How did that "add" up for Ewe Tu? Let's look:

First example:

One box: $300 (30 CDs @$10 each)	×	10 boxes sold	=	$3,000	Net Accounting:	10 boxes or 300 CDs "shipped and sold"

Example with "discount":

One box: $300 (30 CDs @$13 each)	×	10 boxes sold, but 2 given away for "free"	=	$3,120	Net Accounting:	8 boxes or 240 CDs "shipped and sold"

Amazing! Even though both the retail stores and Continental made more money distributing 300 units than they did distributing 390 units, the label only had to pay Ewe Tu their royalty on 240 of them. By just changing the sticker price of the CD, the label made more money selling fewer CDs, and they paid the artist less. This was a much easier way to create a profit than improving their product with something as unpredictable, as, say, artist development.

Stop laughing. All this is true. And it's about to get even more interesting.

(iii) The aggregate number of Records deemed not shipped and not sold under subparagraphs (i) and (ii) above shall not exceed Pacific's standard discount or merchandising plan limitation in effect at the time of shipment of the particular Records, except with respect to special promotions and special sales programs.

(iii) But [*so that you don't get all hissy about us giving away too many records*] the total number that we can say was "not shipped and sold" will never be more than our standard discount described right here in these next few lines, with one exception: those records that are part of "special promotions" and "special sales programs."

Pacific represents that its standard discount or merchandising plan limitation as of the date of this agreement for LP Records on Pacific's Top Line is fifteen percent (15%) with respect to LPs in vinyl disc and analog cassette configurations, twenty percent (20%) with respect to New Technology records, and twenty-three and eight-tenths percent (23.08%) with respect to Singles Records.

We swear on our honor as a record company that our standard discount for records "sold" through major chains and at the top sticker price ($17.98 as of this writing) will never be more than:

15% for 12-inch vinyl and analog cassette configurations,

20% for CDs and Internet stuff (New Technology records),

and 23.08% for singles.

<u>REALITY</u>: This might make you feel a bit more at ease, knowing that there is a cap on how many records they can "give away free." However, what they've done in this clause is set you up, so when you see your royalty statement you'll be accepting of the "fact" that approximately 20%–24% of music sales were "free goods," and you won't be paid for them. Indeed, these types of distributions should be called "free goods," but not because they are free to the retailers, but because they are "royalty free" sales to the label.

The net result is that there is an enormous difference between the amount of records manufactured and the ones you get paid on. You sort of knew this going in, but did you realize that even if every single one of the units manufactured ended up in the hands of a consumer, you'd still only get paid on a reduced percentage of them?

First example:

Units manufactured	–	Units given away for promotion and "free goods"(not to exceed a fixed percentage)	–	Units returned that didn't sell (more on this in the section "The Reserve" on pages 238 and 244)	=	"shipped and sold"

Wrap-Up

Bottom line, the word "sales" as defined here is like a germ in your contract, infecting every clause that it is used in. It means different things when used to describe different records. For example:

"Sales" when referring to CDs means 20% less than you actually "shipped and sold."

"Sales" when referring to 12-inch vinyl means 15% less than you actually "shipped and sold."

"Sales" when referring to singles means 23.08% less than you actually "shipped and sold."

"Sales" when referring to cassettes means 15% less than you actually "shipped and sold."

And "sales" when referring to Internet-related sales (downloads, etc.) also means 20% less than you actually "shipped and sold."

If most of your sales are singles and Internet sales (like iTunes sales), you can expect that to mean about 80% of 83% (or 66.4%) of those actually "shipped and sold." Yes, that could mean (depending on if you catch this super-duper triple-dip) that for every 100 iTunes downloads you actually sell, your label will only count about 66 of them as "sold."

It's a strange piece of Western logic that "sales" can actually mean *not* selling. Where did this madness come from? It goes back to the days when records were made of vinyl, and some of them broke during shipping. Labels would apply a 10% deduction of the "breakage." They did this whether 10% of the records actually broke or not. It was a scam even back then, because records are and have always been sold as consignment items. So if a store can return a record because it didn't sell, don't you think they can return a record because it's shattered? *Duh!*

Nowadays the word "breakage" will only appear in the most amateur contracts. Majors don't use the term any more. Instead they just bury the same concept in the definition of the words "records sold," or "free goods." With Internet sales climbing from 5% of total sales to about 14% since 2003, this practice is starting to sound more and more ridiculous. Will the absurdity stop the labels from doing it? No, they'll just tack on the same deduction and call it something new.

NEGOTIATE

It goes without saying. Get these numbers up. You should try to specify that "sales" always means 100% of the records that never return to the label. *Period.* On downloads it should be absolutely everything that is distributed. When you are a proven artist this will not be hard to renegotiate, but it's hard to be a proven artist with this lead weight around your ankle. Look carefully through the contract, and never assume that if there is no definition of "sales" to be found, that it therefore means 100% of records sold. All terms and expressions used in a recording contract, unless specifically defined in the contract, are subject to the meaning that is commonly understood by those in the industry. The default meaning of "sales," therefore, is 80% to 90% of actual sales.[5]

Another trick that can save you money on an audit, if you should need one down the line, is to make the Special Sales Programs and merchandising deductions the same amount on all types of records. As it is, they're a different amount for each type of record, which never made any sense.

From now on, in this book, as a warning, the word "sales" will be in quotes whenever it is being used as LabelSpeak.

[5] There is a way to fight this, but it will cost ya. If the contract is ever brought before a judge, the law may require that "sales," unless defined differently in the contract, means 100% of records sold. But judges have ruled both ways on this, depending on the state. Plus, in all cases, having a judge decide this will cost you thousands of dollars, even if it does go your way, and will result in breach of this contract. See page 259 for the reason why.

Now that we're clear on how they define "sales," let's go back to learning about "configurations" to see how much they are going to pay for each type of sale you make.

The Meat Grinder:
Different Configurations
for Royalties/Revenue Share

Before we look directly at the clauses under ROYALTIES, we first have to look at the label's definition of what a "record" is. Ugh!! Yes, they have a clause for that too. You saw how cagey they were about the word "sold," so this will probably not be a waste of your time.

Just as in the coffee example at the beginning of the chapter, your royalties will be calculated against several "configurations." Each configuration pays differently. Some pay the full royalty, but most pay only half what is promised. So pay attention!

The anatomy of a "configuration" consists of:

1. The price of that type of record

2. A packaging deduction

3. The royalty percentage that was promised you in the deal memo (14%), and then some deductions to that

Let's look at each part. I recommend you follow along with The Master Chart in the back of the book as you read the next few pages.

1) Types of Records

You probably classify records by format: CD, 12-inch, download, MP3, AAC, streamed, etc. But your contract classifies them by the price and style of how they were "sold." These clauses from DEFINITIONS will automatically define a "sale" as one of four types of records below. **Each type of "sale" will have a direct effect on how much you are paid.** So when negotiating, the first thing you might want to do is consider negotiating these definitions, and get them changed to reflect fairer terms. If you do, they will sanitize other parts of the contract. Many lawyers overlook this strategy and accept that the definitions are engraved in stone. They are not.

"Top Line Record"

A Record released bearing the same Suggested Retail List Price as the majority (or plurality) of the Record releases in the same configuration then in initial release in Pacific's active catalog. (For the purposes of the preceding sentence, a Record release will not be deemed in its initial release if it bears a Suggested Retail List Price lower than that which applied to it when it was first released by Pacific.)

A new release, stamped with a list price that is the same as most other new releases "sold" in that region.

[*In other words, if new releases from top-level artists sell in your region for $15, then "Top Line" is $15. If they sell for $17, then it's $17. Got it? It's important to keep in mind that it's not a fixed number. It changes based on region.*]

REALITY: In major cities, the price is usually $17.98 for CDs, depending on the region. Although few CDs are actually "sold" at this price, even those by major artists, this is the retail price that will appear in your contract as the starting point for how your royalty will be calculated. Since downloads as a rule defy regionalism and have the same price in all parts of the US, "Top Line" usually means the highest price available on iTunes, the most significant store for downloads, or $1.29 for DRM-free singles[6] and hot new releases and $9.99 for Albums.

[6] DRM: Digital Rights Management. The piece of code in the music file that is used for inventory, copy protection, authoring, and licensing purposes. DRM-free files can be copied to different formats. Those with DRM have limitations; thus the lower price point.

(5) "Mid-Priced Record"

A Record, whether or not previously released, bearing a Suggested Retail List Price in the country concerned in excess of sixty-seven percent (67%) and less than eighty-five percent (85%) of the Suggested Retail List Price applicable to the Top Line Record in the same configuration.

A Record (new or old) selling for between 67% and 85% of the list price (SRLP) for most new releases selling in that region.

REALITY: So any record that is selling for a 15% discount from the sucker price—*oops*, I mean, *sticker* price (roughly $13.98 for CDs), will be called "Mid-Priced" and will be paid at the royalty for "Mid-Priced" records (usually three-fourths of the royalty promised in the deal memo). Unless your record is an out-of-the-box hit, it will likely be "sold" at less than the Top Line price. It's a fair assumption that "Mid-Priced" will be the *type* of record you'll be paid on for the majority of units "sold" in the first six months of the record's release. Also, if $1.29 is a Top Line single, that makes 99 cents a "Mid-Priced" record. It should be obvious why this sucks. Most download singles are bought at this price.

(5) "Budget Record"

A Record, whether or not previously released, bearing a Suggested Retail List Price which is sixty-seven percent (67%) or less of the Suggested Retail List Price in the country concerned applicable to the Top Line Records in the same configuration (e.g., long-playing Album, two-disc long-playing Album, Twelve-Inch Single, analog tape cassette, compact disc, etc.) released by Pacific or its Licensees in the territory concerned.

A Record (old or new) marked down to 67% or less of the sticker price of any similar type of record in the same region.

(such as long-playing Album, two-disc long-playing Album, 12-inch single, analog tape cassette, CD, etc.)

REALITY: A long-winded way of saying records sold at a discount when they're still new and the list price is high. For downloads this would be those files that are sold below 99 cents. **If you're not careful, this could be the "type" of record you will be paid on most frequently**.

For those thinking ahead, you might have figured out that Top Line records pay the artist a higher royalty than Budget records. So you want to try and have as many records as possible categorized as Top Line. This means getting the thresholds that separate Top Line, Mid-Priced, and Budget down as low as you can.

So here's our axiom:

The lower the threshold between Top Line and Mid-Priced, the greater your chances to be paid on more Top Line units. The lower the threshold between Mid-Priced and Budget, the greater your chances to be paid on Mid-Priced records.

Thresholds for Top Line, Mid-Priced, and Budget records are completely biased toward the party with the most leverage, and can differ from one contract to the next.

Top, Mid, and Budget, as configured in most contracts.

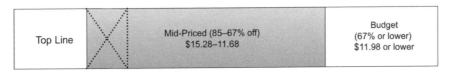

Try to negotiate to look more like this:

As the illustration above shows, because of the way the label places the thresholds for "Mid-Priced" and "Budget," there will be a significant amount of Albums that sell between $15.98 and $13.98 but which will, nonetheless, be paid out at the *reduced* Mid-Priced royalty. Likewise, many records that "sell" at $11.98 will be paid at the *substantially reduced* Budget rate. The area with the "X" shows the crossover. The bottom graph shows how this should be negotiated for the artist.

In some contracts, lawyers have done away with the Mid-Priced records definition altogether, leaving only the two "types" of records: Top Line and Budget. Budget is usually defined as anything that is "sold" at 80% of the list price. The list price is then established on the high side ($19 or $20). This means that any record that sells for about $17 will be defined as a Budget Record, and be paid at the Budget royalty (usually 50% of the normal royalty). This is patently absurd. Whoever heard of a budget record that sold for almost $20? Watch out for this sneaky lawyer trick. It sucks. A persistent negotiator should be able to get the Budget threshold down to around 58%.

And finally, here's the real dandy. Pay attention.

(5)

"New Medium Records"

Records (other than Audiovisual Records) in any software medium (including, without limitation, "digital audio tape," digital compact cassette" and "Mini-Disc" and transmission directly into the home) in which recorded music is not in general commercial distribution in the United States as of January 1, 1997.

Any form of your music (except videos) where a computer is used as an agent for distribution, including digital stuff and MiniDiscs, and any device that gets music piped directly into your house, that was not available before 1997.

REALITY: CDs, in case you didn't know, are a "software medium." Some contracts these days remove CDs from the "New Medium" category, but many still don't. (Apparently there are still a few record executives who are perplexed at how they've managed to smooth out the grooves and make the LP so small and mirrored. So, because it's a mystery to these fossils of the '60s, it must still be "new.") However, don't expect to get downloads out of this category.

Just so we're clear, you *do not* want CDs or downloads to be considered a New Medium. And just so we're clear, the label will try to convince you otherwise.

The following sums up everything so far on "types" of records:

Top Line Sales:	Records/files "sold" at top dollar through the standard distribution methods.
Mid-Priced Sales:	New records/files that are "sold" at a discount.
Budget Records:	New records/files that "sell" far below list price, usually through things like record clubs, or lower-priced digital stores.
New Medium Records:	Any type of record/file that isn't a cassette tape or vinyl disc. (Including CDs and downloads, unless specifically negotiated out of this "type.")

2) The Container Charge, aka the Packaging Deduction

After the "type" of record has been established, the next step in creating the template for a "configuration" is the container charge that will be applied and deducted.

"Container Charge"

The applicable percentage, specified below, of the Suggested Retail List Price applicable to the Records concerned:

A percentage the label deducts from the sticker price for the packaging of the record.

(a) Audiovisual Records – twenty percent (20%).

(a) Music Videos: 20%

(b) Compact Disc Records/New Medium Records – twenty-five percent (25%).

(b) CDs and New Medium Records (i.e., streams, downloads, etc.): 25%

(c) Other Records – twelve and one-half percent (12.5%) on analog vinyl-disc Records in single-fold packaging; fifteen percent (15%) on analog vinyl-disc Records in double-fold packaging and twenty percent (20%) on analog Records in non-vinyl disc configurations.

(c) On 12-inch vinyl with no cool inserts: 12.5%

If it has cool stuff inside: 15%

and 20% on cassette tapes

ROYALTIES

REALITY: Each type of record includes, as part of its definition, a deduction from the sticker price (SRLP) for the packaging that the record comes in:

Music videos:	20%
New Medium (CDs):	25%
12-inch vinyl (no special packaging):	12.5%
12-inch vinyl (special packaging):	15%
Cassette tapes	20%
Downloads	25% (unless you bitch)

[7] See Configuration #6 on page 61. You'll also see that the "Container Charge" for CDs is based on the full retail list price, but the royalty is only figured on the "sale price." This creates a double standard for this configuration, and a second dip into CD Album royalties.

In a fair world, the "Container Charge" would be a percentage of the actual sale price, not the sucker price—*dammit*, I mean *sticker* price—since the sticker price is usually about 15% to 20% higher than the price at which the record actually sells. But it's been this way since the dawn of the industry. The really obnoxious part is that streams and downloads have no packaging whatsoever, but several labels deduct the "Container Charge" anyway, as well as take a deduction for the record being a "New Medium."[7]

And here's another thing to watch out for: There are many indie contracts in which the label takes what it calls a "pressing charge." That's about a $1 fee for the pressing of the record, added on to the packaging deduction. So they are passing the manufacturing cost on to you as well. Majors don't mess around with this sort of thing, but I've seen it on numerous small deals. Get rid of it.

3) The Royalty Base Price

So far we have "types" of records and their various Container Charges. The Definition of "Royalty Base Price" tells you how all this will be applied to each "configuration."

"Royalty Base Price"
(Most records)
(a) The Royalty Base Price for Records (other than Audiovisual Records, compact disc Records or New Medium Records) shall be the Suggested Retail List Price applicable to

(a) The Royalty Base for all records (other than music videos, CDs, downloads, streams, etc.), will be the sticker price minus taxes and the Container Charge.

the Phonograph Records concerned, less all excise, purchase, value added or similar taxes included in the price and less the applicable Container Charge.

(Discounted records)

(b) The Royalty Base Price for Records (other than Audiovisual Records) sold through any so-called "record club" **will be 50% of that for the identical records sold through Normal Retail Channels in the territory concerned.**

(b) The Royalty Base for records (other than music videos) "sold" through super-low discount mail-order catalogs, often called "Record Clubs," **will be half of those same types of records "sold" to record stores.**

(For CDs and other digital mediums)

(c) The Royalty Base Price for compact disc Records and New Medium Records (except those sold through direct transmission) shall be **seventy-five percent (75%) of Pacific's or its Licensee's highest published Suggested Retail List Price** in the category of sale concerned, less excise, purchase, value added or similar taxes included in the price and less the applicable Container Charge.

(c) For CDs, and anything high tech (except downloaded sales) the Royalty Base **will be 75% of the highest sticker price that Pacific sells that record for** minus the Container Charge.

See the following sidebar to learn about another scam to look out for.

6

THE WACKY TACKY NEW TECHIE
WHOLESALE ROYALTY RUNAROUND

All managers, producers, and lawyers in the music industry are now familiar with the "3/4 Royalty," which only pays 75% of the promised royalty for "New Medium" records. But back in the late '70s it was a new phenomenon. Take the story of a band I'll call The Euro-Rhythms. Their records were the toast of the US and England at the dawn of the British New Wave in 1976. By 1980 they had sold enough records to qualify for a royalty rate higher than the usual 12% of retail most artists got then. They were primed for a well-publicized signing with CBS records (now Sony). CBS was eager to give them more than the norm; say 13% or 14% of retail, and to include them in a special release of a new technology called Compact Disc. But the cost, they claimed, was high for this new medium. And who could argue? CDs seemed to sound better than LPs,[8] and so must therefore be more expensive. Plus, these newfangled CDs were going to be priced insanely high, almost $10 each. So, at this new price, it didn't seem fair to give the artist the same 14% royalty for the sale of these new records. What if CDs didn't catch on? After all, the record companies were taking a big risk with this new stuff.[9]

At the time, all record companies were taking a tip from high-tech business by passing the R&D costs for new gadgets onto the vendor (the artist in this case). But The Euro-Rhythms' manager was too smart for that. He wanted a full royalty for CDs as well. CBS claimed that there was no way to track the retail sales price of this new CD thing, since each region was going to charge different amounts. They offered this:

> "The Royalty Base Price for compact disc Records and New Medium Records shall be one hundred thirty percent (130%) of Pacific's or its Licensee's lowest published wholesale price in the category of sale concerned, less taxes included in the price and less the applicable Container Charge."

In other words, 14% of retail or 130% of wholesale. Sounds like a no-brainer until you think about it. Today the lowest wholesale price is usually about $9.98. 130% of that is $12.97. This is actually worse than the way it's configured in the Standard clause, which would yield an "adjusted selling price" of $13.48. (See configuration #1 in the tables below, page 59.)

The Euro-Rhythms took the deal, thinking that this CD issue didn't matter much anyway, since CDs seemed to be too expensive to catch on. And after all, they were still making a full royalty on the sale of LPs and cassettes.

[8] It is the consensus among audiophiles that LPs sound warmer and more natural when played on good stereo systems.

[9] An absolute lie. Major labels engineered the proliferation of CDs.

Starting in 1980, The Euro-Rhythms' CD sales began to edge over cassette sales. Today their songs are hardly available at all in vinyl form, since they've been repackaged as CD box sets. They have never seen a full royalty on CDs because of the deal they made in 1979 on CBS.

This strategy has been so successful for the labels that these days it is still attempted in most record deals, large and small.

REALITY: The "Royalty Base Price" is the amount of money on which your promised percentage will be calculated. In this contract there are only three types of Royalty Bases. I've seen contracts with many more. The more there are, the more difficult it is to audit "sales."

CDs:	75% of the highest sticker price, minus the Container Charge
Record clubs:	Half of the price of the same record sold through stores
Downloads and all other records:	The highest sticker price minus the Container Charge

Review of Configurations in Plain English

Time to review. A "Royalty" is actually part of a "configuration." The configuration is a combination of factors. They are:

1. At what price the records are "sold" (Albums: $17.98, $13.98, $9.99; downloads/singles: $1.29, $.99, etc.);

2. The type of store in which they are "sold" (major chain, digital store, small mom & pop, record club, etc.); and

3. What they're packaged in (jewel case, cardboard sleeve, nothing for downloads)

Just like coffee.

Let's do a typical CD "sale" and a typical download Album, combining everything above.

A newly released CD by a fictional band called the Post Men Apostles is shipped to the store and marked at $17.98, and posted on iTunes for $9.99.

Assuming that it doesn't get returned, become part of a "Special Sales Program," or be marked down, it will sell for the full $17.98/$9.99 and be classified by Pacific as a "Top Line New Medium Record (CD)" for the CD and a "Top Line New Medium Record (Download)" for the iTunes sale. Now you might think that, because the label promised the band a royalty of 14%, that they will earn $2.51 for each CD Album "sold" and $1.39 for each downloaded Album "sold." Not so, because there are a few minor adjustments for each:

1. 25% of the sale price is lopped off the top for the "New Medium" charge on both, making the "sale" price $13.48 and $7.49, respectively.

2. Then the Packaging Deduction will be figured at 25% of the original list price of $17.98 for the CD Album, or $4.49, so that brings us to $8.99. The downloaded Album is spared this deduction because there should be no packaging, and so it remains at $7.49. **These numbers are called the "Royalty Bases."**

3. It's *then* that the percentage promised you in the deal memo (the "base royalty") will be applied—14%.

4. 14% of $8.99 equals $1.25, and for the downloaded Album, 14% comes out to $1.05. (There could and probably will be deductions to this as well. This will be covered below in brief and then again in detail on page 64, "The Sliding Scale Royalty.")

Are you ready to *celebrate*?

In the next few pages are several examples of the most common "configurations," including the one we just did.

The first column describes how the record was bought (including the venue, time of release, and price). The second column designates the label's "configuration" of your record (such as Top Line New Medium, Budget New Medium, etc.). The third column explains the Calculation that was used, including deductions to the base royalty, to arrive at the royalty rate. And the fourth and final column shows your "penny rate"—the actual amount of your "royalty." All of these examples are based on an SRLP of $17.98 for CDs, $9.99 for downloaded Albums, $1.29 for singles, and on a promised *base royalty* of 14% of SRLP.

See if you can figure out the final royalty without looking. Get good at this and you will be on your way to becoming an expert.

Configuration Tables (The Meat Grinder)

If you look at The Master Chart, called the "Road Map of Royalty Deal Points," pages 352–353, you'll find a large section in the middle that's liable to make your head spin. I call it "The Meat Grinder" because large amounts of steak go in, "configurations" are applied, and what comes out the other side are strands of chopped meat, each with its own category, like "Top Line New Medium Record (CD)," or "Budget Record (Cassette)," "New Configuration," or any of approximately 75 other combinations.

Below are some prime examples. Keep in mind that *these are worst-case scenarios.* You're expected to negotiate for better. All are based on a *base royalty* of 14%, which is the industry average for a new artist not on a 360 Deal.

In all equations the penny rate is the final amount in dollars and cents that you're paid for each configuration. The formula for all configurations is:

[10] In older contracts many artists only got a three-quarter royalty on CD sales, so they would only get 10.5% of $8.99, or 94 cents. Check out the clause that does this on page 78.

$$Royalty\ Base \times royalty\ rate = penny\ rate$$

How the Record Was Bought	Configuration	Calculation/Royalty Rate	Penny Rate
1) A CD bought the month of release at Best Buy or other major chain in the US for full price, $17.98 *(As if anybody really does that)*	Top Line New Medium Record (CD) (This is a Triple-Dip configuration. For details, see pages 7 and 13–16.)	SRLP = $17.98 @ 75% for "New Medium" price adjustment: = $13.48 Minus the Container Charge (25% of SRLP)— $4.49. Royalty Base = $8.99 @ 14% royalty rate = $1.25[10]	**$1.25**

How the Record Was Bought	Configuration	Calculation/Royalty Rate	Penny Rate
2) A CD bought about a month after the record was released at a Mom & Pop corner store for $13	Budget New Medium Record (CD) (Based on the same Triple-Dip as above. For details, see pages 7 and 13–16.)	SRLP = $13 @ 75% for "New Medium" price adjustment: = $9.75 Minus the Container Charge (25% of SRLP)—$3.25. Royalty Base = $6.50 @ The budget adjusted rate (50% of the 14% royalty rate = 7%)[11] = $0.45	**$0.45**
3) A CD bought the month it came out for $13.98 on Amazon.com or other online retail service in the US	Top Line New Medium Record (CD) via Telecommunications device in the US (This is a Quadruple-Dip configuration.[12]	SRLP = $13.98 Minus the Container Charge (25% of SRLP—$3.49) Royalty Base = $10.49 @ the telecommunications adjustment (50% of the 14% royalty rate = 7%)[13] = $0.73	**$0.73**
4) Same as above: a CD bought the month of release on Amazon.com or other online retail service, but purchased overseas or in Canada	Top Line New Medium Record (CD) via Telecommunications device, foreign (This is a Quadruple-Dip configuration. For details, see page 52)	SRLP = $13.98 Minus the Container Charge (25% of SRLP —$3.49) = $10.49	**$1.10**

[11] See page 74 for the clause that reduces this royalty.
[12] See page 71 for the clause that reduces this royalty.
[13] See page 71 for the clause that reduces this royalty.

How the Record Was Bought	Configuration	Calculation/Royalty Rate	Penny Rate
		@ the telecommunications adjustment (75% of 14%) royalty rate = 10.5%[14] = $1.10	
5) A CD bought about 10 months after it came out at a second-hand store for about $5	Cutout (For details, see pages 76–77, 100–104, 155, and 342)	Royalty Base: $0.00	**$0.00**
6) An Album downloaded on iTunes the first few months after release for $9.99	Top Line New Medium Record (This is a Triple-Dip configuration. For details, see pages 7 and 13–16.)	SRLP = $9.99 @ 75% for "New Medium" = $7.49 Minus the Container Charge (25% of SRLP) —$1.87. Royalty Base = $5.62 @ New Medium Records rate of 75% of the 14% base royalty is 10.5%[15] $5.62 × 10.5% = $0.52	**$0.52**
7) Same as above figured on a wholesale basis[16]	Top Line New Medium Record	SRLP = $9.99 Minus 33% for iTunes cut leaves: Royalty Base = $6.59 @ New Medium Records royalty rate of 10.5%[17] = $0.65	**$0.65**

[14] See page 71 for the clause that reduces this royalty.
[15] See page 55 for the clause that reduces this royalty.
[16] Most major labels figure iTunes sales on this wholesale basis. The formula for this is 130% of net (the sale price minus the iTunes markup of 33%) times the applicable royalty rate for that configuration.
[17] See page 55 for the clause that reduces this royalty.

Wrap-Up

I know all this must seem horribly unnecessary, but believe me, it's essential. In the rest of this chapter the word "royalty" will be used about 50 times—one cannot understand the full meaning of this word without first understanding that a "royalty" is not really figured against the actual number of records that sold, or the actual sales price, but a "Royalty Base price," which is the result of a "configuration." And a "configuration" is a series of factors.

Then after the "royalty" is calculated, there are the deductions made for the amount of records "sold." You might think that if you sold 500,000 records for $17.98 and have a royalty of 14% of SRLP, that you can look forward to a check for $1,258,600 this year. But the truth is closer to this: only 80% of those records count as "sold," so your actual "royalty" is really only about $1.25 per record, or about $500,000 total. Interesting. And this is assuming you're actually entitled to that 14% "royalty." The contract says you are, but are there loopholes? Let's find out.

From this point forward in this book, "royalties" will be in quotation marks to draw attention to its LabelSpeak meaning.

SNEAKY LAWYER LESSON #2

Encode the following sentence into LabelSpeak:

"We will pay you a royalty based on a complex series of mathematical deductions using 14% of the Album's list price as its basis, applied to 80% of Albums that are sold in the US at their highest available price."

Answer: "You will earn a 14% royalty on 100% of Album sales."

▶The Standard

These clauses deal with how you will earn money through record "sales." They can be found under the subheading ROYALTIES.

Pacific will pay you a royalty computed at the applicable percentage, indicated below, of the applicable Royalty Base Price in	Pacific will pay you a portion of the percentage promised in the deal memo on all the "configurations" in the Meat Grinder. But you'll be

respect of Net Sales of Phonograph Records consisting entirely of Master Recordings recorded under this Agreement during the respective Contract Periods specified below and sold by Pacific or its Licensees through Normal Retail Channels ("NRC Net Sales").

paid only for records confirmed as "sold" (not shipped) by Pacific or its companies when we sell them through the normal ways we do business in the US. And only on records that consist entirely of sound coming from your body that we have approved of and that you agreed to record during the time you agreed to be bound to us exclusively.

(Such royalty shall include your and the Artist's royalties and **all royalties payable** to all other artists, Producers and other Persons which become or may become due by reason of the recording and/or exploitation of Master Recordings recorded under this Agreement. The royalties payable pursuant to the provisions of paragraphs below and the provisions specified in the sub-heading "Joint Recordings" below shall apply to all Phonograph Records except Audiovisual Records.)

(If you are the producer signing this contract for the artist—as in an artist development deal—then, the percentage of money described in the clauses below shall include your share of the royalties, as well as the Artist's share, and **royalties for all other musicians and performers who participated in the recording** [*who may come out of the woodwork demanding a piece of the action for their participation in the recording*]. The royalties below shall apply to all types of recordings in The Meat Grinder.)

REALITY: All types of records go through a matrix of configurations before one of the royalty percentages in the paragraph below is applied. But the most relevant bit of information here is the last part: The label is only interested in paying *one "royalty" for each recording.* If you owe anyone else (like a financial backer), it has to come out of your share (specified below). This even includes the royalties paid to your producer. And to get a decent producer you'll need to give about 3%–5% out of your own 14%.

This raises another important question: How will the royalties be divided among the members of your group? If you write and sing every song, shouldn't you get a bigger cut than the rhythm guitar player, or the DJ? Many a group has split up because of this very issue, but labels insist this is not their problem.

As far as producers go, many prefer to be paid directly by the label. (I guess they realize artists aren't the best accountants.) In order for this to happen, the label must agree to pay the producer's share of the artist's royalties for you. Make sure you carve out an exception that will allow for this in your contract. This can be done with a little legal maneuver called a **"Letter of Direction,"** which instructs the label to pay the producer directly, instead of you having to pay them out of your share, and doing all the nasty accounting that would entail. This can be good or bad, depending on how large a percentage you promised the producer. Many labels don't like Letters of Direction because they create additional hassles. But without one, you will seriously limit your ability to work with the producers you want the most.

The Sliding Scale Royalty

In the deal memo you couldn't help but notice the paragraph where the numbers go up from 14% to 17% with each Album. This is called a "sliding scale," or an "Escalation." The clauses below, from ROYALTIES, show how this will "work":

ON ALBUMS SOLD FOR DISTRIBUTION IN THE UNITED STATES	FOR 10 OR MORE SONGS, RECORDED EXCLUSIVELY FOR US, ASSEMBLED IN A COLLECTION AND THEN PARTED WITH PERMANENTLY, HOPEFULLY FOR MONEY, IN THE UNITED STATES.
1. (i)Master Recordings made during the initial Contract Period or first Option Period: 14%	1. (i) for any recordings we decide to release that you make during the first two to three years after you sign this contract[18]: 14% on all records "sold" in the United States.

[18] See "Terms and Exclusivity," page 280, for why "Contract Periods" have no specific length.

(ii) The Royalty rate pursuant to the subsection above will apply to the first 500,000 units of NRC Net Sales in the United States ("USNRC[19] Net Sales") of each Album consisting of Master Recordings made during the initial Contract Period or first Option Period. The royalty will be:

(A) 14.5% on USNRC Net Sales of any such Album in excess of 500,000 units and not in excess of 1,000,000 units,

(B) 15% on USNRC Net Sales of any such Album in excess of 1,000,000 units and not in excess of 2,000,000 units,

(C) 16% on USNRC Net Sales of any such Album in excess of 2,000,000 units.

2.
(i) Master Recordings made during the second or third Option Periods: 14.5%.

(ii) The royalty rate above will apply to the first 500,000 units of USNRC Net Sales of each Album consisting of Master Recordings made during the second or third Option Periods. The royalty rate will be:

(ii) but this will only apply to the first 500,000 "sold" in the US, and both your first and second Album must consist entirely of performances and material that we have approved. For this, the royalty will be:

(A) For Albums 500,001 to 1,000,000, you get 14.5% on records "sold" in stores and through catalogs,

(B) For Albums 1,000,001 through 2,000,000, you get 15%,

(C) For Albums 2,000,001 and up, you get 16%.

2.
(i) For any recordings we decide to release that you make approximately three to five years after you sign this contract,[20] you get 14.5% of all records "sold" in the United States.

(ii) But this will only apply to the first 500,000 units "sold" in the US through normal retail sales, of an Album that consists entirely of performances and material that we have approved. For this, the royalty will be:

[20] See "Terms and Exclusivity," page 280, for why "Contract Periods" have no specific length.

(8)

(8)

(A) 15% on USNRC Net Sales of any such Album in excess of 500,000 units and not in excess of 1,000,000 units,

(A) For Albums 500,001 to 1,000,000, you get 15% on records "sold" in stores and through catalogs,

(B) 15.5% on USNRC Net Sales of any such Album in excess of 1,000,000 units and not in excess of 2,000,000 units,

(B) For albums 1,000,001 through 2,000,000, you get 15.5% on records "sold" in stores and through catalogs,

(C) 16% on USNRC Net Sales of any such Album in excess of 2,000,000 units.

(C) For Albums 2,000,001 and up, you get 16% on records "sold" in stores and through catalogs.

3.
(i) Master Recordings made during the fourth or fifth Option Periods: 16%.

3.
(i) For any recordings we decide to release that you made for us approximately three to six years after you sign this contract,[21] you get 16% on all records "sold" in the United States.

[21] See "Terms and Exclusivity," page 280, for why "Contract Periods" have no specific length.

(ii) The royalty rate above will apply to the first 500,000 units of USNRC Net Sales of each Album consisting of Master Recordings made during the fourth or fifth Option Periods. The royalty rate will be:

(ii) but this will only apply to the first 500,000 units "sold" in the US of an Album that consists entirely of your performances and songs that we have approved. For this the royalty shall be:

(A) 16.5% on USNRC Net Sales of any such Album in excess of 500,000 units and not in excess of 1,000,000 units,

(A) For Albums 500,001 to 1,000,000, you get 16.5% on records "sold" in stores and through catalogs,

(B) 17% on USNRC Net Sales of any such Album in excess of 1,000,000 units and not in excess of 2,000,000 units, and

(C) 17.5% on USNRC Net Sales of any such Album in excess of 2,000,000 units.

(B) For albums 1,000,001 through 2,000,000, you get 17%,

(C) For Albums 2,000,001 and up, you get 17.5%.

Exceptions to the Sliding Scale Royalty

Feeling comfy? Good. All warm inside? *Excellent*. Now comes the bad news.

4.

The only Net Sales to be considered for the purposes of escalating the royalty rates pursuant to all above shall be USNRC Net Sales. **Without limiting the foregoing,** Net Sales subject to the remainder of this clause hereof shall not be considered for the purposes of such escalations.

None of the foregoing escalations shall result in an increase in any royalty rates contained herein other than the ones directly above, even though other royalty rates may be based on the royalty rates set forth in these paragraphs.

4.

The only actual "sales" that count toward the Sliding Scale "royalty" rates above shall be US "sales" through retail stores, catalogs, stuff like that. **There is no way in hell we are going to apply anything we're about to mention** to the Sliding Scale: None of the "sales" mentioned below count. Nothing, nada. Zero. Zilch.

And *in case you think you're clever,* just because a royalty rate goes up in one category does not mean that your overall "royalty" went up. It's only for that one category. *Dig?*

[Example: If you managed to reach 500,000 in "sales" for one type of record, it does not mean that your "royalty" goes up for all records, just for those "royalties" under that one configuration.]

Now begins a series of "types" of records that even though they "sold," will not be applied to the Sliding Scale.

Foreign and Third World Countries Exceptions

5.

<u>Notwithstanding anything to the contrary contained in this Agreement</u>, with respect to Records sold in Brazil, Greece, Portugal, India, Kenya, Zambia, Zimbabwe, Nigeria and any other territory in which governmental or other authorities place limits on the royalty rates permissible for remittances to the United States in respect of Records sold in such territory(ies), the royalty payable hereunder shall equal the lesser of:

(a) the applicable royalty detailed above or,

(b) the effective royalty rate permitted by such governmental or other authority for remittances to the United States less a royalty equivalent to three percent (3%) of the retail list price and such monies as Pacific or its Licensees shall be required to pay to all applicable union funds in respect of said sales.

5.

<u>Regardless of whatever is said anywhere else in this contract, the following will be the rule</u> for records "sold" in Brazil, Greece, Portugal, India, Kenya, Zambia, Zimbabwe, Nigeria, and elsewhere in the world where the governments are a bunch of tightwads with arcane laws that don't allow for progressive concepts such as royalties and copyrights.

For those records "sold" there, we're only gonna pay you the lesser of either:

(a) the "royalty" discussed above or,

(b) whatever that bone-headed government's foreign policy allows them to pay us, minus 3% of the sale price of the record and also minus whatever union dues those other governments decide to impose on us hardworking free Americans, whichever one is lower.

LOOPHOLE ALERT!!!

EXPLANATION: Well, the Cold War is back. This clause is a great way for Pacific to get out of paying you for what they promised directly above. "…any other territory in which governmental or other authorities place limits on the royalty rates…" is the Loophole Creator. By intentionally not naming all of the countries they're referring to, they can always claim that Germany, for example, never paid them the money they owed on records "sold."[22] And since the label can't pay you, they'll be sports and give you a lame "configuration" that will add up to mere pennies.

Now I ask you: would you do business in a country that was hostile toward you? I think not. So why should the label? I'll tell you. Because all major labels are international and are forced to walk a fine political line. That's okay, but why should you pay for it? Scratch that line out. It's their problem. Don't let them make it yours.

[22] Germany is, in fact, a great example, as one major label recently claimed that the German government refused to forward royalties on account of their socialist laws.

REALITY: This means you could "sell" a *million* records in India, but if you don't "sell" 500,000 in the US, you won't qualify for the Sliding Scale. *Bummer.* (This is demonstrated in configurations 1 and 2 on pages 59 and 60.) We've seen that the sliding scale "royalty" they promised you in the deal memo doesn't apply to "sales" in much of Latin America and Africa. (Basically, about half the globe in land mass.) *Hmmmm* ... I don't remember seeing *that* on the deal memo. Oh well, who cares about Third World "sales" anyway? How many Indians listen to your type of music anyway?[23] (Unless you're Ravi Shankar.) It's America where you earn your gold. Well, let's see.

[23] Roughly about 500,000,000. India has the largest film and recording industry in the world on a per unit and per film basis. (Source: *Farmer's Almanac,* 2000.) It's state-controlled, so artists do get paid.

Giveaways and Charities

In some cases you will not be paid a full "royalty." In fact, as you're about to see, there are more times when your "royalty" is reduced than when you get the full "royalty." Below are situations that will not count toward your sliding scale.

6.
(a) The royalty rate on any Record described in section (1), (2), (3) or (4) of this sentence will be

6.
(a) For any of the following, your "royalty" will be cut in half:

ROYALTIES

one-half (1/2) of the royalty rate that would apply if the Record concerned were sold through Normal Retail Channels:

1) any catalog Phonograph Record sold by the special products operations of Pacific or its Licensees to educational institutions or libraries, or to other SPO clients for their promotion or sales incentive purposes (but not for sale to the general public through Normal Retail Channels);

1) records "sold" to educational institutions or libraries, or to some of our special friends that help us out with promotional problems,

2) any Phonograph Record sold by Pacific or its Licensees in conjunction with a substantial radio or television advertising campaign during the calendar semi-annual period in which that campaign begins or the next such period;

2) records "sold" during the six months after we launch any big radio or television advertising campaign for your record,

LOOPHOLE ALERT ON MAXIMUM!!!

EXPLANATION: Twice a year (Christmas and Spring, when most new acts are released), labels buy bulk TV or radio time to advertise their products. According to the above you receive only a half royalty during these periods, which means that even though the label "sells" records 12 months a year, only those "sold" during what would be the 10 slowest months of the year will have records applied to your Sliding Scale. Also, during the two months when "sales" are the hottest, your royalty will be cut in half. *Nasty*.

NEGOTIATE

You must get rid of this. Here's your defense: You only get a half royalty during the time that the record is released and the label is doing their advertising campaign. When that's over, the list price of the record is almost always reduced to the Budget or Mid-Priced level, and again you only get 3/4 to 1/2 of your promised percentage. So, basically, you can never earn your full "royalty" unless you happen to "sell" a record for full price six months after the initial release. Good luck.

3) any non-catalog Phonograph Record created on a custom basis for SPO clients and,

3) any record that we wouldn't normally release, custom-made for our special clients or sales promotions, and,

4) any Phonograph Records sold by Pacific in the United States through direct mail or phone order or other mail order distribution method.

4) any records "sold" in the United States through direct mail or phone order or other mail-order distribution method. [*Read: record clubs and dot-com sales.*]

DOUBLE-DIP DETECTOR

EXPLANATION: Once upon a time, this clause referred to the label's annoying practice of having telemarketers call people at home to sell them memberships in record clubs. The label had to pay the phone guys an extra commission, a cost they pass on to you. But records are no longer "sold" like this.

This is a riff on the "New Medium" concept identified earlier. As the Internet expands as a distribution system, it will become the main way records will be "sold." With this clause worded as vaguely as it is, the label can interpret the Internet as a "phone order." I wouldn't be surprised if they considered the telephone to be a "new" medium. And, if we are to use CDs as any gauge for how long something remains a "new medium," it will be well into the next century until the Internet is considered passé.

> By using this method, the label shrinks your earnings by switching "sales" from traditional "Normal Retail Channels" (NRC) to ones that use a telephone to sell the product. If you look at the "Royalty Base Price" definition earlier in this chapter, it already includes a 25% reduction in the royalty base price for "New Medium" records. Why cut the "royalty" in half again? This would mean that the configuration for a CD "sold" via a download over the Internet would be only 37.5% of the full "royalty" (about 7%, if the "royalty" is 14% of SRLP). Keep in mind that in a downloaded "sale" there's no packaging at all, and no wholesale distributor. Your royalty should be higher therefore, not lower.
>
> See configuration #3 and #4 in the Configuration Tables above for the "online" calculation.

⑨

NEGOTIATE

The smart negotiator will get this thrown out, or at the very least get the "royalty" up to 85% instead of 50%.

Recordings on Another Label's Releases

Through a variety of circumstances, your recordings may be licensed to other record companies. You will only be paid a half royalty for those records, *and* they do not apply toward your sliding scale.

(b) In respect of any Master Recording:

(1) leased by Pacific or its Licensees to others for their distribution of Phonograph Records in the United States;

(2) embodied on Phonograph Records sold by Pacific's Licensees in the United States through a direct mail

(b) If any of the recordings you record for us:

(1) does not get on the Album, but ends up being distributed by another label [*like, maybe, that first little indie you were on before we scooped you up*],[24] or

(2) is on one of the records "sold" by one of Pacific's "fake" shell companies that do cheesy mail-

[24] This is referring to early demos that you may have accidentally signed the rights away to. Now that you're being distributed by a big company, the original label wants to cash in and distribute them. Pacific will likely try to acquire the distribution rights to these recordings so that the old label is not riding the coattails of Pacific's marketing. The cost for this will be passed on to you with this clause. It also refers to things like *K-Tel's Classic Hits of the Millennium*.

or mail-order distribution method (including, without limitation, through so-called "record clubs"); or

(3) embodied on Phonograph Records sold by Pacific's Licensees in the United States through retail stores in connection with special radio or television advertisements (sometimes referred to as "key-outlet marketing"), **Pacific will pay you fifty percent (50%) of Pacific's gross receipts** (as computed after deduction of all AFM, union and other applicable third-party payments actually made or incurred) provided, however...

if Pacific's gross receipts from such sales are inclusive of manufacturing costs and/or Mechanical Royalties for the applicable Record(s) hereunder, **your royalty shall instead be one-half (1/2) of the otherwise applicable royalty rate** hereunder).

If another artist, a Producer, or any other Person is entitled to royalties on sales of such Records, that payment will be divided among you in the same ratio as that among your respective basic royalty payment percentage rates.

order scams [*like, "Get 10 CDs for a dollar if you buy 10 others for $6 each," or "K-Smells Hits of the Millennium"*], or

(3) ends up on a similar compilation record "sold" by one of our shell labels[25] in connection with an advertising campaign (sometimes referred to as "key-outlet marketing"),

Pacific will give you half of the money it collects on these records after deducting all expenses. But,

Any time one of your recordings shows up on a sister label's imprint, and we are able to collect a mechanical royalty for a song you wrote, then we only pay a half royalty.

If others are entitled to share in that "royalty," as are other artists or writers whose material might be on the record, as well as the producer of those cuts [*count on it*], then all "royalties" due will be divided among all band members/arrangers/producers in relation to what has already been agreed to in this contract.

[25] P&D, "Pressing and Distribution." This would include records that Pacific distributes for other small labels in exchange for a healthy percentage of their profits. In my vernacular, I call these "Two Deep" and "Three Deep" label deals because the small label is two or three levels removed from the main Distributor. See *Confessions*, "What Is a Real Independent Label?" and the "Who Owns What: The Family Tree" charts in the *Confessions* chapter "The Big Picture."

REALITY: If you ever audit the label, they will likely bend on this. It doesn't make sense that you should only be paid a half royalty just because they are required to pay you for songwriting as well. If your song was good enough to get on a compilation Album, that usually means that it was a hit, which is even more reason you should receive a full royalty.

Record Clubs and Internet Sales

6. (b) (3) continues…

No royalties shall be payable with respect to Records given away as "bonus" or "free" Records as a result of joining a record club or purchasing a number of Records from a record club or in connection with any introductory, incentive or other offer made by a record club; provided, however, for the purposes hereof, the number of such non-royalty Records shall not exceed fifty percent (50%) of the total number of Records distributed through such means.

No "royalties" shall be paid for the 10 "free" records that people get when they join a record club for $1, or for ones they buy at the super-low rates used as bait to get them to stay in the club;

however, if this gets excessive and you start "selling" a huge amount of records this way, we will pay you a "royalty" on half of those sales. [*How much is a "huge number"? You'll have to trust us on that one.*]

(c) If Pacific sells or licenses third parties to sell Records **via telephone, satellite, cable or other direct transmission to the consumer over wire or through the air,** the royalty rate will be seventy-five percent (75) of the otherwise applicable royalty rate prescribed above but, for purposes of calculating royalties payable in connection with such sales, **the retail list price of such Records shall be deemed to be**

(c) If we let someone else other than us "sell" records by a direct download over either the **Internet or through some other direct-to-consumer medium, such as satellite transmission or cable,** your "royalty" will be 75% of what it used to be.

But since there is no retail store, the amount used for the SRLP in the Meat Grinder will be the actual sale price that we receive,

9

the actual sales price received by **Pacific** of such records (but in the United States, fifty percent (50%) of the actual sales price), less the applicable Container Charge; provided, however, with respect to Records sold by Pacific's Licensees, in no event shall your royalty exceed one-half (1/2) of Pacific's net receipts after deduction from Pacific's gross receipts of union and all other applicable third party payments actually made or incurred by Pacific.

(except in the US, where it will be 50% of the actual sale price) minus a Container Charge,

But regardless of whether any downloadable records are "sold" by us or by one of our shell companies or fake independent labels, your "royalty" will never be more than half of the money that we make.

DOUBLE-DIP DETECTOR

EXPLANATION: You already paid for this. Remember? On page 55, you already conceded to a reduction in the Royalty Base for "New Medium Records," which includes Internet stuff. Here the record company is taking full advantage of you; they intend to reduce your "royalty" by 27% for most "sales" and 50% for "sales" in the US (as if it costs more to download records in the US than in other countries—if anything, it costs less), and take the same deduction over again, including a mythical container charge when there *isn't even any container.* Neat trick. (See Configuration #1 in the table on page 59.) And as if that isn't bad enough, it won't count toward your Sliding Scale.

NEGOTIATE

This is a Quadruple-Dip. Get it thrown out. If you can't get it thrown out, labels will traditionally push the number up to 100% for worldwide "sales" and 85% for US "sales." There's no legitimate reason why these "sales" shouldn't count toward your escalation to the next royalty plateau, just as there's no legitimate reason why the label should take a packaging deduction when there's no packaging involved.

Budget Records, CDs, Cutouts, Public Domain, and Scrap

More stuff that is a reduced royalty and doesn't count toward the sliding scale.

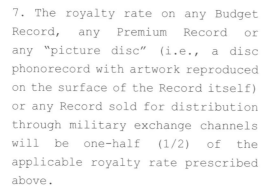

7. The royalty rate on any Budget Record, any Premium Record or any "picture disc" (i.e., a disc phonorecord with artwork reproduced on the surface of the Record itself) or any Record sold for distribution through military exchange channels will be one-half (1/2) of the applicable royalty rate prescribed above.

The royalty rate on any Mid-Priced Record will be two-thirds (2/3) of the applicable royalty rate prescribed above. The royalty on any Premium Record or Record sold for distribution through military exchange channels will be computed on the basis of actual sales price less all taxes and Container Charges.

(i) **No royalties whatsoever** shall accrue hereunder with respect to (A) Records distributed to any Person primarily for promotion or critique, (B) Records sold as "scrap," raw stock or "surplus," which terms shall mean excess inventory of any particular Record which is listed in the Pacific catalog and sold one third (1/3)

Your royalty rate will only be one-half for Budget records, which is any record "sold" for under 65% of the normal price. Your royalty rate will also be cut in half for any promotional records,[26] laser discs, or records "sold" to the military.

The royalty rate on any Mid-Priced Record (one that "sells" for 15% less than the SRLP) will be two-thirds of the normal rate. The royalty rate on any promotional record or records "sold" to the military will be based on the actual sale price minus taxes and Container Charges.

(i) We're not paying you anything at all for:
Promotional records given free to music journalists,
(B) Records "sold" as scrap, raw stock, or surplus. [*Which means the label was unable to sell as many records as they pressed, and no one wants them even at a 66% discount.*]

or less, but not if sold at the same price as of Pacific's then-current sub-distributor price, and (C) which is cut out of the Pacific catalog and sold as discontinued merchandise.

(C) Records "cut out" of the Pacific catalog and "sold" as discontinued merchandise.

BIG SUCK ALERT!!!

EXPLANATION: These are the so-called cutouts. I just have one question: If they are "sold," how can they be *removed* from the catalog, and why shouldn't you get a "royalty"? To understand the chilling, momentous implications of what this clause sets up, see "Is It Really Possible to 'Sell' Records?" page 98.

(ii) If, on any date, the performances embodied on any Master Recording hereunder become **property of the public domain** in any territory of the world so that Persons may reproduce and/or exploit in such territory Records of such performances without license from and payment to Pacific, then, <u>notwithstanding anything herein to the contrary,</u> no monies whatsoever shall accrue hereunder in connection with Records hereunder sold in such territory on and after said date insofar as such performances are concerned, unless Pacific actually receives any such monies in connection therewith, and in such event Pacific shall accrue royalties in accordance with the terms hereof.

(ii) If any of these recordings fall into the **public domain**, anywhere in the world, to the extent that any asshole with a computer can rip and burn a bootleg without paying us, then,

<u>regardless of what it says elsewhere in this contract,</u> we're not paying you a *thin dime* for those records "sold" in that region unless we're somehow able to squeeze a few pennies out of them.
[*This is not likely to happen, but there are some countries where "the people" own everything. It's a foregone conclusion that you will not be getting royalties from those sales.*]

(iii) Notwithstanding anything to the contrary set forth herein, with respect to Net Sales of Records sold in the form of compact discs, the royalty rate shall be **seventy-five percent (75%) of the otherwise applicable royalty rate set forth herein.**

(iii) and one more thing. We're only gonna pay you **75% of your Royalty** for CDs.

REALITY: And there it is. The dreaded "three-quarter royalty" that has become famous for CDs. I put it here so that you will know where to look for it. These days it ain't no big thing to get the label to give you 100% on CDs. Anyone who still insists it's standard to only pay 75% of the Royalty on CDs is an asshole. Walk away.

In the examples given in this book, we're going to assume that you were persistent enough to get a 100% royalty on CDs.

And finally…

The New Configurations Scam

Since every experienced artist's lawyer is now sensitive to the "new technology" deductions that only pay three-quarters of the promised royalty on CDs, sneaky label lawyers have had to become "smarter" at hiding it. The version below is by far the most covert I've seen to date. It's usually hidden in with the ROYALTIES clauses and sometimes goes by the subheading "New Configurations." It's intended to sound like it's filling the gap for any type of record omitted above, and also any new type of record that is invented during the term of the contract, but it's got a little something extra. Read the left column first and see if you can make sense of it without any help from the right column.

(iv) With respect to Net Sales of Records sold in the form of **Record configurations not specifically provided for herein,** Company shall have the option to accrue, at its sole discretion, with respect to

(iv) For any records you "sell" that are **oddball records not accounted for in the Meat Grinder,** we can pay you a Royalty equal to what we would pay you if this was an analog cassette,

each such Record, either a royalty equal to the same dollars-and-cents (or other currency) royalty amount as would otherwise be accrued hereunder with respect to an equivalent Record in the form of an analog cassette, or a royalty computed at the same percentage of the Royalty Base of such other Record configuration as the percentage of the Royalty Base utilized to compute the royalty for an equivalent Record in the form of analog cassette. If the foregoing royalty amount or Royalty Base with respect to an equivalent Record in the form of an analog cassette does not exist, then with respect to Net Sales of Records sold in the form of Record configurations not specifically provided for herein, the royalty rate for such Records shall be two-thirds (2/3) of the otherwise applicable royalty rate set forth in this agreement. For purposes of this paragraph only, the term **"configurations not specifically provided for herein"** means configurations other than vinyl disc, analog cassette, audio-only compact disc, and Audio-Visual Devices.

And if either the Royalty Rate or the Royalty Base of an analog cassette just can't be applied for some reason to the oddball record, then the royalty rate will be two-thirds of your normal "royalty." [*Meaning the Royalty percentage they promised you in the deal memo, minus any applicable deductions.*]

When we say "oddball Records not accounted for in the Meat Grinder," what we really mean is every record "sold" that is not a vinyl disc, analog cassette, or Audio-Visual Device.

REALITY: Anything that is not a 12-inch vinyl LP, cassette, or videotape is considered so weird by the label that they will only pay you two-thirds of your royalty for it. This includes CDs, which sell for about 25% more than cassettes, as well as downloads, ring tones, and streams, which are starting to become the most common type of sales there are. Bottom line, this is the same old devil in a new set of clothes. It's a "new technology" clause being dressed up as an "oddball configuration" clause. Don't fall for it.

NEGOTIATE

If you simply remove the last sentence from the clause, you will already be doing yourself a world of good. Without this last bit, the onus will fall on the label to account for all configurations in the Meat Grinder. If they refuse to remove this, then make sure that everything you can think of is inserted into the list at the end. You risk not getting a full royalty for anything you leave out. **In the examples given here, I'm gonna assume that you were quick enough to catch this, and got CDs excluded from this clause.**

You also need to insist that if "sales" of these oddball configurations start edging past the normal "sales," then you should get paid for them as if they were regular sales. It shouldn't be hard to get the label to agree to a threshold of 30%, beyond which you should be paid 100% of the royalty above that percentage of "sales."

Music Video Deductions

Aside from all the configurations above for Albums, there is also a series of special deductions that come from making your music videos.

8. One Hundred percent (100%) of the production and acquisition costs incurred in connection with any Covered Video will be recoupable from your royalties on sales of Records which do not reproduce visual images ("audio royalties") and one hundred percent (100%) of such costs will be recoupable from all monies otherwise payable to you from the exploitation of such Covered Videos.

All of the money used to produce and promote your music videos (which we call "Covered Videos") will be paid out of your "royalties" on "sales" of records without video portions [*isn't that the same as a CD or LP or tape?*]. (We'll call these "audio royalties" so you can tell the difference between them and royalties you earn off the music portion of the video and from sales of the video itself.)

If any such costs are recouped from audio royalties and additional royalties accrue from Covered Videos subsequently, the latter royalties will be applied in recoupment of those costs and the amount of those audio royalties which were previously applied against those costs will be credited back to your account.

If you pay us back all the money for your videos by using your "audio royalties," and we then earn additional bucks by selling the video itself, all that money earned from video sales will be applied to paying back the video costs. The "audio royalties" that we already used to pay for the video will be credited back toward your normal Album recoupment. [*A mindbender!*]

NEGOTIATE

Many labels can be persuaded to pay for half of the video costs themselves. Fight for this. Fight to have the amount of video costs recoupable *only* from your "*audio* royalties" *if possible*. If a label wants you bad enough, they will absorb the costs for making the video, as they should. It's their promotional expense.[27] They just make you pay for it because they know that in this day and age every artist wants and needs music videos, and so they can get away with it.

Summary of US Sales

PAUSE: Now you can see why I call it the "Meat Grinder." Let's summarize the entire seven clauses above in one-liners.

An introductory paragraph tells us that Pacific will pay the artist a Royalty based on a configuration, and that it will only pay one "royalty," out of which all the artist's vendors will have to be paid, including the producer.

1. Outlines the concept of the "Sliding Scale Royalty" and the benchmarks for each increase from 14% to 16% for approximately the first, second, and third Albums of the contract (the "Option Period").

2. Outlines the "Sliding Scale Royalty" and the benchmarks for each increase from 14.5% to 16% for the second and third Albums.

3. Outlines the "Sliding Scale Royalty" and the benchmarks for each increase from 16% to 17.5% for the fourth and fifth Album.

[27] Getting the artist on MTV (as well as radio) functions as advertising, in my opinion, because those entities are directly or indirectly paid for placement on their services by the label. Technically, however, this is not advertising, it's promotion.

4. Introduces the exceptions to the "Sliding Scale Royalty," stating that anything to follow in the contract does not apply.

5. Details the foreign and third-world countries where copyright laws don't exist or jibe with ours, causing your Royalties to be reduced.

6. Details when your Royalty will be half the usual amount. Specifically on:

   a. (1) Records "sold" to libraries and schools, (2) records "sold" for promotional ad space or on-air time, (3) records custom-made for "special clients," and (4) any records "sold" through direct mail, mail-order, or phone order.

   b. Recording tracks you may have recorded before you were signed to Pacific Records. Specifically: (1) recordings on other labels that end up being distributed by Pacific's parent distributor (a Big Four), (2) sales through Pacific's record club, (3) if Pacific absorbs the "indie" label you started out on and ends up distributing your old basement recordings.

   c. Sales made through data download, satellite transmission, or telecommunication devices, like cable, fiber-optic, etc.

7. Details the Royalty for various configurations of records "sold" far below their "normal selling price." Mid-Priced Records "sold" are paid a 3/4 Royalty; Budget Records (or any record that "sells" for two-thirds of its normal retail price) and 12-inch Singles, Extended Play Records (EPs), etc., are *all* paid a half Royalty. Also, (i) records "sold" for scrap, or anything that is cut out of the catalog, or "sold" for less than 66% of the SRLP, and (ii) records that a court of law says are "public domain" will all be "royalty" free. (iii) Any oddball configuration that does not fit into the previous configurations will be paid out as if it were a cassette. (This is where they will try to slip in CDs at a reduced royalty configuration.)

8. And finally, any money spent on music videos will be recoupable from your "royalty" account. But only half the money earned from the sale or license of videos will be credited to your "royalty" account.

What's left?

REALITY: You can get that "Sliding Scale Royalty" on Domestic Sales, as long as you sell a mountain's worth of records (1) through major record stores, and (2) at the most expensive "selling" price, when the record is released. In addition, the only time you get a full Royalty is when you "sell" cassette tapes (sometimes CDs) or vinyl at Top Line prices in a major record store, and only "sales" realized four to six months after the Album is released. Think I'm wrong? Go back and read it carefully. Here's the axiom:

In most major-label contracts, short of selling cassettes or LPs (and occasionally CDs) at full price four to six months after the Album is released (which is difficult to do), you'll only get 25% to 75% of your promised Royalty/revenue share.

It's a sliding scale all right, but which direction is it sliding in?

If we return to the coffee example at the beginning of the chapter, it's kind of like saying you'll only be paid your full royalty on cups of plain black coffee that are bought without a sip cup, without milk or sugar, and not purchased during the morning rush hour or as part of a breakfast special (i.e., coffee and a roll for $1.25). Anything else is a reduction.

So who actually sees this elusive Sliding Scale Royalty? Major stars with multi-platinum Albums. And even they have problems if they are signed to a production deal and all the money flows through the producer. (See "Advances," page 28.)

Isn't there a way around all this craziness? What about those deals where they just pay you a flat percentage of everything the Album makes? Ah, you mean the 360 Deal. You're right. In those deals you don't have to go through all these calculations and escalations, because they're paying you a flat percentage. But there is a downside. Let's take a look.

360 Revenue Shares

360 Deals (sometimes called "multiple rights deals" or "all-in deals") don't pay "royalties" per se. They pay a percentage of "Net Profits." What exactly are "Net Profits"? Check it out. (Bookmark this page. You'll be referring to it several times in future chapters.)

As used herein, "Net Profits" would mean gross receipts less direct costs (including recording costs, manufacturing costs, marketing costs, distribution costs, a services fee of 6% (to Pacific to be retained by Pacific), **mechanical royalties**, and all monies payable to third parties which may become due by reason of the acquisition, creation, recording, manufacture, distribution, exploitation or other use of the masters, etc.).

"Net Profits" means all the money we collect for the sale or license of your music, minus the costs for collecting that money, like taxes and finance charges, less our out-of-pocket expenses (including recording costs, manufacturing costs, marketing costs, distribution costs, and a vig of 6% that we pay to ourselves for no particular reason other than that we can). We also deduct all **songwriting fees**, and fees to anyone else that gets a slice of this pie which we may owe to others in the future if we get bought out.

LOOPHOLE ALERT!!!

What does this mean? Well the $1 or so per Album they pay you (if you are also the writer) for the rights to sell the song, which is the only money guaranteed to you by law, is about to be taken away. How? Because here they are calling it a "distribution expense" and deducting it from Gross to create "Net Profits." For more on this, see Chapter 4: Controlled Compositions and Mechanical Licenses.

Let's continue…

Included in deductions are Pacific's road costs and freight insurance, hall fees, vendor fees, **and costs of security to prevent bootlegging.**

We'll also deduct whatever it costs us to send you out on the road to promote the music, **oh—and our legal fees that we use to sue college students and grandmothers for BitTorrenting and using Kazaa and LimeWire to steal music.**

In connection with master use licensing, at such times as the Artist's account is in a profitable position, Pacific shall credit Artist's account with 50% of net receipts (prior to such periods 100% of master use income will be applied to the profit split account). In computing net profits, losses from prior accounting periods shall be carried forward. All accountings of net profits hereunder shall be semi-annual, payable within 90 days following the close of such period.

If (after the above) you sell enough to pay back all the money we're laying out and you accrue any "Net Profits," we'll begin splitting all the money we get from sound recordings on a 50/50 basis. But if you owed us money from a past accounting period (like if the first album was an expensive flop) we're going to carry over losses from the past periods where we had to support you. And we'll pay you twice a year, every six months, three months after the end of the accounting period.

REALITY: So, basically every dime they spend on recording the album, distributing the album (including the payments to songwriters, which could be you) and every dime they spend to promote the album, comes off the top, plus a 6% vig. Then you have "Net Profits." Let's see how it breaks down with the top three most common configurations: CD Album, New Technology Album, and New Technology Single. All configurations below are for "Top Line." Which means this is the *most* you would get paid off of these sales. *If you skipped the chapter before this one on "Configurations," now would be a good time to review it.*

	CD Album	iTunes Album	iTunes Single
Top Line SRLP	$17.98	$9.99	$1.25
Distributor's price to retail (Gross)	$12	$6.59[28]	$0.085[29]
AFM's piece of the action[30]	$0.085	$0.085	$0.001
Mechanical license (payments to songwriters: 3/4 rate)	$0.81 (3/4 rate)[31]	$0.81	$0.08
Manufacturing of unit	.80	$0	$0
Duplication/packaging cost (25% of the Top Line SRLP)	$4.49	$3.20	$0.24
Gross profit to labels before overhead	$5.81	$5.85	$0.53
Label's 6% juice	$0.34	$0.34	$0.03
Net Profit Penny Rate	$5.47	$5.51	$0.50
Penny rate if Revenue split is 50/50 for Top Line	**$2.73**	**$2.75**	**$0.25**

[28] iTunes takes 33% of the SRLP as a fee.

[29] iTunes takes 33% of the SRLP as a fee.

[30] The AFM is the musician's union. The label pays them a very small sliver of every sale if that particular title sold over a certain amount. The money goes into a "Special Payments Fund" for pension and health benefits for union musicians.

[31] This is assuming a Controlled Composition License of 3/4 of "12X Statutory." See Chapter 4 for what this is.

The penny rates above will be placed in the artist's account for each "sale." From this the label will deduct marketing expenses, touring, any other advances, and basically anything they can think of, as well as applying "reserve" provisions (see page 238 for what a "Reserve" is).

Also remember that many 360 Deals for new artists don't pay 50/50. They start off paying only 35% or 40% to the artist and only for Top Line "sales." They then use an Escalation to 50% after 500,000 "records sold." On top of this you have to also keep in mind that all the same deductions apply to each configuration in a 360 Deal as they do in a standard deal. You don't get a free pass on those, because each type of "sale" has to be calculated based on the price, type of packaging, and how it's sold, just as in the traditional deal. So Mid-Priced records don't necessarily get split at the Top Line rate of 50/50. They may get split as far less—I've seen 25/75, believe it or not.

If you assume that the average "configuration" you'll realize in a 360 Deal is the same as in a traditional deal—Mid-Priced CD Album—you'll probably be seeing an average penny rate of about $2.00 per "record sold." This, on the surface, seems better than the $0.75–$1.35 penny rates they were paying you with the old-style "royalties" system, but remember that under the old system you also received a separate mechanical royalty for songwriting that in many cases made up for this difference, and now they are also taking pieces of publishing, touring, and other areas that we'll look at in other chapters in this book.

In addition, auditing the label was far easier when all you had to focus on was the sale of records. This basically meant sales receipts, warehouse records, and, if they let you see them, manufacturing records. (See Chapter 8: Auditing for why they don't have to.) All this data could then be compared with an independent bean counter called SoundScan, which is what is used to determine the *Billboard* charts. Anyone can subscribe to their data, so manipulating it is very hard for the label to do.

But in a 360 Deal, in order to see if you're being screwed, you'll have to first know how much they really spent on promotion, artwork, and a million other things that go into the "Net Profits" formula. This is far more data to collect, and guess what—there is no independent bean counter for what the label spends on all these things. You'll just have to take their word for it.

Foreign Sales

So Domestic Sales aren't what you thought they'd be. That's okay, because foreign is where it's at, anyway. Most labels sell about 60% of their product overseas. Let's see how they treat you there.

The Currency Exchange Scam

In addition to deductions to your Royalties and/or revenue share of "Net Profits," the label will pull some more shenanigans when figuring out how much they actually owe you.

The following shall apply with respect to the computation of royalties:

(i) With respect to each particular type of Record (e.g., Singles Record, EP, LP, etc.) sold outside the United States (including Records exported

These are the ways we add up your "royalties":

(i) For all records "sold" outside the United States (including subdistributors[32]), your Royalties will be 2/3, or 66.6% of your normal

[32] Sub-distributors: these are companies that sell to other countries on a massive wholesale basis. Literally tens of thousands of records in each sale. The records are still returnable, and auditing them is next to impossible.

to third parties outside the United States and for which Pacific is paid by such third parties on a royalty-inclusive basis), royalties shall be at sixty-six and two-thirds percent (66-2/3%) the rate otherwise applicable, except seventy-five percent (75%) the rate otherwise applicable with respect to Records sold by Pacific's affiliates under the subparagraphs above. A list of Pacific's affiliates and licensees as of the date hereof is attached hereto. Such royalties shall be computed in the same national currency as Pacific is accounted to, at the rate of exchange in effect at the time of payment to Pacific for such Records, and shall not accrue until payment for the Record sales to which such royalties are attributable has been received by Pacific in the United States in the normal course of business.

Royalty for that configuration (except for records "sold" by one of our "fake" independent labels, for which you will get 3/4, or 75%).

A list of all our shell companies is attached to this contract.[33] Any money earned on sales outside the US will be calculated at the exchange rate of the country where the sale was made, at the time the sale was made, and will not be applied to your account until we actually receive the money from that country [*if ever*].

[33] **This is initially so that if you decide to audit them you know where to start looking. But usually any audit that is to take place is done three to five years later. By then most of these affiliates will have dissolved like a dune in the desert wind.**

RIP-OFF ALERT!!!

EXPLANATION: This one is complicated. See REALITY below.

REALITY: It's important to understand that when labels whine about not being able to collect all the money owed to them from their foreign distributors, they are talking, in part, about another branch of a company over which they have a great deal of control. But aside from that, to really comprehend the evil of this, you need to learn a basic lesson in economics. But first, let's summarize: The above is saying that paying "royalties" or revenue share on sales from some countries is really hard, due to their government regulations about paying foreigners and money leaving the country (especially when it's a country we owe so much to, like China), and our own government's liberal policy of allowing this to persist without threats. And even with countries that are cooperative, you still have to deal with issues of *currency exchange rates.* So to be what the record companies considers "fair," your royalty/Net Profits will be calculated in the currency of the country in which it's "sold" at the official currency exchange rate at that time.

So, for example, let's say the fictitious country of Lilliput has a currency rate that's equal to one US dollar ($1) for every one Lilliputian *garphnog* (¥1). That's a one-to-one exchange. Say a record in Lilliput sells for ¥10, and your royalty is 10%. According to the above, your royalty will be ¥1, which at the time of the sale is equal to $1 US.

But the clause above says that the label won't do the exchange calculation until the money reaches the States. That usually takes six to eight months. In that time, the ratio of the dollar to the *garphnog* will most likely be different, as international currency rates are prone to change. If it goes up half a point, then ¥1 will be equal to $1.50. You score. If it goes down half a point, then ¥1 will be equal to $0.50. You lose. Since no one knows exactly when rates will go up or down, this seems like a fair bet. And it would be, if the record company stated exactly on what date the transfer of money is to take place. But they don't. And since their Lilliputian subsidiary doesn't lose any money, regardless of the exchange rate or when it's exchanged, it's a safe bet that they'll wait until the exchange rate goes down before they transfer any *garphnogs* into dollars. Neat trick. The house has tilted the odds in their favor.

They do this with millions of dollars every day. They do it with employees' payrolls and with loans they owe other companies. For any large global corporation, international finance and currency trading is daily routine. They hire people to sit and watch the exchange rates change, looking for a half-point spread to jump on. It's business as usual.

You, of course, will never catch them, even if your lawyer is alert enough to understand what this clause really says. Sales records for an international audit are inaccessible. And should they ever be accessible, there's a clause in the section on Auditing (see page 235) that waives your rights to see them.

Who's hungry?

NEGOTIATE

There is something you can try. Have your exchange rate calculated at the time of the "sale." If that won't fly, insist that the transfer be made within 30 days of verification of the sale. If the label objects, tell them they are free to hold it in reserve until the money is due to you. This will, at least, restrict the label from continuing to play with the exchange system. The only risk for you is if you happen to sell records when the exchange rate is low. But at least you will have a fighting chance. I would rather let Lady Luck decide these sorts of things than a major-label accountant. Another way to circumvent this would be to insist that the exchange rate be calculated at the highest rate for the Option Period[34] during which the sale is made. I wouldn't hold my breath on this one, but it's definitely worth a try.

[34] For how long an "Option Period" is, see "Terms and Exclusivity," page 280.

The Foreign Licensing Scam

While you're busy trying to figure out all this math, there is a bigger issue that comes right after the one above. What happens if the label receives a lump sum of money for the rights to distribute your record overseas? Do you get some of it?

If, however, at the time such sales are reported to Pacific in the United States such payment is instead applied to recoup an earlier advance received from a third party by Pacific in the United States, then such royalty shall accrue when such sales are so reported and such payment is so applied.

But at the time we get news of your record selling overseas, if we licensed your foreign rights to a company for a lump sum, like an Advance, then those "royalties" will be used to recoup that Advance. Instead of allowing you to share in the Advance, we'll just apply the "royalty" to your account, but the amount figured will be based on the time that we actually received the money, instead of when we pay you. [*Well, that's a relief.*]

If Pacific is paid for Records sold outside the United States but, due to third-party government regulations, Pacific cannot receive such payment in the United States, then Pacific shall, at your

If we get money for foreign sales but, because of that country's Byzantine regulations, we're not allowed to take that money out of the country and give it to you, then, if you tell us to, we'll deposit that money in an account with your name on it in the country that is giving us a hard time.

election and expense, deposit
the royalties payable to you
with respect to such Record
sales in the currency in
which Pacific receives payment
therefrom, and such deposit
shall be made to your account
in a depository selected by
you and located in the country
in which payment to Pacific is
made for such Record sales.
Deposit and notice to you
shall discharge Pacific of the
royalty obligation for Record
sales to which such royalties
are applicable.

Once we do this, we are washing our hands of it, and this money shall be deemed "paid" by us to you.

REALITY: It says that your "royalties" can be used to pay back the Advance the label received from their foreign agent. And until the Advance is paid back, they don't have to pay you any "royalties" at all on foreign "sales," regardless of the fact that you earned them.

WUNDERBAR WONDERBRA

Melissa Wonderbra, a 19-year-old R&B pop diva, had several Top 40 hits. Pacific, wanting to cash in while her iron was hot, put the word out on the street that they were interested in licensing Melissa's Master Recordings in various foreign territories.

A German record company—Das Label—advanced Pacific 50 grand for the rights to license Melissa's recordings in their country, an amount to be recouped against future "sales." Das Label then sold 1,000 CDs, and subtracted $690 in royalties from Pacific's Melissa account. Rather than pay Melissa, Pacific kept the *entire* 50 grand and applied the $690 toward Melissa's debt to Pacific. Melissa then owed Pacific only an additional $49,310 for her foreign license account.

Melissa never saw any of the 50 grand that the label received from licensing her record. But she had to pay it back anyway.

This clause is basically a *mega* form of cross-collateralizing.[35] It should be completely removed. You should have no problem getting it thrown out in its entirety in a Big Four negotiation, but smaller labels will fight you. One expert with 10 years of experience dealing with the accounting departments of labels told me that as a matter of routine, labels only give you about half of the money collected from foreign sales and licensing. Unless you catch them.

Paying Out Your "Royalties"

Buried deep in another section, sometimes called ROYALTY PAYMENTS or MISCELLANEOUS ROYALTY PROVISIONS (and sometimes not labeled at all), is a clause often left untouched. So much of a lawyer's time is spent determining the percentage of your "royalty" that how it gets paid sometimes gets glossed over. But think about it: What's the point in getting a higher percentage if the label doesn't have to pay it to you until you're ready for retirement? This clause deals with the how and when of receiving your "royalties."

Reserves and Scheduling

Monies earned hereunder will be accrued semi-annually and paid, less all Advances and any other charges, during May for the semi-annual period ending in February and during November for the semi-annual period ending in August, in accordance with Pacific's regular accounting practices. Pacific **shall, however, have the right to establish reasonable reserves from returns and exchanges.** The reserve so established shall not exceed, with respect to LP Records, thirty-five percent (35%)

Your "royalties" (and/or "Net Profits" if a 360 Deal) will be added up twice a year and paid to you as follows:
First, we deduct anything you owe us. This includes any money Advanced for parties, limos, hotel rooms, and every little thing we can think of. We'll then pay you once in May for anything you earned up until the last February, and again in November for anything you earned up until the last August. **We still have the right to hold back some money in a reserve.**[36] But it will not be more than 35% of the "royalties"/"Net Profits" earned on all types of records in case some of the Albums are sent back

of all LP Records shipped during each accounting period, and, with respect to non-LP Records, fifty percent (50%) of shipments of non-LP Records shipped during such period, commencing with the second full accounting period after the release of the respective record. **Notwithstanding the foregoing,** if actual returns of any LP hereunder ("Subject LP") exceed thirty-five percent (35%) of the total number of units of such LP theretofore shipped, the reserve for the immediately succeeding LP shall be the actual return percentage of the Subject LP plus an additional five percent (5%).

during that same accounting period, and 50% of the money from all weird types of records (EPs, singles, etc.) that are returned in that same accounting period. We think this is "reasonable." All this will start about seven months after the record is released.

Regardless of what it says above, if the amount of Albums that are returned exceeds 35%, the reserve for your next Album will be the percentage of the returns of your last Album plus 5%.

REALITY: So you're only getting about 65% of your "royalties" or "Net Profits" for a long while. Usually about one to two years (see "Auditing," page 244, for why). You will not be able to get this out of your contract until you are a big star and the label has an idea of the approximate amount of records you might sell in a given year.

There are two really bad problems with this clause, aside from the obvious fact that they hold on to your money. The first is that the label doesn't pay you interest on your money while they hold it. Try to get this changed. I've known of labels who will pay that interest if the artist's leverage is good enough.

The second problem here is that 5% penalty for the next Album. This is a relatively new stanza in recording contracts. It allows the label to go back on their promise of how many records they plan to produce and ship, which they justify by saying your Album didn't sell well enough. But it also creates a foregone conclusion that if your first record was a dog, then your second record will be even worse. If the label does feel that way, why are they continuing to have you make records for them?

Oh, and one other element: 50% on Singles. This is not that big a deal now that we still live in an Album-oriented sales environment, but what happens with this clause when iTunes, and the budding families of digital stores, with their singles-driven sales structure, begin to dominate? This reality may only be a few years away. It means your reserves will soon be in the 50% area. In case you're not screaming at this book already, here's what you probably are thinking: There is little need for a reserve, as records downloaded *never* come back.

NEGOTIATE

Get these numbers down, down, *down*. Especially the 50% on Singles. A viable argument you could make is that since the Internet provides the potential for a substantially higher profit margin (since there's no packaging or middleman wholesaler), the label can afford to be more generous with the reserves. For a complete analysis of reserves and returns, see Chapter 8: Auditing, page 238.

(13)

Each reserve shall be liquidated in equal installments in each of the four full accounting periods after such reserve is established. Pacific shall have the right to establish reserves in excess of such limitations herein if Pacific shall become aware of specific facts, of which Pacific shall advise you, which in Pacific's judgment reasonably create a substantial possibility that the percent limitations provided for herein may be insufficient to cover actual returns. If Pacific makes any **overpayment** of royalties (e.g., by reason of an accounting error), Pacific shall have the **Offset Right** (excluding mechanical royalties) in connection therewith.

We'll be paying you these reserves in increments, as we liquidate the units in the warehouse. We'll do this in equal installments of one in each accounting period. But if we learn anything that clues us into the idea that your records are going to ship back in huge numbers [*bad publicity, poor initial "sales" figures, etc.*], we have the right to take bigger reserves than the ones stated above (in other words, higher than 35%).

And if we've somehow **overpaid** you and have somehow made an accounting error in *your* favor [*and how likely is that?*], we shall employ a nasty little thing called the **Offset Right**[37] to get that money back. In other words, we'll take it out of your next royalty statement, but we won't touch any songwriting fees you've earned if you are the writer of any of the songs (your "mechanical royalties"[38]).

[37] "Offset Right": see page 112 for details.

[38] "Mechanical Royalties" are the fees you are paid as a songwriter on the album, as opposed to the money you get for being the artist. See page 137 for details.

REALITY: Here, after spending several pages establishing a reserve, they then say that they can raise this fixed percentage (35%) to whatever they please. Based on what? Some piece of gossip they hear on TMZ? And how will you know that they are doing this? You can't without an audit.

Selling Your Marker

But wait, the best is saved for last. The following clause gets the label off the hook completely. It's one of the last things you see at the very end of the contract when you are too cross-eyed to even read straight. It's buried deep in a subheading called MISCELLANEOUS.

Webster's Dictionary and Thesaurus defines "miscellaneous" thusly: "indiscriminate, mixed, many-sided; diversified, varied, composed of parts of different kinds."

Tell me if you think this next clause is "miscellaneous":

Monies to be paid to you under this Agreement will not be assignable by you without Pacific's written consent, which Pacific may withhold in its unrestricted discretion, subject to the next sentence. You may assign monies to be paid to you under this Agreement, provided: (a) no more than one such assignment will be binding on Pacific at any time, and if Pacific is notified of more than one it will have the right to rely conclusively on priority of notice to it in according priority among them;

(b) each such assignment will be subordinate to Pacific's continuing right to apply all such monies due or becoming due

Any money we owe you cannot be paid to anyone without our written permission, which we don't have to give you if we don't want to. We've also set up the following roadblocks so that assigning your "royalties" or "Net Profits" to anyone else is even more difficult:

(a) You can assign your "royalties"/"Net Profits" to only one person. No one else is allowed to emerge from the woodwork with his hand out. If more than one creep does show up, only the first one will get paid;
[*In other words, if you owe someone money and you try to assign this contract as collateral, forget it!*]

(b) No matter who you assign your "royalties"/"Net Profits" to, we're not paying anybody anything until after we've recouped *everything* in recoupment of all Advances, loans and other offsets which may be recoupable from your royalties and/or Net Profits, including, but not limited to, those made under agreements entered into by Pacific and you after the date of the assignment concerned; and (c) no such assignment will be effective until it has been accepted in writing by Pacific. Pacific will not unreasonably withhold acceptance of any assignment which is consistent with this paragraph.

we invested in you and then some; and

(c) none of these creeps and leg-breakers gets a dime until we say so in writing. But we'll try to be reasonable about it [*especially while you're refinancing your house*].

REALITY: This is bad. Believe me, you want the right to assign this debt. At some time in the future you may be ready to retire from show business. You've got this voucher from the label saying that you're entitled to money, lots of it, and will receive it as soon as the label is out of bankruptcy hearings. If someone is willing to pay you for that IOU in hopes of collecting it later, you should have the right to sell it to them. But, with this clause, the label's debt dies along with you.

If you think this is something beyond your concern, talk to the families of Elvis Presley, Richie Valens, Marvin Gaye, Selena, Tupac, Biggie Smalls, and just about any other artist who died during the run of his or her career.

TILL DEATH DO US RECOUP—AND THEN SOME

In 1975, Henny Mason, a guitarist of some renown, passed away. Many believed his death was caused by an accidental drug overdose. During his short career he was a sensation on both sides of the Atlantic. When he died, lawyers for his illegitimate children presented Henny's label, Low Life Records, with a will, wherein it stated that Henny left all proceeds from his records and publishing to his two daughters, Julia and Page. Each was looking forward to a steady stream of income generated by the huge rise in record sales due to the publicity from Henny's death.

But alas, they got nothing. When Page and Julia's lawyers met with Low Life, they were shown Henny's recording agreement, which specifically stated that the label doesn't have to recognize any third parties until Henny's account is paid up.

The label calculated Henny's "royalties" in such a way that it was clear that many years would pass before either Page, Julia, or their lawyers saw a dime. And by the time they got a dime, it wouldn't be worth a nickel.

Faced with a contractual roadblock, the girls tried an interesting strategy. Instead of fighting the battle in the courthouse (where they were likely to lose), they invested in a massive PR campaign. They took out ads in *Billboard* and other trade magazines stating the situation.

In less than a month, Low Life settled with Henny's kids for a flat amount that was undisclosed, but rumored to be in the vicinity of $15 million. In exchange for this "Go Away" fee, the girls forfeited future rights to and money from their dad's work.

Henny's records still sell in excess of 500,000 units a year, and his songs are used frequently in movie soundtracks. His catalog is estimated to be worth well in excess of $450 million.

You recognize that the sale of Records is speculative and agree that the judgment of Pacific with respect to matters affecting the sale, distribution and exploitation of Records hereunder shall be binding upon ___ to the terms of this ___thing contained in ___nt shall obligate ___e, sell, license or ___cords manufactured ___aster Recordings ___eunder except as specified in this Agreement.

You knew getting into this business that nobody is really sure of anything. But you agree that, of the two of us, *we* know more. Therefore you must go along with whatever we decide in regard to "selling" your records.

And one more thing: nothing in this Agreement can force us to make, sell, or distribute your Album.

Miscellaneous. Yeah, *sure.*

Wrap-Up

Well, the label *could* make it easy and simply say, "We're only going to pay you about a buck a record." But then a lot of lawyers would be out of work. This way is more precise, don't you think?

Now that we understand what "sales" really means and what "royalty" really means, and what "Net Profits," really means, let's go to the next step: understanding what the label does in its attempt to "sell" your records, and why they make such a big deal out of "records returned."

> Is It Really Possible to "Sell" Records?

Now you might be thinking that all this stuff about Double-Dips and loopholes won't really apply to you because you plan to sell so many records. Well, maybe if it were up to you, that could be true. But when you sign a Thick, you are agreeing to let the label decide how to best sell your records. And as you are about to see, "selling" records is far harder than you could possibly imagine, because the entire concept of how records "sell" to stores is extremely confusing. Here, possibly for the first time in print, the reality of retail record "sales" is revealed. It revolves around a deal between a label's main distributor and one of its subdistributors, called a *One-Stop*.

Read on.

How Normal Brick-and-Mortar Retail Sales Allegedly Work

Example: Pacific has signed and is about to release their newcomer to the alternative rock world: our grunge gang of four, the Post Men Apostles. The Post Men's blend of post-neo-eclectic-trip-hop with a dash of Zydeco is all the rage on college campuses across the Midwest. So much so, in fact, that Pacific has pressed and committed to distributing over 500,000 of their records in the first run. Who will they sell them to?

Before we get the answer to that, let's first get a basic understanding of how things appear to be.

Big Music Chains

Pacific's most prestigious avenue of distribution is the one with big music retailers: Best Buy, Wal-Mart, K-Mart, Costco, etc.[39] Pacific sells these stores records at the highest published wholesale price of between $9.98 and $11.98. These stores will sell many artists' records for a penny above what they pay, in hopes of using the low, low CD price tag as bait to lure people in and sell them other items. These stores contractually agree to only buy Pacific records from Pacific's exclusive distributor (a Big Four) and not through some backdoor, fell-off-the-truck, five-finger-Eddie discount deal.[40]

Why would these stores lock themselves into paying top dollar and only buy from Big Four distributors? Because they get two things in exchange: 1) They get all the top releases first—those records riding the wave of multimillion-dollar publicity; and 2) they get to return records for a 100% refund after a specified amount of time (usually about four months).[41]

Apostle gets their full royalty for these sales because they are considered "Top Line Record sales."

One-Stops

What about small Mom & Pop record stores? A Goliath like Pacific doesn't deal directly with them. It's too nickel and dime. Instead they ship records to a subdistributor/middleman called a One-Stop, which services smaller record boutiques.

Why do the Mom & Pop stores need these One-Stop guys? Why don't they just buy from the majors and avoid extra fees? If you were going to open a record store of your own, you would have to contact many different entities: all the major label's distributors, blank tape supply companies (for your customers who like to make compilations), T-shirt companies, and many others. You would have no choice but to deal with many different distributors. Between research, billing, accounting, and inventory, a small shop owner could spend his or her entire existence doing all the paper and phone work. The One-Stop is hassle free. They satchel everything together, including records from all the major and indie labels, and ship them to your store. You only have to make "one stop" and pay one bill. You can order small quantities, and don't have to maintain a relationship with a big, impersonal, multinational conglomerate like Pacific, who will likely laugh at your petty inquiries. For this service the One-Stop charges a premium, like any broker.

[39] In the 2001 edition of this book, this sentence read, "Tower Records, Spec's, HMV, Sam Goody, Virgin." My, how things have changed.

[40] In theory. If you see a CD with a little hole cut in it at one of the big chains, you can be sure that the store manager has a liberal philosophy about where he gets his products. He's probably a good candidate for you to approach about stocking your self-distributed CD. These days there's a lot of controversy about labels "bullying" stores into selling records at high prices. The large chains hate this practice, as it reduces their competitive edge against the Mom & Pop stores.

[41] Records that ship back are called "Returns." See "Returns, Reserves, and Cutouts" in *Confessions.*

The One Stops, ironically, are more powerful than the big chains—even though you probably couldn't name one—because they collectively move over twice as many records. Majors don't want to alienate the One-Stops, lest they dirty their fingernails with the nitty-gritty of the record sales themselves. One-Stops buy most CDs from Big Fours for $9.98 and sell them to the Mom & Pops for $11.98, making a two-dollar rip. Like the chains, they get to return anything they don't sell for a *full refund*.

Can you imagine all the paperwork and banking involved in refunding money on the hundreds of thousands of records that are returned? Well, here there's almost none. Because big labels don't actually send the One-Stop or the Big Chain a check for their refund; it's done in the form of a *credit*. The label "pays" the One-Stop only in a computer, just like a debt that you might owe your brother. No actual money changes hands.

Let's say that a One-Stop is distributing the Post Men Apostles' new record. Now the tide turns, Clifton Chenier makes a comeback, he swallows up the Zydeco niche with a spicy Cajun single that races up the charts, and the Apostles soon sound *so yesterday* that they're a joke. Overnight they're forgotten. The Mom & Pops ship 100,000 Apostles records back to the One-Stop for a refund, and the One-Stop ships the 100,000 CDs back to Pacific. Pacific puts a note in their computer saying that the One-Stop is owed a credit on 100,000 records. The One-Stop will save this credit for the next hot new Lady Gaga release, which they can get without laying out *any additional cash*. Neat.

Rack Jobbers and Used Record Stores

Ever wonder how the record clubs and used record stores can sell records so cheaply when other stores are still "selling" them for full price? Allow me to explain.

Weeks after its release, when the big chains and the One-Stops return thousands of the Apostles' records, Pacific will try to sell them at any price to whomever is desperate enough to buy them. Enter the Rack Jobbers, always happy to lend a helping hand. These are the ones who scrape the bottom of the barrel and buy returns for about a dollar a unit. They sell these to "discount stores," where they rent floor space to display revolving racks of CDs, LPs, etc. (thus the name "Rack Jobber").[42] They also sell to recycling plants and to some record clubs (those "Buy One CD, Get 10 for $1" guys). Rack Jobbers are Pacific's last chance to make money on the Apostles' record.

[42] In the past, it appeared that Walmart itself was selling the music, but it was, in fact, only renting the floor space to the Rack Jobber. Today, "Big Box" (like Best Buy, Costco, etc) stores have started to recognize just how much profit there is in CDs, and several of them have done away with Rack Jobbers, using CDs as "loss-leader" items to lure in business themselves. This has caused quite an uproar, because they've destroyed big chains like Tower, Sam Goody and others.

However, unlike big chains and One-Stops, Rack Jobbers *cannot return their merchandise to the label.* If they don't sell it, they eat it. In the artist's contract these are called "Budget records," and the Apostles' "royalty" is close to zero. If the records are "sold" as scrap for under 65% of the published wholesale price to these Rack Jobbers, they are considered "cutout sales," and the artist is paid *zilch* because the label is "selling" the CD or tape at below the label's cost (or so they say). Reasonable?

Study the diagram below to get a feel for how the two-way flow of merchandise works:

Brick-and-Mortar Retail Sales Chain (How It Should Work)

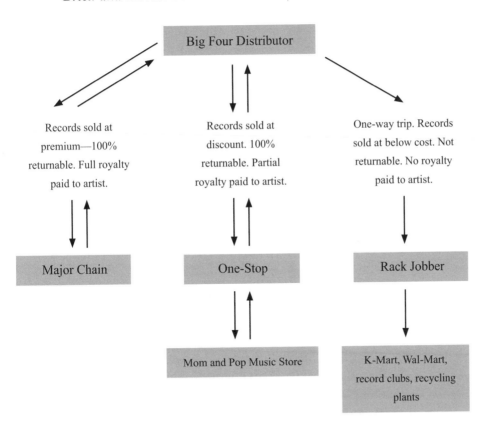

This illustration shows how CDs, tapes, and LPs flow from the main distributor to the various brick-and-mortar retail outlets. Notice that when sold to the rack jobber it's a one-way trip.

How Normal Brick-and-Mortar Retail Sales Really Work

Okay, so now that you understand the tooth-fairy version of this system, let's learn how it works in the *real* world:

The first thing you may have noticed is that the One-Stop only makes about $2 by "selling" the Apostles' CD through the Mom & Pop, but can get a full $9.98 credit toward any new release by returning it to the label. *Amazing*. There is a greater incentive to return records to Pacific than to try to sell them to the stores. If only they could somehow get a truckload of the Apostles' CDs from various other sources, they could exchange them for more credits toward Jay-Z.

This would be great work if you could get it: Return the "difficult" records and stockpile credits so you can cherry-pick the easy releases; something that the big chains can't even do.

Where can a One-Stop get large amounts of Apostles CDs that don't come from Pacific? How about from the Rack Jobbers? Study the diagram below while you read the next sequence to have your mind blown by this devil of commerce.

1. Weeks after the initial release, One-Stops and Big Chains return huge quantities of the Post Men Apostles' CDs to the label.

2. The label concludes that it's over for this band, discontinues their CD, and then sells the whole stock to a series of Rack Jobbers for $2 each, paying no royalty to the Apostles for these sales.[43]

   [43] For why an artist gets no money on these sales, see page 77.

3. The Rack Jobber can't return them to the label, but can sell them to someone else who can. They immediately flip the entire stock of Post Men Apostles CDs to a One-Stop for $4, realizing a $2 profit on each CD.

4. The One-Stop doesn't even bother trying to sell them to the Mom & Pops, because they know that Pacific is now accepting "returns" on the Apostles. They send the entire stock back to Pacific for a $9.98 credit on *each CD*, which they trade for an equal amount of a new, much-anticipated release. They've just paid $4 for a premium item worth about $10 wholesale.

It gets better.

Pacific, desperate to clear all the Apostles CDs out of their warehouse, once again sell a batch of them to another Rack Jobber for another $2 a CD, who in turn flips it to another One-Stop for $4, who returns it to Pacific for a $9.98 credit. During the three-week window common for most returns, this can go on and on if properly orchestrated, with the same records rotating through the system. Two or three times is not unheard of. This little dance is called "stock rotation."

Stock Rotation

Records keep revolving through the system, making money for everyone but the artist.

Why doesn't anybody put a stop to this? Don't the labels lose money "selling" CDs for below cost, and giving out credits to One-Stops? Not really. Look at the net result of the same CD passing three times through the system:

1. The three One-Stops collectively made almost $30 worth of credits for a $12 investment.

2. The Rack Jobbers collectively made $6 in profit for each unit (roughly $600,000 on 100,000 records).

[44] If you refer
to Egghead
Box #4 in the
Confessions
chapter "The
Major Label Deal
from the Label's
Point of View,"
you'll see that
stock rotation
is substantially
more profitable
than selling
records the
"traditional" way.
It should also
start to become
clear why labels
are insistent that
new artists write
all their own
material. They
don't want to
be stuck paying
mechanical
license fees to
other writers each
time the CD goes
through rotation.
See "Controlled
Compositions,"
page 154.

3. Pacific, by selling the same CD three times to a Rack Jobber, has realized a gross income of $6 per unit ($600,000 on 100,000 records) on a CD that supposedly "wouldn't sell." And they don't have to pay the artist or the writers anything.[44]

And there's a bonus for Pacific: the One-Stop basically paid $9.98 to Pacific for a product but, because they were waiting for a hot release to cash in their credit, didn't actually get the product until months later. So, in essence, they loaned Pacific money, which Pacific didn't mind.

The truly frustrating part of the above is that it is completely legal. No one is breaking the law, and culpability on the part of any single party is nearly impossible to assign, even with an audit (see "Auditing," page 254).

Record companies claim this only happens "occasionally." You be the judge. The good news is that things will likely change soon, but not due to any complaints by artists. In the past few years, stores like K-Mart and Best Buy have increased their record divisions and are now selling most of the physical product.

How do you beat this system today? Only sell downloads? That's one way, but impractical, as CDs still make up over 80% of most artists' sales. Another way is to start your own record label and distribute yourself. No big advances, no limousines, no frills. Okay, it's true that no single artist has "sold" over a million records by self-distribution, but at least you're the master of your own domain.

❯ Conclusions

It's all about "selling" records. But, as we can see from what we just read, doing so can be rather difficult. When your recording contract says that you will only be paid "on records sold," what that really means is any CD, tape, or platter (LP) that has managed to beat their "return" system and made it to a store without being part of a "Special Sales Program" (read: "discounted"). Or it could mean downloads, which bypass most of this craziness, but only make up about 10% of your sales.

So we've learned quite a bit today. We learned that a "sale" does not necessarily mean that you "sold" anything or are entitled to money. We've learned that a "Sliding Scale Royalty" can slide both ways. We learned that getting it to slide *up*—which is what Pacific held out in the memo—is only achievable if you "sell" enough units to reshingle the South Bronx or fill Google's hard drive.

We learned that a "royalty" is actually an equation that, at its heart, has a percentage, but whose anatomy is mostly made up of a complex and varied number of other deductions based on records "sold." And we learned that there is an annoying maze of math (which I call the "Meat Grinder") that ultimately reduces your Royalty to a "royalty" or your profit share to "Net Revenue," and is worth mere shekels. From this amount you will be expected to pay back hundreds of thousands of dollars that you owe the label. And if you don't pay it back, you don't get any more money, except whatever's left of your next Advance.

A FORMULA FOR SUCCESS

So what is a "royalty"? Is it the actual percentage of a "sale" price that you receive? Maybe. But it includes, as part of its matrix, all deductions, Double-Dips, and loopholes. To make it simple, here's the basic formula:

Royalty Base   **Royalty Rate**
(SRLP – deductions)   ×   (Royalty – deductions)   =   "royalty"

Well, if that's the way this works, then your Advance is starting to look far more important than it did a chapter ago. Holding onto as much of it as possible will become your primary goal. This being the case, let's look a bit closer at how you will be required to spend that Advance in the next chapter: "Master Quality and Delivery."

Turn the page.

CHAPTER 3

Master Quality and Delivery

or "How much do I gotta spend to make them happy?"

"To retain respect for sausages, one must not watch them in the making. This goes for records, too."

—Otto von Bismarck (slightly altered)

Master quality" is one of those ambiguous terms that sounds more majestic than it really is. What is master quality? An analysis of its semantics is covered to the degree of its importance (about two pages) in *Confessions*. I won't repeat myself here. Suffice it to say that "master quality" is whatever the label says it is. From a legal perspective, however, its importance to the artist is significant, because the label will have specific qualifications in the contract as to how you must spend your $250,000 Advance to produce these "Master Recordings." If you thought that you'd get to pocket that cash and deliver a homespun recording, forget it. If you don't watch how you negotiate your contract, you'll have to spend a major portion, if not the entire Advance, on recording costs. The clauses we're about to examine are designed to make sure you do.

Why This Clause Exists

If you look in the "Glossary of LabelSpeak," you'll see that the definition of "delivered" is "a commercially satisfactory master, or a finished recording, that the label decides is easy for them to 'sell.'" It's not what you think sounds cool.

Therefore, the label could dispense with all these clauses and simply say, "We (the label) do not have to accept anything you record if we don't like it. You shall continue to record music until we, in our sole discretion, decide that you've fulfilled the requirements of the contract, which is to create, for us exclusively, hit songs that we can easily exploit."

Well, that sounds a bit too brutal—no artist would sign that. So instead, the label uses many mind-numbing words to say the same thing. By the time you figure out what you're reading, you'll be too tired to argue about it.

"Master Quality" boils down to five issues, with a clause or two dealing with each:

1. Control of material

2. Control of budget

3. Control of the production (called "Administration")

4. The producer's role and responsibilities

5. Terms for "Delivery"

There are two important primers for decoding these clauses you should be familiar with: **"Option Period"** and **"Commitment Album."**

"Option Period" and "Period" – the initial period, or any Option Period, of the term hereof (as such Periods many be suspended or extended as provided herein). Something referred to herein as Option Period or Initial Period.

"Option Period" or "Period": an amount of time during which you are working exclusively for us making records. These amounts of time may be lengthened or shortened at our discretion. There are places in this contract where "Option Period" or "Initial Period" are used interchangeably with "Option Period."[1]

[1] See Chapter 10: Terms and Exclusivity, page 280, for more details on the length of the "Contract Periods."

Most Option Periods are generally about 10 to 14 months long, followed by a two- to four-month grace period, during which the label can decide if it wants to engage the artist for another "Option Period." In case you didn't guess, the "option" is the label's, not yours.

There will usually be one Album per Option Period, making it sound like five option periods is the same as a five-year contract with one Album per year. But as you'll soon see, there are many special circumstances that allow the company to extend or shorten the length of time, so that this phrase, "Option Period," becomes a red flag that really means "that amount of time the company wishes to keep the artist bound to the agreement."[2] Since "Option Period" sounds so standard and finite, the phrase is used liberally, without drawing attention to the fact that it really means any length of time.

The next term, "Commitment Album," is a little easier to understand. This definition can be found either in the DEFINITIONS section of the contract, or hidden in plain sight right up front in the clause called RECORDING COMMITMENT. I say "hidden," because the definition is intentionally worded so benignly that one can easily gloss over it without a care. No reference to it is made again anywhere in the DEFINITIONS section, which is where attorneys look for loopholes. Clever contract drafters strategically placed certain definitions where they could be overlooked during rushed negotiations.

[2] Chapter 10: Terms and Exclusivity, page 282, is dedicated to the exact meaning of "Option Period."

"Commitment Album" – Each Album required to be recorded and **Delivered** by you hereunder is herein sometimes referred to as "Commitment Album."

A "Commitment Album" is any collection of no less than 10 songs **that we approve of**, that you are required to create for us.

And now we put all this together into the clause called RECORDING COMMITMENT.

During each Option Period, you will perform for the recording of Master Recordings sufficient to constitute one (1) Album and cause those Master Recordings to be produced and **Deliver** them to Pacific (the "Recording Commitment"). Each Album required to be recorded and Delivered by you hereunder is herein sometimes referred to as a "Commitment Album."

About once every 10 to 14 months (the Option Period), you will spend however much time it takes to record enough material to constitute 8 to 10 songs **that we approve of** (one Album). (This is called the "Recording Commitment.") Sometimes it will show up in this contract as "Commitment Album." [*It also goes by the name "Minimum Recording Obligation" in some contracts.*]

You will fulfill the Recording Commitment for each Option Period within the first five (5) months of the Option Period.

You will make this Album within the first five months of each Option Period.

[3] All these are record company property. See page 124.

Each Commitment Album (or other group of Master Recordings) Delivered to Pacific will consist entirely of **Master Recordings** made in the course of the same Album (or other) recording project, unless Pacific consents otherwise. Pacific may withhold that consent in its unrestricted discretion.

And this Album (and any outtakes or improvised jams that you came up with, while in our studio[3]) will **consist entirely of your performances.** If you want to use your buddy to add anything, it can only be with our written permission.

And we don't have to give it to you, and we're not obligated to give you any explanation, either.

SNEAKY LAWYER LESSON #3

Translate the following bit of LabelSpeak:

"You will deliver 3 Albums within the Option Period."[4]

The answer is in the footnote.

[4] "You will record and finish, under our guidelines, three Albums of no less than 8–10 songs that we approve of. The period of time you are bound to us (Contract Period) will end when you finish all three Albums."

❯ The Standard
What You Have to Pay for—Exactly

You are required to pay for a host of things out of your Advance. The greatest expense of all will be your recording costs. But what constitutes a recording cost? If you order pizza for the band while laying down tracks, is that included? Your contract specifies the criteria regarding what the label considers to be bona-fide recording expenses in a section that starts with an introductory clause like the one below, taken from the subheading called RECORDING COSTS.

You shall be responsible for, and shall promptly pay when due and owing, all costs and expenses whatsoever in connection with Master Recordings hereunder, including, without limitation, all transportation, hotel and living expenses necessarily incurred by you and/or Artist and/or Producer in connection with such Master Recordings and for all costs of delivering to Pacific the fully edited Master Recordings and other items which you are required to so deliver hereunder ("Recording Costs").

Without limiting the generality of the foregoing, you shall be solely responsible for the payment of (i) any union scale payments (including, without limitation, fees or royalties) or any other payments required to be made to Producer and all Persons (excluding Pacific personnel) whose services are rendered in connection with the Master Recordings delivered hereunder; (ii) all expenses relating to cartage, instrument rental, concert hall rental, technical equipment and personnel, including, without limitation, all engineers for the purpose of recording, editing, mixing, remixing, mastering, re-mastering and re-recording the Master Recordings hereunder; (iii) all amounts payable pursuant to the

You have to shell out for *all* costs and expenses whatsoever involved in the making of your record, including transportation, hotel, and living expenses for you and your band and your Producer [*and their entourages*] as long as you're working on your record. You'll also be picking up the tab for all costs related to meeting our requirements for "delivery" (as outlined below). All of which we call "Recording Costs."

Interpret this next sentence in the way it could hurt you the most: You alone are responsible for paying (i) any money for doing sessions, and any "royalties" that might or will be owed to the Producer and anyone else [*your band, the orchestra you hired because sampled strings just wouldn't do, etc.*];

(ii) cartage, instrument rental, concert hall rental, technical equipment, all engineers for the purpose of recording, editing, mixing, remixing, mastering, re-mastering and re-recording the tunes you record under this contract;

(iii) all money that the unions require you pay to performers on the record

requirements of any applicable collective bargaining agreements based upon or calculated by reference to union scale payments; and

[union scale is about $125 per hour, as of this writing]; and

(iv) all advances or fees payable to any Producer or any other third party (including, without limitation, advances or fees payable to third parties for **"sample" clearances**); costs for immigration clearances, trademark and service mark searches and clearances; and all travel and living expenses (including per diem), if any, required for recording session participants.

(iv) whatever money [*or services*] your Producer demands to keep him or her happy. You also have to pay fees to the owners of all those samples we heard in your demos. These are called **"sample" clearances.**

If someone in your group is from another country, *you* have to pay to cover their immigration expenses. You also pay for the cost of making sure that the cool logo on your posters is actually owned by you and not some other local band. You also have to pay the out-of-pocket, day-to-day walking-around money for any out-of-towners that come to work on your record.

You agree that all costs, charges and expenses referred to in this Paragraph will be paid for by you when they are due. If, however, Pacific pays any such costs for which you are responsible, then, without limiting Pacific's rights you will indemnify Pacific, as outlined below, and Pacific shall apply and Pacific shall have the **Offset Right** (as hereinafter defined).

You must pay everything above *immediately* when the costs are incurred. But if you're a bit light [*seeing as how you've probably been using all the shekels you saved from your day job to do foolish things like buy musical instruments and things like that*], we'll front you the cash. If we do, however, don't think it means that you are off the hook—we still have the right to apply a little thing we call the **Offset Right,** defined in the contract, which simply means we can take money for sample clearances out of your "royalties."

What's an "Offset Right"?

Buried deep in the back of the contract, under the DEFINITIONS subheading, (which is where many loopholes live), we find the following:

"Offset Right" means Pacific's right, with respect to certain monies to which the Offset Right applies hereunder, to demand reimbursement from you of such monies (and you shall immediately make such reimbursement) and/or the right to charge such monies against and/or deduct same from any sums accruing or becoming payable hereunder. **In the event that any such deduction is effected against an advance otherwise payable hereunder, such deduction shall not impair Pacific's right to charge and recoup, in the manner herein provided, the entirety of the advance which would otherwise have been payable hereunder.**

"Offset Right" is our right to demand that you pay us back any money we shelled out for you, or we'll deduct it from any money you make off this contract.

If we choose to take that money out of your Advance, you will still owe us the entire Advance amount that we should have paid you but didn't.

⑬

DOUBLE-DIP DETECTOR

EXPLANATION: This last bit is insane. You are being asked to pay back money you never received—twice. And even if they take that money from your Advance, you still owe them the full amount of what your Advance would have been. Look at the table of Advances on page 23, and you'll see that this could get expensive.

As mentioned in the Introduction, these are the worst clauses I could find, so hopefully you won't see versions as bad as these in your contract. But always look carefully. The previous one came from a BMG (now Sony) contract.

REALITY: Everywhere else in this contract it says that if you go over budget and the label pays the difference, they will recoup that money *only* from your "royalties." But the definition of "Offset Right" says that it can come out of *any fund* (including the money you earn as a songwriter—which is supposed to be a separate fund). These are the seeds of Cross-Collateralization.[5] The math here is simple: Let's say that the budget for both Albums 1 and 2 is $250,000 each. If you went over budget by $50,000 on your first Album, then you're only getting $200,000 for your next Album instead of $250,000. But you still have to pay back the *full amount* of the Advance for Album #2. The label has paid out a total of $500,000, but you owe $550,000. A nasty Double-Dip.

[5] Cross-Collateralization: See *Confessions* for a complete explanation.

NEGOTIATE

Some contracts call it something else, but in most recording agreements there is some covert technique, functioning as an Offset Right, to deduct money from *all* earnings rather than deducting it only from your "royalties." You must do a search and destroy on this. At the very least, you should have that money taken from only one place (preferably "royalties"), and let your mechanical royalties remain cherry. (I will be referring to this "Offset Right" in other places, so become familiar with it. It's a major *mudda fugger*.) In 360 Deals this is moot, because the entire contract is basically an "Offset Right," since you only make money on "Net Profits," which already has all these deductions as part of its definition (see page 83).

Another clause to have inserted is something that limits how the label applies this deduction. For example, disallow things like costs incurred with respect to remixes and/or re-mastering after you "deliver" the record. Most labels will agree to this.

More good news is that in many major-label contracts the Offset Right is used less liberally than their bulldog language would suggest.[6] But in smaller One-Deep and Two-Deep "Indie" deals, they go to town on this sort of thing. Most contracts don't spend much page space on it. However, most major-label contracts will break up the above clause into smaller, more anal clauses that get into serious detail. The strategy is to lull the lazy attorney into thinking this is more repetitive crap. In fact, a few land mines have been inserted here just for *you* to trip over. Continue ...

[6] But you will have to catch them in the auditing stage. Then they will give in on the point.

Control of Material and Sessions

Step One in clipping the artist's wings is making sure that you "deliver" something that sounds approximately close to the demo that inspired them to sign you in the first place. Here's how that will be approached. These clauses can be found in the subsection called RECORDING PROCEDURE.

1. You will follow the procedure set forth below in connection with Master Recordings made hereunder:

1. You will do the following when recording for us:

Except as expressly noted otherwise in this Agreement, prior to the commencement of recording in each instance, you and Pacific shall mutually approve each of the following; provided, however, in the event you and Pacific shall not be able to reach an agreement, Pacific's decision shall be final, except where otherwise noted herein:

Unless it says so elsewhere in the contract, before you begin to record anything, we have to get a few things straight. If, however, you disagree with anything specified below, we have the final say. Cool?

i.) As and when required by Pacific, you shall allow Pacific's representatives to attend any or all recording sessions hereunder at Pacific's expense. (Those expenses will not be recoupable as Recording Costs.)

i.) Whenever we say so, one of our people [*probably an A&R person*] will be stopping by the studio [*unannounced*] to see how you're doing and make sure you're complying with everything in your contract. It might only be one session, but it could be all of them.[7]

A) **Selection of Producer.**
_____ is pre-approved as producer on a maximum of four (4) tracks delivered in connection with the first Commitment Album.

A.) It is strongly recommended [*and you don't want to disappoint anyone*] that you use _____ as your producer for at least four songs on the first record. We like him, and he's never let us down.

[7] Note: Even though I put this clause right up front, it's usually buried in "Recording Procedure" or "Miscellaneous," and sandwiched between two completely irrelevant clauses.

B) **Selection of material,** including the number of Compositions to be recorded, provided that in the event that you and Pacific cannot agree, Pacific shall have final say with respect to two (2) Controlled Compositions demoed by the Artist and Delivered to Pacific. You will advise Pacific of the content of each medley before it is recorded. Unless Artist is solely an instrumentalist, no Master Recording made hereunder shall embody solely an instrumental Performance. Pacific will have the right to disapprove and reject any material which in Pacific's reasonable, good faith opinion is patently offensive, constitutes an obscenity, violates any law, infringes or violates the rights of any Person, or which might subject Pacific to liability or unfavorable regulatory action. You shall not record a Multiple Record Set without Pacific's consent, which may be withheld for any reason.

C) **Selection of dates** of recording and studios where recording is to take place, including the cost of recording at such studios. You shall not begin recording any Commitment Album within five (5) months after the **Delivery** of the prior Commitment Album. Pacific may disapprove a studio if it is not a first-class recording studio, if its

B) You will record at least two songs that were on your demo. We get to pick which ones, with *no argument* from you. As for the rest of the material…

You will tell us exactly what's in each song before you record it. No Recording will be an instrumental. [*Unless, of course, you're a strictly instrumental artist, like Kenny G. or something.*] We can and will reject any material that we think is offensive, obscene, or brings any whacko political groups out of the woodwork.

You are not allowed to make any double Albums unless we say so. And we probably won't.

C) You can't begin your second Album until five months after **we've decided the first one is ready for the street and easy to sell.** We may disapprove of any recording studio if it doesn't have a lot of fancy equipment [*most of which you won't use*], or if they don't pay to have their garbage picked up by the right people, or if we think that use would require expenditures inconsistent with the approved recording budget, and not any other reason. The scheduling and booking of all studio time will be done by Pacific, in accordance with your requests and the approved recording budget.

D) **Each Master Recording hereunder shall be subject to the approval of Pacific, and Artist and Producer shall, if necessary (and Pacific, at its election, may), re-record material** in order to obtain a Master Recording technically and commercially satisfactory to Master Recordings delivered in connection with LPs subsequent to the First LP. These shall be deemed commercially satisfactory if of a quality, concept and style (allowing for the natural progression of Artist's musical direction) reasonably consistent with that of Master Recordings previously delivered to and accepted by Pacific hereunder.

E) Nothing in this Agreement shall obligate Pacific to continue or permit the continuation of any recording session or project, even if previously approved hereunder, if Pacific reasonably anticipates that the Recording Costs will exceed those specified in the approved budget or that the Recordings being

they're just too damn expensive. That's all; no other reasons.

We'll book all your recording sessions for you, and we'll do so according to the budget we approved.

D) **We get to approve or reject every recording you make. If we don't like something and want it redone, you and/or your producer will re-record it till we decide it's good enough.** We call this a "commercially satisfactory master."
Any recordings you make for this Album will be considered commercially acceptable by us only if the quality, concept and style (allowing for a natural evolution of your chops[8]) is close enough to that of your last Album which we released. [*In other words, we want you to grow as an artist, but not too much so soon that we can't figure out how to sell your new record.*]

E) Nothing in this contract can force us to fund a loser. If your recording sessions are going badly, if production expenses have become a runaway train, or if your record simply sounds like *shit*, we're gonna pull that old proverbial plug.

[8] Chops: Slang for technique for playing a musical instrument.

produced will not be technically and
commercially satisfactory to Pacific
for the production, manufacture and
sale of Phonograph Records.

REALITY: Well, this is a much different tune than the one the A&R guy was blowing in your face backstage at your gig before you signed with the label. "Yo," he said, "we want to give you *everything* you need to complete your vision. We're a hands-off label, *yo*. And we think you're *phat*." Now it seems like you can't even go to the bathroom unless Pacific okays the toilet, the toilet paper, and the lock on the door. Believe it or not, this is *standard*.

Budget Control

Step Two in the label's process of taking control of your life is based on the epitome of stereotypical American corporate thinking: *More expensive means better*. Here the label actually says that they will not approve your budget unless you agree to spend almost all the money they give you.

2. A proposed budget (which you will submit to Pacific sufficiently in advance of the planned commencement of recording to give Pacific a reasonable time to review and approve or disapprove it at least fourteen (14) days before the planned commencement of recording). A recording budget (inclusive of Producer advance and/or fees) for any Commitment Album which does not exceed ninety percent (90%) of the amount of the **applicable Recording Fund** described herein will not be disapproved by reason of its overall amount.

2. You have to submit a budget at least two weeks before you start recording [*so that the label can check it out and make sure you're not screwing them with kickbacks to your friends, or to people who work for them*].

We'll only approve this recording budget (which must include the Producer's advance and/or fees) if it's not more than 90% of **whatever amount of money we think your next advance should be.**
[*This refers to the range of money in the table on page 23 in "Advances," which is reprinted below for convenience.*]

	Lowest amount of money you could get	Highest amount of money you could get
Current LP	**Floor Amount**	**Ceiling Amount**
First LP	$250,000	$500,000
Second LP	$250,000	$500,000
Third LP	$300,000	$600,000
Fourth LP	$325,000	$650,000
Fifth LP	$350,000	$700,000
Sixth LP	$375,000	$750,000
Seventh LP	$400,000	$800,000

Typical advances for the first through seventh Album on most major labels.

REALITY: If you were hoping that you could put some of the Advance money for your next recording budget in your pocket, this clause will put a stop to that.

Look closely at the table above. In the paragraph you just read you agreed to submit a budget that will not be more than 90% of the "applicable recording fund." But they never define how much that "applicable recording fund" actually is, nor do they ever specify if that 90% is based on the Floor or Ceiling amount. If you recall back in the chapter on Advances, you agreed that your next advance would be equal to two-thirds of the royalties you have accrued up to this point (see page 22). But as you'll see in the chapter on auditing, **you're not allowed to see the label's records without starting an audit. You must, at this point in your deal, trust that they're telling you the truth about the actual amount of royalties you've accrued.** Therefore, your 90% is based on a dollar figure that is *completely* generated from data you don't have access to. And how come if this is a "recording fund," your budget is only 90% of it? What happens to the other 10% of your recording fund? Here's one theory:

Clever lawyers usually assume that the amount of money applied will be the Floor Amount (or "Minimum Amount"), because the conventional wisdom is that companies like to spend as little money as possible on their product. But this is not necessarily so in Major Label Land. I have known of several situations in which an A&R person tells an artist to submit an inflated budget with the intention that once the artist gets their funds, they would pay the A&R person money under the table.

[9] Many labels have all their artists collateralized into a single Advance from the parent company that is financing the One-Deep or Two-Deep label. Under this structure, no artist gets "royalties" until the label, as a whole, turns a profit. See page 350 for more on this, or the *Confessions* chapter "Super-Duper Cross-Collateralization."

[10] See "Kickbacks" in *Confessions*.

[11] Card Rate: A term used to define the highest amount of money that a studio advertises for their hourly rate. It's usually only charged to outside clients on high-budget projects. Pop acts typically pay about half the "card rate," so for a label to charge you full rate does not coincide with the "you're in our family now" philosophy they've been touting up till now.

Many new artists are so hungry for the deal that they agree to do this. They figure they're only stealing out of their own pocket, so there's no victim. Wrong. There are plenty of victims. Every other artist on the label pays for this graft.[9] This is a conspiracy that goes far beyond stealing pencils from the supply closet. This is how, in my experience, certain unethical A&R people have turned artists into thieves. It's appalling.[10] And even if there is no covert kickback, the label might own their own studio facilities and charge you the full card rate[11] for their use.

However, in a less paranoid world, one could just attribute this to the same kind of corporate waste that goes on in all businesses. Large corporations feel secure when they're spending money on "the best." Of the three scenarios above, this is the more common.

NEGOTIATE

Try to have this clause thrown out completely. The label already has enough control over your songs, how they're recorded, who records them, etc. There is no need for them to put a restriction on how much you have to spend. In my experience labels will toss this clause if the artist agrees not to record the Album in his basement or his cousin's recording studio, where he's getting a kickback.

If you can't get it thrown out, then have a clause inserted that specifies that the 90% figure be based on the minimum number *only* and that if they insist that you record in a studio owned by them, that you be charged the minimum hourly rate.

Producer Stuff

To further ensure that more money than necessary gets spent (or that the kickback is designed with a middleman to deflect suspicion), the label will now dictate that you hire a producer who will shepherd you through the recording process.

Once upon a time this made sense. Recording was an enigmatic process that you could only experience in an expensive studio. Those days are long gone. Now just about everyone can afford more sophisticated equipment in their home studios than the Beatles had when they recorded *Abbey Road*. I have yet to meet a competent recording artist that didn't understand what an overdub was, or how reverb enhances a performance.

These days there are essentially two camps of producers. There are those who do everything for the artist—they make all the musical decisions, and basically run the show. The other kind are producers who are little more than consultants, giving advice from a distance as the artist makes her own decisions and runs her own sessions. Both kinds, taken to an extreme, can be a source of real frustration for artists, as the producer becomes little more than a puppet of the record company.

This clause, sometimes called YOUR RELATIONSHIP WITH PRODUCER, outlines how this works:

You warrant and represent that:

a) You shall enter into a binding contract with each Producer prior to delivery of the applicable Master Recording hereunder (collectively the "Contracts") which shall grant to you all rights necessary for you to fulfill all of your obligations hereunder which relate directly or indirectly to Producer. If you do not enforce any of your rights under the Contracts, Pacific may, without limitation of Pacific's rights, enforce such rights in your name and/or the name of Pacific. If you should breach any of the Contracts, then Pacific may, without limitation of Pacific's rights, cure such breach on your behalf and at your expense. No modification of or amendment to the Contracts will be made which would directly or indirectly diminish any of Pacific's rights hereunder. **You shall be responsible for prompt payment of any payments which are payable to Producer** as a result of the services performed by Artist and Producer in connection with this agreement.

You swear that:

a) You'll sign a legal contract with a Producer before you "deliver" the Masters to us. In this agreement the producer must agree to grant you all his rights to the recordings (such as if he was one of the musicians, singers, or co-writers who worked on the record[12]), so that you can transfer the rights to us.

If you do not enforce that contract, we can take it upon ourselves to sue the bastard in your name or the name of Pacific. If you breach the contract with the producer (if you don't pay him his "royalty" or any money you owe him) and the producer sues you or us, then we may solve the problem on your behalf by paying him whatever we settle on, and charging it back to you. And nobody is allowed to say otherwise and we're not changing a word of this agreement to satisfy his needs. If your producer doesn't like our terms, get a new one. **You and you alone are responsible for prompt payment of any money owed him for his work.**

[12] **Producer's rights:** The producer is technically and legally an author of the record. Obviously this right must be transferred to the label so that the label is free to exploit the records. For a deeper understanding of this producer as author thing, see the *Confessions* chapter "The Major Label Deal from the Producer's Point of View."

(13)

b) You will, upon Pacific's request, furnish Pacific with a complete copy of Producer's Contract and any modification of the Contracts.

c) Each Contract shall contain a provision (the "Flow-Through Clause") as follows: Upon the occurrence of any Default Event, **Producer shall perform directly for Pacific** each obligation herein described as your obligation insofar as the same relates to him or requires any action, forbearance, cooperation, warranty or representation by Producer.

b) You have to make sure we get a copy of the producer's contract...

c)...and it has to contain a clause that allows us to contract him directly [*in case we like his work and you try to fire him*]. We call this a "Flow-Through Clause," which works like this: As soon as we learn that there's some problem between you two, we can execute this clause, and **engage the producer *directly* to finish the Albu**m with or without your consent.

REALITY: So the label can request that you hire a producer, but in reality, it's more than a request, it's a *requirement*. And furthermore, you can't fire him, even if he starts screwing up your record. It's obvious who this guy works for, regardless of the fact that *you* are responsible for paying him. This has always been the way it is. Producers are paid for by the artist, but they are there to protect the record company's interests. Period. That doesn't mean a producer is a waste of money. Many a producer has saved a lousy album. But just as many have screwed one up.

NEGOTIATE

Forget it. It's not a battle worth fighting. Just make sure that the label gives you a list that includes five to 10 "approved" producers, instead of insisting on one and only one person.

What the Hell Does "Delivered" Really Mean?

We've seen the word used about 50 times in the past few chapters. Now let's look at it close up.

(a) You shall cause Producer to perform all services customarily rendered by producers in the record industry, including, without limitation, (i) timely furnishing Pacific with complete written Musicians Contracts (AFM Form B-4), W-4 forms and AFTRA Reports for recording sessions,

(ii) timely submitting to Pacific in writing complete label copy, liner notes and credits (including complete and accurate writer and publisher credits), sequence and final timings, and all consents or clearances required by Pacific in relation to the use of the Master Recordings hereunder (including, without limitation, mechanical licenses in a form acceptable to Pacific (attached hereto as Schedule "B") with respect to non-Controlled Compositions and "sample" clearances), and (iii) securing and timely delivering to Pacific necessary immigration clearances for all persons performing services in connection with Master Recordings hereunder, including without limitation, INS Form I.

(a) You are responsible for making sure that your Producer performs all services one would expect from a producer in the record industry, including (i) getting us all the contracts, W-4 forms and all that report-shit-AFTRA-union nonsense for the recording sessions that we need [*as if you're supposed to take notes and keep reports when you're trying to record your music*].

(ii) giving us, on time, a complete list of credits for the liner notes (including a complete list of all writers and their publishers), the order of the songs and the length of each one, and all contracts permitting us to release the record (including licenses for all the cover songs you didn't write and any clearances for "samples" that you may have used),

and (iii) giving us the necessary immigration clearances for anyone performing on the record who is not a US citizen.

9. **Without limiting the generality of the foregoing**, Producer shall, within two (2) weeks prior to mastering of the applicable Master Recordings hereunder, deliver to Pacific the names and addresses of the publishers of such non-Controlled Compositions.

(b) You shall deliver to Pacific two (2) reference master files of the master two-track. Written approval of master file shall constitute its approval. Following such approval, Producer shall prepare and you shall deliver to Pacific the master files and two (2) equalized copies thereof, and the "instrumental version" and "TV track" of the master two-track accompanied by the appropriate digital tracking information.

All work parts (including, without limitation, any out-takes or tracks recorded during the same session as the recording of tracks contained in Master Recordings delivered hereunder) shall be subject to all restrictions outlined herein[13] below and shall, at Pacific's election, either (i) be delivered to Pacific or (ii) be retained in the studio under Pacific's control.

9. Within two weeks of mastering this Album, your Producer has to give us the names and addresses of the publishers of every sample and cover tune used on the Album. **We really mean every single one.**

(b) When doing your final mixes, make sure you mix and deliver instrumental versions of everything (your tracks mixed without vocals) onto a master file. You must also give us a master file of the full final mix for our approval. If we give you our go-ahead, the Producer will supervise the final mastering of the recordings, and you will give us a two-track master and two mastered copies, and all the track sheet info must be included.

You will also give us the files of any bits and pieces left over from your sessions, such as outtakes, spontaneous jams, or other performances that occurred during the making of this record. These will all be exclusively owned by us as outlined below.[14]

If we decide, all this stuff will either… (i) be brought to our office or (ii) be kept in the recording studio under our account and control.

[13] See Chapter 6: Merchandising and Rights in Recording, page 195, for complete details.

[14] See Chapter 6: Merchandising and Rights in Recording, page 195, for details on what this is.

If Pacific so requests, you shall at your expense have prepared and you shall deliver to Pacific a safety copy of the master files. You shall also deliver to Pacific as part of your delivery obligations hereunder, a track-by-track list ("Personnel List") of all featured vocal performers, background vocal performers, and instrumental performers on each Master Recording, identifying their performances.

If we instruct you to make copies of everything (as a safety) and then give them to us, you must do so at your own expense. Along with that, make sure that you include a track-by-track list ("Personnel List") of all featured vocal performers, background vocal performers, and instrumental performers on each song, identifying who played each part on every track.

Without all those things, your Album is not considered, by this contract, "Delivered."

(c) (i) You shall, and shall cause Producer to, follow Pacific's procedure as described below, with respect to samples embodied in any Master Recording delivered hereunder. You shall cause Producer to warrant and represent that all information supplied by you and Producer to Pacific in that regard shall be complete and correct.

(c) (i) There is a list directly below that the Producer must follow regarding samples. It's up to you to make sure he does. If he doesn't, it's your ass.

In your contract with the Producer, you have to make sure that he's certain all information supplied by both of you to us is complete and accurate.

(ii) As part of Producer's delivery obligations, and **prior to Pacific's acceptance of Master Recordings hereunder** as completely and satisfactorily delivered, Producer shall deliver the following:

ii) Here's the list:
Nothing is considered "delivered" until we get the following:

(A) One (1) fully mixed (but not mastered) copy of each Master Recording embodying samples, together with each sample, recorded separately;

(A) One (1) fully mixed (but not mastered) copy of each song that has a sample in it, together with a separate recording of the sample itself,

(B) A detailed list of any and all samples embodied in each Master Recording;

(B) A detailed list of any and all samples you buried in each mix,

(C) A written clearance or license for the perpetual, unrestricted use of each such sample in any and all media from the copyright holder(s) of the master recording and the musical composition sampled; and

(C) A written letter saying that you have the right to use each sample and distribute it everywhere in the known universe,

(D) Any and all necessary information pertaining to credit copy required by the copyright holder(s) of each sample embodied in each Master Recording.

(D) The names of all writers and performers on the sample so that we can include them in the liner notes.

REALITY: Now you can't ever say, "I didn't know that sample was in there, the *producer* was supposed to take care of it." Record companies have been burned with this excuse before. This plugs that leak and makes it abundantly clear that you, the artist, are responsible, even if, one night while you were crashing on the couch, the producer tinkered with the mix, got creative, and slipped a sample in there, figuring no one would ever know where it came from, so it's cool.

It ain't cool. Someone *will* catch it and then you are in a world of shit. But this clause protects their relationship with a hit producer—a precious commodity— and makes you the fall guy.

NEGOTIATE

Of all the things above, the only one worth fighting over is the recurring theme of the label owning all your outtakes and inspirational ideas that came up in recording. They should have the right to hear them and decide if they want them on the Album, but if they plan to shelve those recordings, the artist should retain the rights.

And what about the reverse? What if the label decides to release the outtakes on a separate record without your permission? Unless there is a specific clause that says otherwise, they can do that. I recommend inserting a sentence that prohibits the release of any outtakes without your prior written approval. This should not be hard to get.

The other thing they slipped in there while you were dozing off is the part about copies of all the recordings being made at *your* expense. This is overreaching. Have it thrown out, if possible. If the label wants copies, let them pay for it.

Administration and Union Junk

"Administration" is yet another function the label insists that the artist fulfill, forcing you to be a secretary, a labor attorney, and an accountant. The artist will usually hire someone else to take care of these things, or have the producer do it. Either way, unless you accomplish all of the following requirements, your "Master Recording" can't be considered "delivered."

You shall notify the appropriate Local of the American Federation of Musicians in advance of each recording session.

It's your responsibility to make sure the musicians' union (the American Federation of Musicians) knows about each recording session in advance.

i) In connection with the requirement of the U.S. Immigration Law, you shall not engage or permit the engagement of any Person to perform services with respect to any Master Recording unless and until you have caused such Person to properly complete an INS Form I-9, you have executed, completed and signed the employer verification section thereof, you have attached copies of documents verifying employment eligibility,

i) According to US Immigration Law, you can't use anyone on the record who is not a citizen and who has not filled out INS Form I-9. Since you are technically considered their employer, you'd better make sure that you're not breaking the law. You can be sure *we* won't be responsible for what happens if any laws are broken.[15] You have to personally sign each form for each of your employees and get those to us within 72 hours after each recording session.

[15] See "Indemnification," page 263.

and you have delivered same to Pacific with respect to each such Person within seventy-two (72) hours after the applicable Person first renders services with respect to Master Recordings hereunder. You will comply with any revised or alternative employment verification procedure of which Pacific advises you in the future.

If we have any of our own employment paperwork, you will fill that out as well.

You shall timely supply Pacific with all of the information it needs in order: (1) to make payments due in connection with such Recordings; (2) to comply with any other obligations Pacific may have in connection with the making of such Master Recordings; and (3) to prepare to release Phonograph Records derived from such Master Recordings.

Whenever we ask, you will give us everything we need: (1) to make sure all your employees get paid;

(2) to get us off the hook with any government agency; and

(3) so that we can release your masterpiece to the public without the INS or anyone else shutting us down.

Without limiting the generality of section (2) of the preceding sentence:

Consider every way that Section 2 of the last sentence could screw you and then consider this:

1) You shall furnish Pacific with all information it requires to comply with its obligations under its union agreements, including, without limitation, the following:

1) You must give us all information we require to get the union off our back, including the following:

i) If a session is held to record new tracks intended to be mixed with existing tracks (and if such information is requested by the American Federation of Musicians), the dates and places of the prior sessions at which such existing tracks were made, and the AFM Phonograph Recording Contract (Form "B") number(s) covering such sessions;

ii) Each change of title of any Composition listed in an AFM Phonograph Recording Contract (From "B"); and

iii) A listing of all the musical selections contained in Recordings Delivered to Pacific hereunder; and

2) You will deliver to Pacific all AFM or AFTRA session reports, tax withholding forms, and other documentation required by Pacific within seventy-two (72) hours after each recording session hereunder so that Pacific may timely make all required union payments to the session musicians and other employees concerned, if any.

3) You hereby warrant and represent that, if Artist's and/or Producer's services come

i) If new takes are to be tracked and mixed with older takes (and if the union requests it), you must supply us with a list of all dates and places of the original tracks, as well as Form "B" from the AFM (American Federation of Musicians) that goes with that session;

ii) If you've changed the title of any songs, you must also list those changes in the Form "B" mentioned above; and

iii) A complete list of every song you record for us; and

2) You will give us all AFM or AFTRA (union) session reports, tax withholding forms, and other documentation within 72 hours after each recording session. This is so that we may comply with our obligations to the union and pay your band members (or group members, soloists, background singers, side players, etc.) right away.

3) You hereby swear on Notorious B.I.G.'s grave that if your own work, or that of your producer, your

within the scope of any agreement between any union and Pacific, you shall cause Artist and/or Producer (if Artist and/or Producer are not already a member of any such union) to join such union within thirty (30) days after Artist and/or Producer first render services hereunder that are subject to such agreement(s). You further warrant and represent that Artist and/or Producer shall remain a member in good standing of such union so long as Artist's and/or Producer's services hereunder are within the scope of such agreement.

musicians, or band members falls under the jurisdiction of the AFM, you must insist that they all join the union within 30 days from when they performed on the record. [*How you're supposed to do that is left to your imagination.*]

You also guarantee to us that these people will remain in the union [*and continue to pay due*s] as long as you are under contract and intend to use them on your recordings.

[16] In *Confessions*, I outline the exact costs of a typical major-label recording budget, and the union scale wages required. See "The All-In Deal."

[17] Singers are included in the category of "musicians" according to the AFM. They usually get paid double the amount of other musicians hired on the same job.

[18] On most professional records, the singer works for an average of three hours per track.

[19] Fly in: A recording term that means recording one take on a track, sampling it, and then inserting that same take in other places. Most commonly done with background vocals. It's a big time-saver.

REALITY: If you thought you were going to save money by using your friends (who aren't professional musicians but who would fall all over themselves to play on your big label record), forget it. Each of your friends will be required to join the union. "Pressured" is actually a better word.[16] The union scale you'll have to pay them for the hours they spend trying to get their parts right will add up to thousands of dollars. You can use your friends, but do the math. Make sure they're really worth it.

How you are supposed to force your friends to join the union and pay dues is not mentioned. Nor is a non-payment penalty mentioned, though it does exist. It's presumed that if the union shakes down the label for dues, the label will pay them and charge that cash back to you.

The label (and your lawyer) will likely say that this is a good clause because it assures that you will be paid about $100 an hour for your work on the recording.[17] Your lawyer or manager will say that, since your Advance is low, you should welcome this. But he doesn't have to help you pay your bills. It's important to realize that most bread-and-butter work taken by the average musician are not union jobs. Plus, you don't really get $100 for each hour you spend in the waiting room of the studio, only for the time you are actually performing.[18] (This will add up to far less money than you think, especially in regard to things like background vocals, which are almost always performed once and then sampled and "flown in."[19]) It's a lousy trade-off.

The good news is you won't see this language in an indie contract, since indies don't have strong ties to unions. But since all the majors are in bed with the unions, there is little you can do about this clause, except to take some solace in the fact that it's rarely enforced. More good news is that the union is so relaxed that they probably won't know if you do a non-union gig on the side. But I cannot endorse this in print, as it is illegal to be a union member and accept "scab"[20] work in the US.[21]

[20] Scab: When a union person performs for a non-union gig.

[21] "Right to Work" states are the exception here. There are currently 22 states with this provision. Florida is the biggest.

Sample Clearances

The clauses below are assembled from several sections, sometimes called: RECORDING PRODUCER OBLIGATIONS, LICENSES FOR MUSICAL COMPOSITIONS, CONTROLLED COMPOSITION, and RECORDING PROCEDURE. They are written with the intent that the person reading this is either the artist, or a producer with any artist signed to his production company. Generally this is done because the producer knows more about what's really in the recording than the artist. This first one comes from the subheading RECORDING PROCEDURE.

You shall comply with Pacific's policies with respect to samples, and you and Artist hereby warrant and represent that all information supplied by you or the Artist to Pacific in that regard is and shall be complete and correct. As of the date hereof, Pacific's policies with respect to all samples embodied in any Master Recording (including remixes of Master Recordings, regardless of whether such remixes will be commercially released) are as follows: Prior to Pacific's authorization of pre-mastering (e.g., equalization and the making of reference dubs or the

We have a few rules about samples that we think you should know. First you must guarantee to us that you'll keep a perfect record of all samples that you use in the recordings, and give it to us when the record is done.

As of today, Pacific's "Sample policy" [*which includes remixes, whether we release them or not*] is as follows: Just before you finish each record, you have to give us the following:

equivalent thereof in the applicable configurations) for a particular set of Master Recordings hereunder, you shall deliver the following to Pacific for the applicable set of Master Recordings:

1) A detailed list of any and all samples embodied in each Master Recording;	1) A complete list of any and all samples mixed into each track;
2) A written clearance or license for the perpetual, non-restrictive use of each such sample interpolated in each Master Recording in any and all media from the copyright holder(s) of the Master Recording and the Composition sampled;	2) Proof that you have received worldwide permission for the ongoing use of the sample from the copyright owners of the Master Recordings that you sampled, and from the copyright owner of the song that is sampled (which may or may not be the same person);
3) Any and all necessary information pertaining to credit copy required by the copyright holder(s) of each sample interpolated in each Master Recording.	3) Any and all credit information for the liner notes of your record.
4) No Master Recording will be scheduled for release and no Master Recording shall be deemed to be Delivered to Pacific hereunder (and no Advances due on Delivery, if any, will be paid) until such written sample clearances (including credit copy, if any) have been obtained and approved by Pacific.	4) No recordings will be considered "delivered" until we get all the paperwork (known as "clearances"). And if you're supposed to get a chunk of money from us when you complete the record (like the balance of your next Advance), guess what? You ain't gettin' it until we get the damn paperwork.

REALITY: This is going to be more work than you realize right now. If you want a taste of what I'm talking about, take a record that has a song that you want to sample, then look everywhere on the liner notes until you find the main publisher of any particular song. Here's a hint: it's not ASCAP or BMI. Give up? Well, don't feel bad. Often the parent publishers and administrators are not named. So how are you supposed to get permission when you can't find the guy giving out the hall passes? Tracking down administrative rights is not something most artists find the time to do. They generally hire a pro—a lawyer, manager, producer, or consultant who knows the lay of the music publishing land.

Now that you're one step closer to getting your license,[22] you need to write the song's publisher and the label to get a sample clearance[23] for your major-label release. This has the same effect as walking into a restaurant and asking them what they would charge to host a wedding reception.

The minute you use a key word like "wedding," or in our case, "major label," the price goes up. Once you have a license from the writer/publisher, that's only half the battle. You still have to get the record company's permission. That label will be even less excited about giving a discount to one of their competitors. In exchange for a license, count on giving each party a piece of your new recording's publishing. It can get very expensive.

Date of "Delivery"

Finally, after doing tons of paperwork, and after giving up a significant percentage of your royalties to a producer, and after spending almost all the money that the label gave you, you are ready to "deliver" your masterpiece. But there are conditions for that as well.

Delivery Schedule – You shall fulfill the Minimum Recording Obligation as follows:

a) as to the First LP, no later than July 1, 2000.

b) as to the Second LP, no earlier than nine (9) months and no later than fifteen (15) months after delivery of the First LP.

Delivery Schedule: You must "deliver" the recording as follows:

a) You'll have six months to comply with *all* the above and "deliver" your first Album.

b) You'll have nine months after that to do all the paperwork and "deliver" your second Album. [*But if you're more than six months late, it's gonna cost ya. See "Advances," page 27.*]

[22] There is also a website linked to the Harry Fox Agency that will act as a search engine and get you started. ASCAP and BMI also have free databases to help you find publishers.

[23] A complete sample clearance consists of licensing two copyrights, each usually owned by separate companies. The first license is for the composition (the songs), and is owned by the publisher. The second license is for the sound recording of the song, and is owned by the record company.

c) as to each of the Third LP through the Seventh LP, within one hundred and twenty (120) days following the commencement of the Option Period in which such LP is required to be delivered.

c) As for the rest of the Albums that you will record for us, we're not going to use a specific amount of time that you are bound to us exclusively. **Instead, we're going to base it on when we renew the option on your contract.** So after we notify you that we are keeping you on the label, you will have four months to complete and "deliver" each new Album. (See "Terms and Exclusivity," page 284, for when that is.)

d) Pacific shall send you written notice of acceptance of delivery of the applicable Product LP and the date such notice is sent shall be deemed the date of delivery for purposes of this Agreement. If Pacific fails to send such notice, Artist may, in writing, request that Pacific send such notice, and if Pacific fails to do so the date of such request shall be deemed the date of delivery.

d) You will know that we accepted your Album because we will send you a written letter stating so. The day we send the letter is the day it is considered "delivered." If we forget to send it, you can send us a reminder. If we still forget, than the day you send the reminder shall be the day the Album is considered "delivered."

DOUBLE-DIP DETECTOR

EXPLANATION: Why is there all this crap about sending a letter to say something is "delivered"? Who cares? Isn't it obvious that the files are "delivered" if they're sitting right there on the A&R person's desk? Well, the label cares about this because, if you remember in "Advances," page 27, you agreed that if you were late "delivering" your Album, the label could reduce your next advance by 5% for each fraction of a month that it is late. Now that clause is gonna bite you in the ass, like a bulimic Piranha on a binge.

REALITY: Indie contracts rarely have language like this. They usually function on a one or two Album deal. But majors really care about this stuff because they are obligating themselves to consider seven Albums. So here's how it will likely play out, based on the above clauses. In order to keep things simple, we are going to use the following dates:

THE "DELIVERY" DATE FROM HELL

1) January 1, 2011	1) You sign the contract.
2) June 1, 2011 The Label has 90 days to approve your masters.	2) You hand over the masters for your first Album to Label.
3) September 1, 2011	3) Label tells you that you need to record more material. (You have, therefore, not "delivered.")
4) October 1, 2011 The Label has 30 days to approve.	4) You turn in more material.
5) November 1, 2011	5) Label accepts the new material and sends you notice that your first Album is officially "Delivered."

Net result: You are *five* months late "delivering" your first Album. Your next Advance will be reduced by 20%, or $50,000 (as per the clause on page 27). This will leave you with a recording budget of only $200,000, but, as per the clause on page 22, you'll still be required to spend about 90% of the Floor amount ($250,000) of your next record (presuming you've negotiated a specific clause that says that the 90% budget will be based on the Floor amount and not the Ceiling amount), which is $225,000. The other $25,000 you will have to make up. This means that the label only gave you $200,000 of actual money for the second Album, but you will have to pay back $250,000. *Smooth!* It's just like a credit card at 20% interest. In reality, if you need the money to complete the Album, it won't come out of your pocket now; the label will Advance it to you. But you will, of course, have to pay it back eventually.

This is where your lawyer can earn his fee. There are many ways to stop this insane Double-Dip from working. One way is to force the label to accept 10 out of 13 songs that you turn in, if you turn them in on time. Another is to make sure that, if the label reduces your Advance, the amount added to the recoupment is the actual amount Advanced, not the amount that appears in the Table. Some relief I might offer is that if you do audit your label, they will usually "forgive" this extra debt as a way of seeming "reasonable."

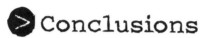 Conclusions

So we learned a new word today: "delivered." You might have thought it's the same as when you order a pizza. But what we find out is that this pizza is not "delivered" until: 1) It arrives; 2) You open the box and check to make sure the order is done right and that the bill is correct; 3) You check the immigration papers of the person "delivering" it to make sure they are a US citizen; and 4) You make them responsible for not only the pizza, but for ensuring that all the ingredients in the pizza were purchased and used legally in compliance with USRDA standards. (Imagine the headache if you had ordered Chinese!)

From this point forward, the word "delivered" will always be in quotation marks whenever it's referring to the LabelSpeak definition.

Now we know that much of the Advance is spoken for, and that "royalties" or "Net Profits" are something of a remote gamble. But what about the money you earn if you are a songwriter as well as a recording artist? The law says the label *has* to pay you, and can't get around this. Do you believe it for a second?

Turn the page.

CHAPTER 4

⯈Controlled Compositions and Mechanical Licenses

or "How much are they (not) paying me for my songs?"

I f you are an artist who writes her own songs, then this just might be the most important chapter in this book. If you are an artist who doesn't write his own songs, after reading this chapter you will see why you should begin to do so. At which time this will become the most important chapter in this book for you as well.

Ninety percent of all new artists never learn what a "mechanical license" or a "Controlled Composition" is until they see the clause in their first record deal. By that time it's usually too late to play catch-up and learn how to protect yourself against one of the most clever and insidious ways that record companies convince artists to give up their money.

Why This Clause Exists

Songwriters have a huge advantage over artists who don't write. Artists get paid mostly through record sales, personal performances, and endorsements. This can be a risky endeavor. What if you don't "sell" many records? What if the tour loses money? What if you're too ugly to be a Nike spokesperson?

So what leverage do writers have over labels? *Plenty!* Even if the artist is a flop, the writer(s) can still get paid thousands from labels because the law requires record companies to pay them *immediately.* (Well, within four months of releasing their material to the public.)

The special payment record companies (and indeed any company wishing to use a song for commercial purposes) cough up for the use of a song is called a "mechanical royalty," or as it's referred to in the biz, **"a mechanical."**[1] When a song is being published (which literally means "made publicly known") for the first time, the writer can charge whatever they want for the mechanical license, but when it's been published once, and someone wants to use it again, then the law sets a minimum amount that the copyright holder must license the song for to any record company. Currently that amount is 9.1 cents per song on a standard sound recording (CD album, download single, stream, etc.), and a special rate of 24 cents for ring tones.[2] These amounts are often called **"the statutory rate(s),"** because it's written in the law, or **"the compulsory rate,"** because the law *compels* songwriters to issue a license to any one who wants one. They can refuse no one. (This is why you don't need to ask permission to do a cover song on a CD—just pay the licensing fee of 9.1 cents.)

Though it's only a few pennies, this can result in hundreds of thousands of dollars even for a moderately successful venture. Think outside the box of the record deal for a second, such as greeting cards that play a tune, and how many thousands are sold over the holidays, each one paying 9.1 cents to the writer.

Publishers spend all day negotiating these licenses with toy, game, and greeting card companies. They represent the songwriter in these negotiations. But when the songwriter is being courted as a recording artist, they lose most of their leverage. Why? Because now a big major label wants to license a song and potentially release tens of thousands of CDs (each paying 9.1 cents), as well as downloads (each paying 9.1 cents), and give the song radio and TV exposure— far greater hit potential than a toy license (usually).

If the song(s) the label wants has *never* been published (as is usually the case with a new artist/writer), they must pay whatever price the writer sets for his or her work—even $10 a copy. This would be cost prohibitive for the label. So when the writer is the artist, the label uses their leverage to get them to agree to waive their "first use" rights and license the new songs for the minimum statutory rate of 9.1 cents. *Remember: Once a songwriter gives up this "first use" right, they can never get it back.*

Here's a dialogue as example:

Scene: *A music lawyer's office. A lawyer is seated on one side of a desk, with many platinum records on the wall behind him, and an artist on the other side with his manager sitting next to him.*

Lawyer: Well, it looks like we struck oil. Pacific wants you bad.

Artist: Yeah? *Cool!* How bad?

Lawyer: Well, it looks like an advance of about $300,000, plus a seven-album deal.

Artist: *Cool!*

Lawyer: Yeah, they want you real bad. They want to use all *your* material. No covers.

Artist: *Really?*

Lawyer: Yup. This is great. With all 14 songs on the record written by you, you stand a better chance of having a hit.

Artist: *Cool!*

Manager: Sweet!

Lawyer: Now, we have a serious thing to discuss. How much do you want to license your songs for to the label?

Artist: How much? I don't under–

Lawyer: The songs. They are your songs, right?

Artist: Yeah, they're mine.

Lawyer: And none of them were published before, right?

Artist: Right…

Lawyer: Good. That means that no one else has the rights to them.

Artist: I own everything, I think. I haven't signed anything with anybody.

Lawyer: Good. Those songs are your property, and the law says the label has to pay for them. How much do you want?

Artist: Well, I don't know. What do you think I can get?

Lawyer: About nine cents.

Artist: (*silence*)

Lawyer: Nine cents per song is good! That's all any label will pay. It's "the statutory rate." But it's cool, because it means you get nine cents for every song for every album you sell! If you sell even 100,000 records and you have 14 songs on the record, think about how much you're gonna make!

[*Manager begins punching numbers on a gold-plated calculator.*]

9.1 cents per song	×	14 songs on a CD	=	$1.27 cents	×	100,000 CDs sold	=	$127,400

Lawyer: And that's not even counting your 14% royalty for being the artist on the record. That's just for songwriting. Plus you're probably gonna sell way more than that. And you *do* want this deal, right?

Artist: (*getting nervous*) Yeah. I think I do.

Manager: Sweet!!![3]

[3] This dialogue is totally exaggerated to make a point, but I have heard very similar versions of it.

WHY DO WE NEED THE GOVERNMENT TO HELP US SELL A SONG?

Now I know you think it's cool that the label owes you all this money, but the truth is that they're taking advantage of you. How? Well, think about it: You own the damn songs. You wrote them. Why is the government setting a price for how much you can sell your work for? And only nine cents! Do they set minimum rates telling doctors or lawyers how much they can sell their work for? Do they tell farmers how much (or how little) they can charge for their food, or tell dentists how much they can charge to pull a tooth? Of course not. That would be illegal. So what gives?

The reason is that there's a long-standing tradition of hating monopolies in this country. The Founding Fathers decided that monopolies lead to tyranny, and they put stuff in the Bill of Rights that makes it possible for the law to prevent such things. In the past few years you may have heard of large companies being investigated and broken up by the government because they have too much control over technology or a precious natural resource. Well, believe it or not, this same principle applies to songs. Your government feels that you shouldn't have the right to completely own something valuable without being forced to share it with anyone who wants to license it from you. (Power to the people.) To ensure that you don't completely control your hit song, they make you issue a license to anyone who wants to do a cover of your song. The license is called a "Compulsory License." "Compulsory" means the same as "mandatory" or "required." Many artists think that this was done for the benefit of writers, because it is a license that the label is required to pay. Wrong. It's a license you are required to give, and it's about nine cents a song. Still think it's cool?

The government is not stupid. They know that if everything belonged to the people, then the incentive to create new works would be quashed. So a compromise was reached—something like a temporary monopoly. That's what a copyright is, as well as a patent and a trademark. They are temporary monopolies that the government allows so that creators can be compensated for their work.

This applies to many forms of intellectual property. Most patents, for example, are only good for 17 years before they become public domain. In the case of songs, songwriters retain a copyright for each song they write, which is essentially a temporary monopoly (the life of the author plus 75 years). But you can only dictate how much you will charge for its use *before the song is published*. After that, anyone can cover your song without permission as long as they pay the minimum mechanical royalty to you, and by law you are "compelled" to give them this license. That minimum amount is the statutory rate. It was established by the Copyright Office of the United States in 1976 at 5 cents per song, and goes up every couple of years to adjust for inflation.

At the time of this writing (early 2010) it's frozen at 9.1 cents due to the downturn in the economy in 2008. However, they have added other rates, such as a ring tone rate of 24 cents, and minimum rates for ad-revenue models that may fluctuate in time.

If your music generates 200,000 downloads, and 100,000 ring tones, and 100,000 CD "sales" (not uncommon for a mid-size major-label artist), there will be so much songwriter cash that the label is hopping you (or your lawyer), that you'll forget about the fact that you were entitled to license this first-time song for as much as you wanted.

Labels want to have their cake and eat it too. They want fresh material, but they want to pay less than the rate for a cover song. Why doesn't the label just offer you nothing? They seem to have a lot of leverage. Why not just say, "Hey, if you want a deal, give us all your songs for free." They could, but at some point the government would be asked to intervene by the Songwriters Guild and/or the National Music Publishers Association, claiming that the Big Four cartel is using its leverage to rip off writers (this would be in the form of an anti-trust suit). So, as a *gimme*, the labels voluntarily regulate themselves and agree to pay an amount that is equal to the statutory rate to keep Uncle Sam off their backs. Since 2007, that rate is 9.1 cents per song per record distributed, and 24 cents for ring tones. (The statutory rates for subscription services are too small to discuss here, and ad-revenue-generated royalties also have statutory rates, but they are not, in practice, compulsory. They are negotiated, and so the label does not have to manipulate you into a deal.)

A Runaway Train

The downside for the label in agreeing to pay 9.1 or 24 cents a tune per copy should be obvious. This can become a runaway train for the record company. What if the market price of ring tones goes down to 20 cents and they still have to pay 24 cents to the songwriter? They will lose 4 cents on each ring tone they sell. What if they sign an artist who then wants to put 20 songs on her CD album? The label would have to pay the artist 20×9.1 cents, or $1.82 for every CD they manufacture (in addition to the artist's "royalty"). Or what if an artist decides that he wants to put 30 one-minute cover tunes on his CD (they would have to be Ramones songs in this case)? The label would be required to pay $2.73 in mechanical royalties alone. Plus, depending on when the label plans the release of the record, they might have to make this payment even *before* they ship the CDs. Plus, the statutory rate often goes up every couple of years to adjust for inflation. Do they have to pay the new rate? In this book's first edition, in 2001, the rate was 7.7 cents. That's a 25% cost increase to the label in less than a decade, yet the economy for record sales has gone down. Where does the madness end?

The answer is that it doesn't end unless the label clips the artist's wings a bit and limits two things:

1. How many songs they have to pay for with each Advance (or on each Album); and

2. The amount that they will pay for each song.

The way they do this is by constructing a series of clauses, collectively called a "Mechanical License," that caps the amount of your mechanical royalty. As we'll see soon, if you are not careful with negotiating this license, you could actually end up owing your label money for every record you "sell." Think I'm joking? I *never* joke about money owed to writers. Numerous famous recording artists have filed bankruptcy due to a badly negotiated version of this clause. So pay attention.

⊘ The Standard

In your contract, the header for this section might be labeled one of two ways: CONTROLLED COMPOSITIONS or MECHANICAL ROYALTIES. Either way it's going to look something like this:

Defining the "Controlled Composition" and the "Statutory Rate"

In the DEFINITIONS section of the contract you will find the key primers of all clauses relating to your songs. They are "Controlled Composition" and the "Statutory Rate." Each contract defines them a bit differently. Below is the Standard, but watch out for clever and subtly altered versions of these words.

(a)As used herein:
(i) "Controlled Composition" means a work which is written in whole or in part by Artist and/or Producer or which is owned or controlled by you and/or Artist and/or Producer or in which you and/or Artist and/or Producer have (has) an interest in the income to be derived therefrom or from the copyright thereof.

(a) In this contract:
(i) "Controlled Composition" means a song you wrote, co-wrote, or "control"; i.e., have the right to collect money from. [*Usually this is one that you wrote.*]

This is easy enough to understand, or so it seems. But this next term is the real sneaky one.

(ii) "Statutory Rate" means, with respect to each musical work recorded and embodied in a Record

(ii) Used in this contract, "Statutory Rate" means the smallest amount the law requires someone to pay a

⑭

[4] The Copyright Royalty Tribunal Reform Act of 1993, Public Law 103-198, eliminated the Copyright Royalty Tribunal and replaced it with a system of ad hoc Copyright Arbitration Royalty Panels (CARPs). The panels are administrated by the Library of Congress and the Copyright Office to adjust the copyright compulsory license royalty rates (including the mechanical rates for the making and distributing of phonorecords) and to distribute the royalties collected by the Licensing Division to the appropriate copyright owners. In 2004 the CARP was shortened to just CRB. Too many "crap" jokes.

[5] See the comparison on the next page for what they've agreed to pay you in the near future.

hereunder, the minimum fixed (without regard to playing time) mechanical royalty in effect pursuant to the United States Copyright Act or the Canadian Copyright Act

or

the generally accepted rate negotiated by record companies and music publishers in Canada (as the context so requires) at the time of manufacture of such Record.

writer as a mechanical for the use of their previously published song. This is required by the United States Copyright Act and the Canadian Copyright Act.

Or it could also mean:

an amount of money universally agreed to by leaders of the recording industry that songwriters can get as a mechanical. This amount is fixed at the time the recording is manufactured.

REALITY: So instead of just saying that the "Statutory Rate" in the contract means the same thing as the "statutory rate" established by law, now they are saying that it's the rate established by law *or* whatever the record industry decides to pay. Which do you think will be lower?

A peculiar trend in the music industry is that instead of using the rate that Congress created, a panel of record industry execs gets together once every couple of years with a panel of judges. The panel is called the CRB (Copyright Royalty Board), and together they decide what the rates will be.[4]

In your contract, be aware that "Statutory Rate" (when capitalized) does not mean the same as the statutory rate required by law, but rather the rate that a committee of record industry executives agrees to pay. Currently it's 9.1 cents per song. (I guess we should thank them.)[5]

It's a very sneaky way of allowing you to think that "statutory rate" is the same as "Statutory Rate." The first is an amount set by statute or law; the second is an amount set by this contract. The former goes up every couple of years; the latter one ***never changes***.

> *If your record becomes a hit and sells for a decade or so,*
> *you will never get more than the Statutory Rate locked in*
> *at the time you sign your contract.*

"statutory rate"	"Statutory Rate"
An escalating rate established by Congress for previously published songs to be paid to the writer on the reproduction of each unit distributed, within four months of its distribution. (Since 2007 it's been 9.1 cents per song.)	An amount of money (usually the same amount as the current "statutory rate") fixed at the time you sign the Thick that you will be paid for "first use" of your songs, only on "records sold." (Since 2007 it's been 9.1 cents per song, and 24 cents for a ring tone was added in 2008.)

NEGOTIATE

You should try to get the definition of "Statutory Rate" in your contract to duplicate its actual definition in the Copyright Act as closely as possible. The label will fight you on this, because the version they've created is a term so similar (yet so different) that you are bound to get confused. My experts tell me that they've never seen a situation where a Big Four has changed this. But there's always a first time for everything. Recent events have shamed labels into changing a few things about their business practices; perhaps awareness on this issue will do the same. At the very least you should push to get the "fixed" elements out of the definition, if there are any.

When and How You Get Paid for Your Songs

The Copyright Act has specific guidelines for payment of the statutory fee. They involve payment to the writers or publishers not more than four months after the song's release, accountability for each sale, and some other things that keep the writers happy. Labels, of course, have their own spin on this. All of the clauses in this section come from the clauses titled either MECHANICAL ROYALTIES or LICENSES FOR MUSICAL COMPOSITIONS.

[6] A middleman agency that routinely audits record companies to collect mechanical license fees. They charge a 5% commission for any money they collect that you were supposed to get and didn't. They also issue licenses for cover songs if you want one on your Album.

(b)(i) Pacific shall be responsible for the payment of **mechanical royalties** directly to the copyright proprietors of the musical works embodied on the Master Recordings hereunder. Artist and Producer agree to assist Pacific in entering into mechanical licenses with such copyright proprietors, which licenses shall be consistent with the terms and conditions hereof but which shall otherwise be in the general form utilized by the Harry Fox Agency, Inc., or in a form otherwise acceptable to them:

(ii) Except with respect to previously recorded material on Artist's LP, you, Artist and Producer warrant, represent and agree that Pacific shall receive, with respect to all works embodied in all Master Recordings hereunder, "**first use**" mechanical licenses as such term is understood in the record industry.

(b) (i) Pacific shall be responsible for the payment of any **mechanicals due writers and publishers for songwriting**. You agree to accept these terms for payment, as outlined below, and [*if you didn't write all the songs yourself*] to get any of your co-writers (or other writers, if you used any outside songs) to accept these terms, which are consistent with the Harry Fox Agency, Inc.,[6] form for such payments:

(ii) You swear that, aside from demos, this is the first time you have recorded these songs for *any* record company, with the intention of widespread distribution (which in the industry is called "**first use**"). And that you're giving us the right to reproduce these songs for the **first time**.

REALITY: What's the point of this? Well, by swearing that this is the first time you are licensing these songs, you remove any opportunity later down the line to claim that you didn't realize that you gave up your "first use" rights when you licensed them for 9.1 cents each to the label. You are also agreeing to cooperate with the label to make sure that writers are paid for all the songs that you didn't write that you record under this contract.

(c) With respect to Controlled Compositions licensed hereunder for the United States, Pacific shall render quarterly statements and payments therefrom of all

(c) For all songs that you wrote and which we are able to distribute in the United States, we'll send you a statement every three months showing how much money you have

mechanical copyright royalties payable as set forth herein, within sixty (60) days after the end of the applicable quarters ending in May, August, November and February (in accordance with Pacific's regular accounting practices), for each quarter for which such royalties accrue pursuant to the terms hereof. **Pacific shall have the right to withhold a portion of such royalties as a reasonable reserve for returns and exchanges.** The provisions regarding auditing of royalty statements stated herein throughout shall be applicable to accountings rendered pursuant to this subparagraph.

made. We'll pay you within 60 days after we send the statement. These accounting periods end in May, August, November, and February.

For each group of three months that you earn these mechanicals, **we're going to keep a portion of your money as a reserve, just in case your records ship back or distributors want to exchange them** [*for an artist who is more popular than you*]. If you want to check our math, the same conditions for auditing your "royalties" apply here.[7]

[7] See "Auditing," page 235, and "Royalties," page 37.

REALITY: So even though the law says the label has to pay this money within four months of distributing the records (which could mean selling or giving them away), they want you to agree to let them hold this money for a good long while. How can they do that? Did you miss it?

The reserve. The reserve is a special account where your money is held in case the records ship back. The company doesn't want to pay you too much on units that may ship back for a refund (God forbid), so instead, they hold on to some of the cash they owe you (usually about 35%), and then, when they're sure those records are never going to ship back, they "liquidate" the reserve and pay it to you. They apply this reserve even to downloads (which cannot possibly ship back), because, on rare occasions, there are refunds granted on downloads for corrupted data, misleading advertising, etc.

How long till you get the entire amount you're owed? It says how long in the clauses on page 247 in the chapter on "Auditing." But to save you the trouble of flipping back, it's about two years. So this means that the money the label is supposed to pay you *by law* within four months will only be paid in part, and part will be withheld from you for up to two years. Will they pay you interest on the money they hold? Probably not, but you should ask.

In calculating your Advance, the label applies a special reserve calculation that is less than the "reasonable" Reserve they use for calculating "royalties." In "royalties" it's 35%, but for the Advance it's only 15% (see page 23). Perhaps they could do the same thing here. A reserve of only 15%—especially for downloads, which they should consider carving out completely—that sounds reasonable to me. No? They could also agree to liquidate the reserve in six months instead of two years. Most companies do this as a matter of routine, and will tell you that regardless of what's written, it's their policy to liquidate every six months. If that's their policy, let them put it in writing.

Adjusting and Fixing the "Statutory Rate" (the "Three-Quarter Rate")

Step Two in the label's attempt to get you to be "reasonable" about your mechanicals is their creation of a clause that says they're not going to pay you the full "Statutory Rate." Instead they want you to agree that they only have to pay you 75% of the "Statutory Rate," or 6.8 cents and 18 cents for ring tones, and they're going to **lock that rate in for the life of your contract, even if that rate goes up in the future.**

d) You, Artist and Producer agree that each Controlled Composition recorded hereunder is **hereby licensed** to Pacific, for the United States and Canada, at the following rates:

(i) With respect to Records sold in the United States or Canada through Normal Trade Channels on Pacific Top Line or Mid-Priced Records: **three-fourths (3/4) of the "Statutory Rate."**

d) For the United States and Canada, you give us permission to pay you as follows for **the entire length of this contract:**

(i) For new material on a record "sold" for between 100% and 60% of the highest list price in a region, we're only gonna pay you: **75% of the bullshit statutory rate.**

REALITY: So even though your material is new, Pacific wants to pay you like these are old, previously recorded cover songs. And not even that—they're only going to pay you three-fourths of the bullshit statutory rate, not the real one. This is what is called in LabelSpeak "the three-quarter rate." There are several things referred to as the "three-quarter rate" in the record biz,[8] but this is the most severe one with the most serious effects for songwriters, because this three-quarter rate has become the standard throughout the industry. What the label is hoping you forget is that a seven-Album deal will likely stretch out for about seven to 10 years. (See thecharts on pages 285, 287, and 288.)

NEGOTIATE

In regard to the "fixed rate," even though this is "standard," it's just plain crazy. There's no legitimate reason why the rate should stay fixed in time, except that the label feels that they can leverage you into it.

If there's any language at all regarding "fixed" rates in your contract, cross it out. If the term "licensed" is used in this regard, as above, then add language that creates an adjustable rate that increases each time the copyright office (or the CRB) increases the actual "statutory rate." Believe it or not, there are songwriters who have old hits still selling in stores, but who are paid on the "Statutory Rate" that was payable when they signed their contracts back in the '70s. So, for the sake of your children, negotiate this.

The other tactic you should try is to simply ask for a higher "Statutory Rate." This obvious strategy is often overlooked, because the word "statutory" seems to imply that it's a law, which is the desired effect. But it's not. **It's an arbitrary amount.** So ask for more. It can't hurt. And:

> *Don't listen to a lawyer who tells you that this "Statutory Rate"*
> *is the amount the labels are required to pay by law.*
> *That's a clear sign that he's either dishonest, confused,*
> *or too lazy to educate you.*

Getting a higher rate is difficult, but maybe if everyone starts asking for it, someday the labels will agree.

[8] **Three-quarter rate: "New Technology" deductions in royalties for record sales are sometimes called "three-quarter royalties," and are often used informally in an interchangeable manner (see page 78).**

THE "STATUTORY RATE" INCREASES AGREED TO BY THE BIG FOUR FOR THE YEARS 2000-2010

YEAR	STATUTORY RATE	STATUTORY PER-RATE MINUTE
2000	7.55¢	1.45¢
2001	7.55¢	1.45¢
2002	8.0¢	1.55¢
2003	8.0¢	1.55¢
2004	8.5¢	1.65¢
2005	8.5¢	1.65¢
2006	9.1¢	1.75¢
2007	9.1¢	1.75¢
2008-	Frozen @ 9.1¢ and 24¢ for ring tones indefinitely	Frozen @ 1.75¢

There are two rates: one on a per-song basis that is used by record companies for each sound recording of a single song, and another that is calculated by length. This second rate is used by the film and TV industry, and is more applicable when the composition in question is longer than four minutes. These rates were once set by the Copyright Office of the United States, and are now set by a committee composed of record executives and judges called the CRB. As of this writing, the rates have been frozen at the request of labels as a sort of economic stimulus to offset alleged losses from Internet piracy.

More Deductions to the "Statutory Rate"

(ii) (A) With respect to Records sold in the United States or Canada as premium Records: one-half (1/2) of the "**Statutory Rate.**"

(ii) (A) For Records "sold" through record clubs [*those "Get 10 CDs for a $1" guys*], we'll pay you half of **the bullshit statutory rate**.

(B) With respect to Records sold in the United States or Canada as **Budget Records:** two-thirds (2/3) of the "**Statutory Rate.**"

(B) For records that **"sell" for anything below 67% of their original SRLP,** we'll pay you two-thirds of the **bullshit statutory rate.**

REALITY: If you recall from Chapter 2: Royalties, I showed you how the Budget Records scam really works (see page 102). Therefore, you can count on most of your mechanicals being calculated at the rate in "B" above. Only hit artists in the first three to four weeks of a new release can sell many hundreds of thousands of records at the full rate. If you recall in "Royalties" on page 50, the term "Budget Record" was defined as:

"Budget Record"

A Record, whether or not previously released, bearing a Suggested Retail List Price which is sixty-seven percent (67%) or less of the Suggested Retail List Price in the country concerned applicable to the Top Line Records in the same configuration (e.g., long-playing Album, two-disc long-playing Album, Twelve-Inch Single, analog tape cassette, compact disc, etc.) released by Pacific or its Licensees in the territory concerned.

A Record (old or new) marked down to 67% or less of the sticker price of any similar type of record in the same region.

(such as long-playing Album, two-disc long-playing Album, 12-inch Single, analog tape cassette, CD, etc.)

When the original statutory rate was created, it was done with the intent that the owner of the song was licensing it for use on a record. The price of the record was not relevant. Guess what? The label just made it *very relevant.*

If you followed my suggestion and got the threshold lowered to 50%, you'll be very happy right about now.

STATUTORY RAPE

Some of my lawyer acquaintances who work for major labels claim that I rant too much—that there is no real difference between the "statutory rate" in the law and the one the labels create in The Thick. They claim that both "function" the same way, and that I'm completely overreacting. You be the judge.

The real "statutory rate"	The new and improved bullshit LabelSpeak version called the "Statutory Rate"
1. Goes up from time to time.	1. Never increases.
2. Established by Congress.	2. Decided by a cartel of labels and three judges (CRB).
3. Applies only to remakes.	3. Applies to all songs, new and old.
4. Is paid on all copies.	4. Is paid only on records "sold."
5. Is paid in full four months after distribution.	5. Only 65% is paid four months after being "sold", 35% about two years later.
6. Does not go up and down with the price of the record.	6. Is adjusted based on the price of the record.

What's the difference between "statutory rate" and "Statutory Rate"? Not much? Really?

Killing the Three-Quarter Rate: The Co-Publishing Scam

The label has by now whittled your promised payment of 9.1 cents per song down to a mean average of 6 cents per song. They've also fixed it in time so that no matter how much the rate goes up in the future or how much inflation increases, they never have to pay you more. How can you get out from under this? Well, the label will try to induce you to sign with one of their sister publishing companies as one method. *Behold*:

iii)   **Notwithstanding anything to the contrary contained in subparagraphs (d, I) above,** if Artist enters into an agreement with a publishing affiliate of

(iii) **In spite of what it says in the paragraph above**, if you enter into a publishing deal with the publishing arm of Pacific, we'll pay you 100% of

Pacific granting rights in and to Controlled Compositions, then with respect to Records sold in the United States or Canada through Normal Trade Channels on Pacific Top Line or pursuant to the subparagraphs above, each Controlled Composition subject to each agreement will be licensed to Pacific at one hundred percent (100%) of the **"Statutory Rate."**

the bullshit statutory rate on records "sold" at the highest possible retail price for that region in the United States or Canada in traditional record stores.

REALITY: So you get offered a trade-off: If you allow the label to take 25% of the money you earn from songwriting (standard co-publisher share), then they'll let you earn 25% more per song. Interesting, except it's not a fair trade for two reasons:

1. Publishing deals typically allow the Publisher to take an additional 10%–15% off the top for administrative fees. This means that you're actually giving up more like 35%–40% of your songwriting money in exchange for an extra 25% of the "Statutory Rate." And, as you'll see later on in this chapter, the label will find other ways to take that 25% back anyway, especially if it's a 360 Deal, through deductions to "Net Profits" and the "Offset Right."

2. Notice that it says they'll give you the full rate, but only for records "sold" at the highest possible retail price and only through normal trade channels. What the F are those? Whatever the label says they are, and in most cases they do not consider iTunes to be a "normal trade channel." So what about all the other records you're going to sell in digital stores at 99 cents (which are not "Top Line" but "Mid-Priced" records)? Guess what? You're back to the three-quarter rate, and back to getting jacked, but now it's from both ends—the "sales" end *and* the publishing end.

Yet many artists opt for this offer, not because of the increase in the amount of their mechanicals, but because these publishing deals generally come with another Advance that is almost as big as the recording fund. But with this Advance there are no recording expenses, so *you get to keep it all*. For an artist with a family to provide for (or an expensive habit—you know, like stamp collecting), that's a heavy inducement.

The Controlled Composition Clause

If you thought, "Well, who cares about all this statutory crap? So they decrease the amount of money they pay me per song; so what? I got *lots* of songs. I'll just put two more tunes on the record. They don't even have to be good ones. I get paid the same either way." Wrong. Now that the label has put you in a more "reasonable" frame of mind, it's time to lower the boom.

(e) **Without limiting the payments outlined in subparagraph (d) above**, it is agreed that the maximum copyright royalty which Pacific shall be required to pay in respect of a Record embodying Master Recordings recorded hereunder shall be the aggregate of (i) the number of Controlled Compositions on such Records times the applicable rate described in subparagraph (d) above, and (ii) the number of works on such Record which are not Controlled Compositions times the "**Statutory Rate**"; provided, however, that in no event shall the aforesaid maximum copyright royalty exceed an overall limit of (iii) ten (10) times the "Statutory Rate" for an LP, (iv) one (1) times the "Statutory Rate" for a Single both in physical media and sold through any digital medium, or (v) five (5) times the "Statutory Rate" for an EP, (vi) one (1) times the

(e) **There are no limits to the payments outlined in "d" above. This is the fact** [*even if you sign with our sister company for publishing*]: The largest amount of money we will ever pay for a song or group of songs (like an Album) will be the total of:

(i) the number of songs you wrote (or co-wrote) in that Option Period (or on that Album) times the three-quarter rate of 6.8 cents per song and
(ii) the number of songs you didn't write or own, times **the bullshit statutory rate.** But this will have a limit that is *never* more than:

(iii) 91 cents for an Album,

(iv) 9.1 cents for a single, download or otherwise, or

(v) 45 cents for an EP,

"Statutory Rate" for a section of any master used for cellular network identification, specifically a so-called "ring tone," "mastertone," "ringback," etc.

(vi) 24 cents for a ring tone.

(f) No mechanical royalty whatsoever shall be payable for

(f) We're not giving you any songwriting money for:

(i) Records cut out of the Pacific catalog and sold as discontinued merchandise or Records sold as "scrap," "overstock" or "surplus";

(i) Discontinued records that we no longer promote ("cutouts"), which are usually sold as "scrap," "overstock," or "surplus";

(ii) any work which is non-musical;

(ii) spoken word stuff, silly in-between-the-cuts chatter, or other recordings the label deems "non-musical";

(iii) records distributed by Pacific which are not "Records sold" as defined herein (except, with respect to Controlled Compositions, mechanical royalties shall be payable on fifty percent (50%) of LP Records distributed by Pacific hereunder pursuant to Pacific's standard discount or merchandising plans in effect at the time of shipment of the particular Record);

(iii) Records that are not "sold."[9] (Although we will pay you songwriting money on half of the records we ship as part of any marketing plan.) [*For example: a plan in which the label says, "Buy five boxes of this new artist and get one box of an established artist 'free.'" (Free Goods.[10]) This seems to say that you'll get a mechanical for half of the giveaways. But it doesn't really add up to that.*]

[9] For the actual definition of "sold," see "Royalties," page 39.

[10] See "Royalties," pages 41–47, and "Auditing," page 250, for more on Free Goods.

[11] They will simultaneously trick the artist into agreeing to produce over 12 songs. See "Master Quality and Delivery," page 135, giving them free masters for the fixed price of 10.

REALITY: In plain English, no matter how many of your songs you put on your Album, the label will only pay an amount equal to 10 of them at the three-quarter rate of 6.8 cents/18 cents per song.[11] No matter how many they manufacture for "distribution," you get no money for records they give away as promotional material, or sell at a loss. Only those they "sell."

The *most* that a label will pay you is:

1. Three-quarters of the "Statutory Rate" times the number of songs you wrote on the Album. For a record with 10 songs, that would be 68 cents.

    Or, if you've signed a publishing deal with their sister company,

2. The full "Statutory Rate" (9.1 cents per song), provided that it's never more than 10 times 9.1 cents, or 91 cents per Album.

    Industry shorthand for both 1) and 2) above is: "10× Statutory."

This is what a "Controlled Composition" clause is, and it saves the label mega bucks. It's a way for them to get out of paying money that the law says they must pay. And it stops the potential runaway train mentioned earlier.

EXAMPLE: Let's say that the label was not satisfied with the first 10 songs you tried to "deliver" and asked you to come up with more. You then got to work writing and recording four more. And what do you know, they actually came out better than some in the first batch! Now the hard part is deciding which 10 to give them. But the contract says that the label has the right to choose, and they can choose all 14 songs if they want (see page 109). Even though you're only going to be paid for 10, because you just agreed to a mechanical that has a limit of 10 × Statutory. And they mean to hold you to it. Sorry. Look at the chart below:

Record Company *Should* Pay		Record Company *Will* Pay		You Lose the Balance
$0.068 (three-quarter rate on 14 songs) or 14 × Statutory: Total: **$0.95** per album	−	Total limit you agreed to, or 10 × Statutory: **$0.68**	=	Over the limit by **$0.27** per record sold

If you "sold" a million records, the label only pays you $680,000 instead of $950,000. You lose $270,000. (Still, not a bad problem to have.)

NEGOTIATE

In some major-label contracts, the mechanical has been increased to 12× Statutory for CDs. I'd suggest trying to get a sliding scale that specifies that after you sell half a million units, the rate increases to 100% of the "Statutory Rate." Most 350 Deals offer this up front. But remember, any sliding scale is going to have a series of clauses right after it that disqualify many units. (For examples of this, see "The Sliding Scale Royalty," page 64.) I've seen WEA contracts that have paid as much as 15× Statutory to compensate for this.[12]

Summary

In order to comprehend the pure evil of what's about to come, you must understand the concept of a "Controlled Composition" clause. Let's recap before we get into the really scary stuff.

The label has limited their overhead and created a *standard payment* for every collection of songs you create during an Option Period (often, but not always for an Album). This is called a **Mechanical License,** or **Mechanical Royalty,** both of which are referred to in LabelSpeak as "a mechanical." In this way, every Album you make for this deal will have the same license, regardless of whether you have 13 songs or 10 songs on the CD. You can make less by having fewer than 10 songs on your record, but you will never be paid for more than 10 songs (unless you were able to negotiate for more). The license is also fixed from the date you sign the contract and will never go up, even though the real statutory rate goes up every few years (in a normal economy).

Okay, got it? The roller coaster is about to go over the hill.

Oldies and Reprises

To thwart this system, artists in the past were often tempted to record acoustic versions of tunes they had already recorded, or modern versions of old folk tunes (*John Barleycorn* by Traffic, for example), rather than give up more of their own arsenal of original material. So labels got wise to this, and created the following clauses to keep this very thing from happening:

[12] In a WEA contract the 9.1 cents figure is called the "Non-Controlled Rate" rather than the "Statutory Rate."

(iv) any work which consists of an arrangement of a work in the public domain; or

(iv) any cover tune of a public domain song [*like "The Star Spangled Banner"*], or

(v) any more than one use of any work on a particular Record.

(v) any second mix or reprise of a tune already on the record [*like a sparse acoustic version of an otherwise fully produced tune on the record*].

REALITY: Along this same line of thinking goes your plan to do an Album with 10 versions of "Billy, Don't Be a Hero," ranging from an acoustic version to an opera on a single "Concept Album." If you did this, you'd receive no mechanicals at all for two reasons: 1) it's a cover tune; and 2) each track is a reprisal of the first. If you actually did this, Pacific would have to pay for all 10 of these versions individually to the song's author/publisher, because as far as the law is concerned, you recorded 10 versions, and each requires a statutory rate fee to be paid to the publisher who controls that song.

So to make your life easier, you agree to *only* record *original* songs for the label, or ones where you personally know the songwriter and know that she will agree to be paid the way it has been outlined in the previous chapters. Okay? Are the labels happy now? No.

Now, this is important. *Read carefully*:

When the record company pays this "Statutory Rate" to writers *other than you*, who do you think they are paying? They are paying another record company. Well, publishing company, really, but in the Big Four arena they're really the same thing, because often it's the publishing arm of another company in the major-label cartel. This we could understand—labels compete with each other and should pay each other when required to—but what if the label you're on *owns* "Billy, Don't Be a Hero"? Do they still have to pay? You *betcha!*

They save 58 cents per Album they "sell" by paying the money to themselves.

From the label's point of view, you are the perfect artist; one that will record a 10-or-more-song Album of all cover material that the label already controls through its publishing arm.[13] Could you be any more perfect? Oh, yes. The fun is just starting. Continue...

[13] In the early days of the industry, most artist's agreements specified that they had to record songs from the catalog of the label that signed them if they wanted to record a full LP. Thank God this has changed a bit. But what is odd about this is that if you did two versions of the same song, then they can charge you twice. This makes little sense since, as stated in the clause above, you're not allowed to collect from them for the same song appearing twice.

(g) **Without limiting Pacific's rights**, if for any reason Pacific is required to pay any mechanical royalties in excess of the limits specified in this Paragraph, Pacific shall have the **Offset Right**.[14]

(g) **No matter what,** we will never pay more than the limit you agreed to above, and if for some reason we have to pay more than the limit, Pacific shall deduct it from the money we owe you for songwriting, or **anywhere else** for that matter **("Offset Right")** [15]

[14] See "Master Quality," page 113, for the definition of "Offset Right."

[15] See "Master Quality," page 113, for the definition of "Offset Right."

LOOPHOLE ALERT ON MAXIMUM!!!

EXPLANATION: This is not the first time we are seeing the term "Offset Right," but now is where it will really be a ball-buster. It basically means the label can take deductions from any account of yours that they have control over. Check it out. This clause is the setup for a major Double-Dip that will be revealed below.

REALITY: The one really serious problem with this concept of a Controlled Composition creating a limit for the mechanical has just surfaced. What about songs that you want to put on your CD that you don't control in which the songwriter wants the full amount of the *real* statutory rate? (9.1 cents.) Like a cover tune of a previous hit, for example. Pro songwriters want the full rate in the hope that someone will take their "oldie" and make it a hit again. Or what if the label teams you up with a hot songwriter to "round out the Album with a single," and that well-known writer doesn't accept the three-quarter rate. How does this work then?[16]

What will happen is that the label will pay that outside songwriter three-fourths of the 9.1 cents (which they were going to pay to you if this were your song). **And you have to pay the other one-quarter out of your pocket.**

Do you still want that cover tune on your record? Even if it's a hit?

Check it out in the sidebar called "A Tale of Two Writers":

[16] This happens so often that it is something that many artists should count on. For details on the dynamics of how this works, see the *Confessions* chapter "9-to-1 Publishing, or Why Is There Only One Good Song on the Record?"

A TALE OF TWO WRITERS

What happened to teenage R&B pop diva Melanie Wonderbra in the 1990s is a common tale. Melanie had just finished recording 10 songs for her first Album on Warner Brothers, *I'm So Cute, My Smile Could Crack a Mirror*. She had a standard controlled composition clause which created a license of 10 × ¾ Statutory Rate (7.7 cents per song back then), which meant that the mechanical licence could not exceed 57 ¾ cents per album (let's call it 58 cents to keep it simple). Unfortunately, the A&R gal[17] didn't hear a hit that could cross over to the adult contemporary market. So they decided to only put nine of Melanie's songs on the record and bring in a ringer—a pro songwriter with a catalog of tunes in need of an artist—to write the 10th song.

Melanie and her A&R gal fell in love with a song by a writer we'll call Mustang Sal. Mustang was a seasoned, hard-nosed veteran, and didn't feel he had to license his material at three-quarters of the bullshit "Statutory Rate." Also, he didn't have a deal on a Warner Bros. publishing imprint (like Warner/Chapell). He was with a competing label's publisher, EMI, and on top of it all, he hated Melanie's whole teen-vixen vibe. So Warner had little ammunition to persuade him to compromise on the licensing fee. He wanted almost double that actual statutory rate—14 cents. Not only that, but if they wanted to reprint Mustang Sal's lyrics in the liner notes (as Melanie wanted to for all the songs on her Album, along with a fold-out patchouli-scented photo of her in a halter), Sal wanted an extra 6 cents, meaning that the license for his song was going to be a total of 20 cents.[18]

So the total mechanical for Melanie's Album now cost Warner 72 cents. That was almost 15 cents over the limit Melanie agreed to in the Mechanical License clause of her contract, which set a limit of 57 3/4 cents per Album "sold" (10 times three quarters the statutory rate at the time she signed the deal). If the Album sold 100,000 copies in the first few months of release, Warner would have to actually write a check to EMI for the "overage." And this could go on and on for every year that they continued to "sell" that record.

Therefore, because this overage was an actual cash-out-of-pocket expense, a check would need to be cut once every four months by *Melanie* to cover her spread (poor choice of words—sorry). Warner knew that Melanie's only source of income at that time was the money she made working part time at the local ice-cream parlor. So they agreed to front the cash to pay off Mustang Sal's publisher and to take it out of Melanie's "royalties" with use of the "Offset Right" (page 113).[19]

[17] **A&R: "Artist and Repertoire."** The A&R person guides the artist through the major-label process.

[18] Lyrics are handled separately from the composition, and most writers and publishers allow lyrics to be reprinted gratis, as a courtesy if you license a song from them. Some writers charge an extra rate to reprint their lyrics.

[19] Which means it could end up affecting Melanie's next Advance. See page 113.

Record Company Must Pay		Record Company Will Pay		Melanie Pays the Difference
Melanie: 52 cents (3/4 rate on 9 songs) *and* Mustang Sal: 20 cents (14 cents for the song and 6 cents for lyric reprint permission) Total: **72 cents** per album	−	Mechanical License limit Melanie agreed to: (10 × 3/4 Statutory) **57 3/4 cents**	=	Over the limit by **14.25 cents** per record sold

If Melanie sells 1,000,000 records, she will owe the label over $140,000.

NEGOTIATE

Often, if the label doesn't feel your material is strong enough, they may insist you record a cover tune that they feel has commercial appeal. If they do, then you should specify that they pay the extra money for this, not you. Sometimes, if the cover tune has a new arrangement that's so fresh that the label knows it will be a hit, they will agree to pay the additional money. Ask for this. *Always* ask for it.

Also, **if extra money is to be paid to a third-party publisher for use of one of their songs, it's vital that you insist that this money not be taken out of your next Advance.** It's bad enough that it will come out of "royalties" and/or "Net Profits." You should try like hell to keep these accounts separate, meaning that the label can't pay back the deficit created by Advances with mechanicals. Many major-label contracts used to have this separation of accounts included, but since the 360 Deal, this is one of the first things to come off the top when calculating "Net Profits" (see page 84 for what "Net Profits" means). You must scour through the contract and carefully examine every mention of "Mechanical Royalties," "Offset Rights," and "recoupment" to make sure that this cross-accounting is not allowed.

Greatest Hits

Notwithstanding the foregoing, the "Statutory Rate" with respect to the selections embodied in a particular Greatest Hits Album shall be determined as of the date of the initial release of such Greatest Hits Album in the United States (rather than as of the date of initial release of the first Master embodying each selection therein), but only with respect to sales of such Greatest Hits Album and any singles released in connection therewith.

Regardless of what it says above, about [*the label being cheap bastards and*] the rate not changing and all, well, we'll give you this: if you're lucky enough to have a string of hits to the point where we put out a Greatest Hits album, well, then (*okay, okay*) when we release your Greatest Hits Album, we'll figure out a new bullshit "Statutory Rate." [*Though they don't say what it will be. See below.*] But this applies *only* to this Greatest Hits album, on a song-by-song basis. It's not retroactive to the original releases, so don't get any ideas, *y'hear*?

REALITY: This seems awfully generous, considering the label's overall attitude. Well, they're not that kind. This is where confusion over "statutory rate" and "Statutory Rate" can come in handy for the sneaky lawyer. The clause above is intended to make you think that when the greatest hits record is released that the mechanical license for the songs will be at whatever the new statutory fee is at that time. This is bound to be more than the rate at the time of initial release, because the rate historically has always gone up (although there's no legal reason why it couldn't go down). So you are happy. Right?

But remember that "Statutory Rate," when capitalized, means *whatever* they want it to mean. In this contract it means a fixed amount "inspired by" the amount established by the law *or* whatever the record industry cartel agrees to pay. In 2008, for the first time in history, the Copyright Royalty Board that sets the rates agreed to throw the labels a bone to stop them from whining about losing money because of the Internet. Usually they establish what the escalation of rates will be for the following 10 years. This time they simply said, "We're going to set the rates for 2010–2020 something down the line. So, all bets are off as to what the future of the Statutory Rate will be. Right now it's frozen until further notice at 9.1/24 cents."

So this means that they'll negotiate in good faith at that time to determine what the new rate will be for the Greatest Hits album.

In addition, the fate of the CD Album is also uncertain, and thus the fate of "greatest hits" compilations, although we can bet that some version of it will always be in play.

NEGOTIATE

Make sure that the Greatest Hits album (which may be a combination of other people's songs and your songs) has the same rate applied to *all of your songs*. The sneaky lawyer may try something like, "We'll pay you 25% more than the old 'Statutory Rate' for your Greatest Hits Album." But if one of your songs is about 10 years old and another of your songs is a year old, the difference between these two will be drastic. Level the playing field.

Sampling Rights, or "Y'mean, I gotta pay for that, yo?"

What about tracks in which you use samples from other songs? Yes, the Controlled Composition clause applies to them as well. Fights over samples have been in the pages of *Billboard* ever since Vanilla Ice had to pony up mucho bucks to David Bowie and Queen for use of a sample from their song "Under Pressure" in his 1990 hit, "Ice, Ice Baby."

The concept of "borrowing" someone else's music to build your own "original" master recording is a source of ongoing debate. Is it stealing, or true artistic expression? The courts decided it was stealing some years ago, and a whole new set of clauses dealing with this issue were introduced into the recording contract. Here's the rule:

The label has no intention of paying anything extra over 10 × "Statutory Rate" (91 cents per Album) to buy you samples.

SAMPLE THIS

Remember Melanie from the last sidebar? Well, she used three samples in her version of Mustang Sal's tune (for which she was already going to have to pay 14 and 1/4 cents). Two samples came from a James Brown record (owned by Universal) and one from a jazz record on Blue Note Records. Neither of these catalogs are owned by Warner Bros., which was Melanie's label. Now each of the other publishers, Universal and PolyGram, wanted 25% of Melanie's copyright on her recording of Mustang Sal's song for the use of samples from their catalogs. Although this was fairly standard, it meant that each publishing company wanted a quarter of the 7.7 cents of Melanie's allowance, or 1.9 cents per sample. Let's call it two cents a sample to keep it easy (see the footnote[20] if you don't get the math).

Melanie would have to pay for the three samples out of her allowance of 58 cents per Album, which meant that just for the samples on this song, Melanie would owe the label 4 cents on *each copy of the song that the label sold*. This was in addition to the 14 cents she already owed Mustang Sal for the song. Melanie's parents quickly figured that the "overage" above and beyond the 58-cent limit she agreed to was not going to cover her, because she owed a total of 20 cents on the Mustang song alone, and still had to figure out what to do about all the samples she was putting on the other nine songs on the Album. Before long she would go broke putting out this record. To cut costs, she ditched the Mustang Sal tune and decided to budget herself. She limited each of her jams to between two and five samples a piece. Here's Melanie's sample licensing breakdown:

Song #	Status	Mechanical cap	Deduction	Remaining
Song 1	2 Samples	3/4 rate = .058	4 cents	$.54
Song 2	2 Samples	× 10 songs	4 cents	.50
Song 3	3 Samples	= .058 allowance	6 cents	.44
Song 4	3 Samples		6 cents	.38
Song 5	5 Samples		10 cents	.28
Song 6	4 Samples		8 cents	.20
Song 7	2 Samples		4 cents	.16
Song 8	3 Samples		6 cents	.10
Song 9	4 Samples		8 cents	.02
Song 10	3 Samples		6 cents	-.04
Total	**31 Samples**	**$0.58**	**$0.62**	**-$0.04**

Better. But Melanie still had to reimburse Warner Bros. 4 cents for every CD they sold to make up for the deficit caused by what they paid out to the other publishing companies.

[20] The breakdown for this is given in *Confessions* in the chapter on publishing. Basically, the "publisher's share" consists of 50% of the song's revenue.

The example in the sidebar "Sample This" only uses 31 samples in an entire Album. I've worked on many records with five times that many samples. Remember, your rate is "fixed." What if you wanted to use a sample from a record released last year on a song on your fourth Album? If you're on your fourth Album in 2010, that means you probably signed this contract about seven years ago. Since the sample was from last year, the "Statutory Rate" for it would be based on a different "Statutory Rate" than yours. A much higher one. *HA!!!*

Now, labels have a good argument: why should *they* pay any extra mechanicals just because you want to use all these samples? Well, I'll tell you why. Number one: since they heard your demo before they signed you, they already knew that your music was "sample intensive." Therefore, they should take the risk along with you, or at the very least, offer to facilitate the acquiring of the sample clearances free of charge (most major labels charge an administrative fee if they do it for you).

Number two: **If you're signing with a major label there is a better than average chance that most of these samples come from records** *that they already own*. Yes, it's true. So they're charging you for something that, in most cases, they could *give* to you. Which puts this clause in the "Big Suck" category.

Controlled Composition clauses were originally designed to prevent you from recording a ton of songs and remakes. Each song you don't control would require the label to pay the full rate. But no one could have anticipated, before the advent of samples, that in drafting these clauses the labels would give themselves an extremely effective way of taking back the money they are required to pay songwriters by law and simultaneously creating a new revenue source for themselves.

First, the label encourages you to use your creative genius and sample, sample, sample. **Then they charge you for each one.**

NEGOTIATE

Most people don't make an issue out of this for the main reason that many don't catch it or comprehend it. You can see how covert it was.

Try to have the label create a separate line item that comes from the recording fund to pay for samples. You should only have to pay for the use of the sample up front, instead of as a percentage of "royalties." Use the argument that samples are a necessary element of the finished product (unlike a cover tune, which is a bit of a luxury). In other words, it's no different than buying a guitar. It might work in a standard deal, but forget about this negotiation in a 360 Deal. These costs are most definitely coming out of "Net Profits."

Another thing that has worked in standard deals and 360 Deals is asking for an increased mechanical if you use many samples right up front. Say 15× Statutory instead of the usual 10 or 12× Statutory.

You should also have the label agree that if any of the samples are part of their catalog or a sister company's catalog, that they pay the songwriter and waive their cut of the publisher's share. This would cut the "Offset Right" or "Net Profits" deduction in half.

Have a clause put in your contract that clearly states that if the sample comes from a catalog that they have any control over that there will be no deduction from mechanicals. And if the sample comes from a competing label's catalog, then the business affairs department of your label will assist in acquiring these licenses for no charge.

If the sample does *not* come from the label's catalog and they say that they will have to pay for it, add a clause that allows you the last right of refusal to reject the label's "best effort" negotiation to secure the sample.

HOW TO BOIL A FROG IN YOUR RECORD AND NOT GET CHARGED FOR IT

How do you go from having all these rights and liberties to owing the label money? It's like magic. Here's the trick: It's like the story of the frog in boiling water. If you throw him right in, he'll leap out. But if you put him in lukewarm water and turn up the fire very, very slowly, he'll never hop out, and will boil to death. Here's the Mechanical License version of that. This is how they get you to be so "reasonable."

They convince you that:

- You should not charge them more than the "statutory rate" for your new material.

- The "Statutory Rate"" is the same as the "statutory rate."

- You should let them pay you the same way they pay your normal "royalties" and hold between 35% and 50% for up to two years.

- You should not insist they pay you anything on records they give away for "free."

- You should let them pay you only on records "sold."

- You should take a small deduction of 25% (three-quarter rate) in this license because it's "standard."

- A limit is in order so that you don't take advantage of them. (And because it's "standard.")

- If you go over your limit, you will pay the overage out of your "royalties."

- You should put elements in your Album that you don't own or control (like cover songs and samples). And they neglect to mention that they own these other elements, but can get you a "good rate" on them.

- You should let them bill you for the overage.

- You should let them collect your publishing money and charge you an additional 25%–50% for this.

- You should smoke a fatty.[21]

> Conclusions

Now, when labels boast, "It's our creative philosophy that a song should be recorded by the person who writes it. And that's what we look for in an artist," you will have a new perspective on this way of thinking. Although you are entitled to receive as much money as you want for your songs, the record companies stampede over the law and convince you to let them pay you only a percentage of what the law provides. Your lawyer plays a culpable role in this if she does not educate you on your rights and instead toes the party line, so you'll sign the deal and she can get paid.

As if that's not bad enough, the label then introduces a series of nasty pocket-picking extras that whittle your due money down even further, often to less than zero, thus putting you in a deficit. It's that simple.

Do you want to make money? Put only original songs that you write completely on your Album and don't use samples. Then you'll get three-quarters of what you're entitled to. Or better yet, think you're a rebel? Try this:

Don't agree to license your never-before-released songs at the mechanical rate. Convince the label your material is worth more. And get more.

[21] Smoking a fatty could, under these circumstances, also be considered a recoupable expense, since it is accomplished during the course of business.

This wraps up the chapters on what you will be paid and how. Starting with the next chapter, "Promotion," we will see what the label is claiming they will do to make you rich and famous. Since, as we've learned, they intend to squeeze every nickel and dime they can out of paying you, you should be very interested in what they are planning on doing in exchange for that—i.e., make you into a hit so that you can earn money from other sources, such as endorsements, movie deals, etc. Let's see if they have any intention of keeping their word.

Turn the page.

CHAPTER 5

●Promotion
or "You mean, I got to pay for my own video and tour?"

I n the old days of rock 'n' roll, managers (who used to negotiate contracts) would tell their benumbed clients that they fought with the label to get them full-color artwork on the album jacket, black light posters, and a special tour bus. They would neglect to mention the part about it being recoupable. Only after a year or two went by, and the artist tried to make sense of their royalty statements, would the truth hit them like Wile E. Coyote's Acme anvil falling from the heavens. Then it was too late.

Artists are far more savvy these days. As a result, their lawyers and managers have had to move up a peg in their rationalizations as well.

Why This Clause Exists

Labels are well aware of their star-making ability. A hit record means a lot more than "royalties" for an artist; it's prestige, and can generate opportunities for many other sources of revenue. Mark Wahlberg is the best example that comes to mind. From Funky Bunch singer to film star. Might he have achieved his screen success without his previous fame? Maybe, but it could never be argued today that one had nothing to do with the other.

Labels are well aware that as the artist grows he or she will be sought after. So, in the early stages of your career, when you're desperate for a break, they will make you agree to equity in parts of your career that are outside of recorded music. This was the major-label viewpoint even before CD sales started to drop in 2003. Thus was born the concept of the "360 Deal," a deal that capitalizes on all aspects of a recording artist's revenue, touring, mechanicals, acting roles, and of course publishing (which was covered in the last chapter). With that, let's learn some new words.

This Matter of "Agreement," "Approval," "Consent," "Mutually Determined," and Being "Reasonable"

The entire strength of the clauses that govern promotion center around three words: "reasonable," "approval," and "consent." Many sentences in these clauses sound like this: "Label must get artist's approval to..." or "an amount of time that is reasonable..."

We've already been introduced to the word "reasonable" from the reserve clauses in the past chapters. But, like other words that you thought you knew, "approval" and "consent" have unique meanings in LabelSpeak. You thought they meant that the label has to get your permission before they do something that will either 1) cost you money, or 2) make you look stupid.

Both are untrue.

I usually show you loopholes in this book as they come up, but here the loophole is created by burying the real definition of "approval" and "consent" in a short little clause that is sometimes not even labeled. If it is labeled, it's called something like WAIVERS, or if they are feeling generous, they might call it AGREEMENTS & CONSENT.

Let's have a look at this, up close:

1) As to all matters treated herein to be determined by **mutual agreement**, **or** as to which any approval or consent is required, such agreement, approval or consent will not be unreasonably withheld.

1) **Whenever we need to agree on anything**, you better not give us a hard time about it.

2) **Not withstanding anything herein contained to the contrary**, your agreement, approval or consent, whenever required, shall be deemed to have been given unless you notify Pacific otherwise within five (5) business days following the date of Pacific's written request to you therefore.

2) **Forget what it says anywhere else in this contract; this is the actual rule:** whenever we require **your cooperation** to do *anything*, you will only have five days after we notify you to make up your mind before we can make up your mind for you.

REALITY: I've worked with artists and pop bands for about two decades, and I've never seen one who can make up their mind in five days about anything. Joking aside, some of the things for which they will ask your "consent" are simple, but most are not. Consider the group photo showing four players. One thinks he looks best in shot "A." Another thinks he looks better in shot "B." A third doesn't like the outfit in shot "B" and wants the color of the shirt changed using Photoshop (so they don't have to reshoot).

These kinds of decisions can take a *lot* more than five days, and the label knows it. And this is assuming that they only give you one critical issue to think about at a time. Usually, decisions about tours, videos, singles, and cover art are all made within a short 30- to 60-day window. The label has weeks, even months, to plan their "suggestions." You have five days to respond.

Finally, the term "mutual determination" needs to be examined when used with "reasonable." You often see these phrases living next to each other in sentences that look like this:

```
"By mutual determination, Pacific will make such changes in
the Album Artwork that the Artist reasonably requests."
```

The only problem is, unlike the words "consent" and "approval," "reasonable" is not defined. So we assume the label is referring to the common use of the word, as in, "C'mon, Joe, you're the club manager; be *reasonable* about making us lug all this equipment to the backstage door when our van won't even fit in the alley."

The word "reason" as the root implies that some form of logic will be employed in creating a standard. But, as anyone who's been in a debate with Joe, the club manager, will tell you, what is "reasonable" exists only in the eye of the beholder. And who is the beholder in the recording contract? The label. So "reasonable" becomes just about anything they want it to become, because few people relish spending the money to go to court to ask a judge what is "reasonable."

So unless you want to be the first artist in history to take a record company to court for breach of contract for "not being reasonable," for the sake of simplicity, just assume that everywhere you see the word "reasonable" or "mutual" below, it means "whatever we [the label] think is best."

And now, with this in mind, let's look at the Standard and see exactly what you will have to be "reasonable" about.

>The Standard
The Marketing Plan

Pacific shall conduct with you in a good faith, meaningful manner on creating and developing a marketing, advertising and promotion plan for each Album delivered hereunder (this sentence shall not be interpreted to require Pacific to increase the video commitment or alter the release commitment made in this Agreement). In connection therewith, **Pacific will obtain your approval** of the general concept and theme of each national or other major advertising, marketing and promotion campaign in the United States relating to such Albums (**which consent may not be unreasonably withheld**) provided that you shall not have the right to frustrate Pacific's ability to release any Album in a timely fashion.

Subject to your reasonable availability and Pacific's actual time constraints, you shall have the right to approve the visual elements, concepts, ideas, wording and design of posters, advertisements and other marketing materials which are under Pacific's control in the United States, but once you have done so Pacific will not be obligated to obtain your approval

We will keep you posted and give you periodic opportunities to object to the plan to promote your record.

(this does not mean that we will have to make a music video for each Album you "deliver" or even release any record that you "deliver.")

But we will **get you to agree with us** on a general concept for how to best market you on any national campaign. [*Notice there's no mention of* underline*international marketing anywhere, and you won't find any, either.*]

(You can object to our suggestions, but not too strongly) as long as you don't [*keep changing your mind and*] piss us off by forcing us to push back the release date of the Album.

If you can tear yourself away from the studio, and we're not under any deadline [*they always are, however*], we'll show you all the artwork, and tell you where we plan to advertise and how. You can make comments and suggestions at that time, but we don't really have to listen to them. [*If they just nod and pretend that they care, it will be enough to satisfy this contract and*

of any specific advertisements or other related materials or of any specific placement of advertisements, but such advertisements, related materials, and placements will be consistent with the **approved general concept** and theme, and will incorporate the pre-approved design. Subject to your arranging same, you may have a representative present at major marketing/promotion meetings in the U.S. held to discuss the marketing/promotion of Albums recorded hereunder.

constitutes "consulting with you."] After that, we don't have to tell you shit about how we might plan to plaster your face everywhere and anywhere we think will help "sell" records,

as long as we stay **somewhere in the neighborhood of what we showed you.** [*It's a big neighborhood if they want it to be.*]

Assuming you remember to tell us when you're available, we'll try to schedule our marketing meetings around you. You can send a band member, or your manager down to the meetings to watch your back.

REALITY: The nodding and miming like they give a hoot, described above, is truer than I can describe here with mere words. Art Department people are well trained to pacify artists. Don't be angry with them. It's the higher-ups that are to blame if you don't like the way you are being marketed.

DON'T NEGOTIATE

Save your legal bullets for more worthy battles. This is one area where I think most artists should let the label have control. "Selling" millions of records is what they do best. This is why you're signing with them and putting up with all this. Let them do their magic and turn you into a legend. Save your moxie for the things below.

Album Cover and Poster Art

1) In preparation for the initial release in the United States during the term hereof of each Commitment Album, Pacific will consult with you

1) While you are [*very busy*] finishing your recordings [*which is tedious, due to our annoying standards for "delivery"*], we

regarding the "Album Artwork" (as herein defined). As used herein, the term "Album Artwork" means all artwork, photography or other graphics and related materials for the packaging of the applicable Album. You shall have the right, after such Album Artwork has been made available to you at Pacific's offices for review and comment, to disapprove such Album Artwork. Unless otherwise provided in this paragraph, Pacific will make such changes in the Album Artwork as you reasonably request.

2) Pacific will not be required to make any changes which would delay the release of the applicable Album beyond the scheduled date or which would require Pacific to incur any Special Packaging Costs. Any premium charges incurred to meet the release schedule because of delays in approvals by you will constitute Advances and may be recouped by Pacific from any and all monies becoming due to you hereunder.

will, from time to time, invite you down to the office [*even though you probably live in another city*] and casually flash in front of you ideas we have for your album cover art, and other stuff we think is best for the promotion of your record. (These include posters, mobiles, and anything else that those wacky guys in promotion can think of.) This is what we call a "consultation." You have the right to object to anything we show you within five days. If you request changes at that time, we'll make them if we feel like it.

But:

2) If any change you request pushes back our deadline for release, we don't have to do it. If we do go ahead and do it, it's called a "Special Packaging Cost," and the cash required to fulfill your little ego trip will be considered an Advance. That means it will be taken out of future "royalties" (or "Net Profits") from this Album, or any other money we owe you [*count on any changes you want to make to be considered "Special"*].

EXPLANATION: This was already charged to you in the form of the "Packaging Deduction" (see page 53, in "Royalties"). This should be removed *completely*.

Upon completion of the Album Artwork, Pacific will determine and advise you if the costs for the manufacturing of the packaging would require Pacific to incur Special Packaging Costs. If you notify Pacific of your objection to such Special Packaging Costs in connection with such Album Artwork, and Pacific nevertheless uses such Album Artwork, Pacific shall not recoup Special Packaging Costs hereunder. No failure to so advise you will be deemed a breach hereof, provided that if Pacific fails to so advise you, Pacific will not recoup any such Special Packaging Costs.

3) **Pacific will not be required to make any change which in Pacific's reasonable, good faith opinion** is patently offensive, constitutes an obscenity, violates any law, infringes or violates the rights of any Person, or which might subject Pacific to liability or unfavorable regulatory action. All matters

After we complete the Album Artwork, we'll let you know if we went over budget and had to apply Special Packaging Costs. If we did go over budget, you have five days to object. But if we fail to notify you that we went over budget, it's no skin off our back; we just won't recoup the Special Packaging Costs from your "royalties." [*But there's a good chance that we'll just call the extra expenses something else and deduct them anyway. So in case you have any thoughts about trying to have a say in this process, check this out.*]

Also:

3) **No matter what you say, we're not obligated to make any changes** that we feel are obscene, unlawful, or offensive in any way (*or which might bring out of the woodwork right- and left-wing radicals with nothing better to do than litigate the First Amendment, subjecting Pacific to Big Brother interventions*).

relating to Pacific's trademarks, legal obligations, notices or disclosures deemed advisable by Pacific's attorneys or other requirements will be determined in **Pacific's sole discretion.**

Oh yeah, and one more thing: Whenever our lawyers say that associating our name or trademark in a particular situation could reflect poorly on us [*such as an obscene album cover*], we will **assert complete control.**

LOOPHOLE ALERT!!!

EXPLANATION: Have you ever seen an Album cover where the label's name did not appear? I thought not. Any time their name appears, they have say over what the Album looks like, not you, regardless of the three pages of gobbledygook before this last sentence.

NEGOTIATE

Try to just cross it out. They may not even care. Their ass is covered six ways to Sunday on this issue anyway.

REALITY: Well, this is not my beautiful house. This is not my beautiful wife. What happened to all that peace, love, and granola the label offered back when they were still sucking up to you? Now it's all ass. The reality is this: No matter what they tell you up front, there's *no way in hell* that a new group gets to say what their Album cover art will look like, because they've made it patently impossible for you to actually have a say. The only time the label agrees to "consult" is when they know you'll be far too preoccupied to focus. And even if they do "consult" with you, they don't have to listen to your input, as they can always claim that it's just too late and any changes you want will cost extra. It's a complete brush-off.

There is one thing you can do. Everywhere where the contract says, "Notwithstanding anything herein contained to the contrary…" in the clause that outlines what "approval" is (see page 170), have your lawyer change that wording to: "Except as otherwise expressly provided in this Agreement." This puts the burden on the record company to customize each clause in which they want to screw you with this five-day bullshit. They'll still try to do it, but you've made it a bit harder for them.

You can also try to get provisions inserted in your contract that allow you to extend the five-day period. Make sure it's at least five *business* days, and that you can take part in "consultations" with the art department, even if you are in a different city than the record company. There's a lot that you can do with FedEx and by sending files through e-mail. The best thing to do, though, to make sure the label doesn't screw you with some lame Album cover, is to maintain a good, *close* relationship with them. This is what your manager is paid to do, but it doesn't hurt if you take this matter into your own hands. Get to know the Art Director at the label, get chummy with the VP handling your account. Here's another axiom for you:

A good relationship is worth 10 times more than an expensive lawyer.

So that's how they treat you when it comes to artwork. Do you think they're any more generous when it comes to picking the Single? Let's see.

Singles

Major-label contracts go out of their way to be vague about Singles. They know it's a touchy area. They also know that every artist's lawyer asks for guarantees regarding this. Who doesn't want a hit song to their credit?

However, labels have always been cagey about this issue, since they know that any band they sign today might not seem so hot 10 months later, when they "deliver" their first album. Trends can change by then, and the label might feel the band hasn't come up with a track that's good enough to be released as a Single. The band will undoubtedly think otherwise, but it's the label that decides what can be considered a "reasonable" Single.[1]

[1] For an interesting and often true example of this phenomenon, see the sidebar "A Tale of Two Writers" in the previous chapter.

Even more common is when the label and the Artist don't agree as to which song on the Album should be the Single. Many artists have had their careers ruined by a poor selection. So lawyers representing artists have become smarter in this facet of negotiation. If you look in the subheading that is sometimes labeled MASTER RECORDINGS, here's what you get these days regarding Singles:

1) You and Pacific shall mutually determine the selection of Singles Records to be released from each Product LP hereunder, however, in the event of a dispute, Pacific's decision shall be final.

1) We'll ask you your opinion about which songs should be released as Singles off the record. We hope you agree with us on this. But if you don't, we'll just go with our decision. *Cool?*

2) With respect to each Singles Record, Pacific shall have the right to edit and/or re-mix the Master Recording for the purpose of releasing a Singles Record which is commercially satisfactory and of a suitable playing time acceptable for broadcast on commercial radio. Such edits and/or re-mixes shall be **subject to your approval, not to be unreasonably withheld.**

2) Regarding each Single, we will determine if it needs to be remixed [*or cut into a dance version or a Muzak version, or whatever*] so that it's not more than 3.5 minutes long, and in case it contains any four-letter words, we want you to remove them. **We'll ask you your opinion on these changes, but you can't disagree without a really good reason.**

REALITY: Same concept, different clause. The label will always make the decision for the artist regarding a first Single. If an artist objects strongly, the label will oblige them, but it will never promote the artist's choice as heavily as their choice. In this way the label creates a self-fulfilling prophecy. They don't promote it with the same enthusiasm, and then when it fails they can turn to the artist and say, "See, you should have listened to us." The artist will sooner or later buckle to this circular reasoning. It's unavoidable, in most cases.

Hopefully, you will agree with your label on what should be the Single. One way to ensure that you do is to talk about it before you are signed. A&R people are well trained to avoid this subject with comments like, "Well, let's see what happens on the record. Maybe you'll come up with something that's even better than the demo." This is sidestepping. I've never known a label to make a recording commitment to a new artist without a preconceived notion about what song on their demo will be the Single.

In the same way that you can't get the public to buy a record that they hate (no matter how hard you push it),
you can't get a record label to promote a record they disapprove of.

NEGOTIATE

For the reason above, many artists let the label do what they will here. But there are a few things you can do that they might not cry over. For example, if you can't "agree," let them pick the first two Singles and give you the final decision on the third and fourth Single off any particular Album. Or they get to pick the Single off the first Album and you get to pick the Single off the second.

Also, no matter what, make sure there is a sentence in there that says basically this: "If the artist [you] and the label cannot come to an agreement over which track to release as a Single, to release no single is not an option." I call it a No Cop-Out clause.

Independent Promoters

In the book *Hit Men*, Fredric Dannen tells a series of tales that everyone should be familiar with: how the major labels gladly paid Mob-tied extortionists called "Independent Promoters" to sell (or push, might be more accurate) certain records to key radio stations.

Several people got caught after a government sting, and as a result the labels no longer take responsibility for these expenditures. Instead they push it off on the artist, saying that "we don't force you to spend money on this, but we strongly endorse it." They'll give you a "signing bonus" of about $50,000 with the "expectation" that it will be used for this express purpose. Every artist wants a hit, and so many buckle. Some try to hire smaller, allegedly more honest, promoters. But trial and error has taught most in the business that the more honest you are, at least in this area, the less likely your chances of success.[2] The label provides for this contingency in the contract with a clause often found under PROMOTION. It goes like this:

[2] See the *Confessions* chapter "Airplay."

[3] Contrary to popular belief, there is no law against paying a radio station to play a particular song or artist. "Payola" is when that financial agreement is not disclosed to the listening public. You may remember that the launch for Limp Bizkit used paid air time. Likewise, it is not illegal to feed answers to contestants on a game show; it's only illegal to fool the viewing public about it.

[4] As you will see in "Terms and Exclusivity," the "Option Period" is not a specific length of time, but rather a period that starts when you sign the contract and ends in conjunction with certain events. The key event is the "delivery" and promotion of your Album, which you can't do quite as well if you're in jail or under indictment. See page 268.

[5] See the *Confessions* chapter "Airplay."

1) Any promotional efforts or expenditures made by or on behalf of you in connection with any Records hereunder shall be in accordance with applicable legal standards, including Sections 317 and 507 of the Communications Act of 1934, as amended. In the event you are in breach of the preceding sentence, Pacific may, without limiting its rights, terminate the Term forthwith by sending you written notice of such termination.

1) We can't cop to you breaking the law [*even though it might be necessary*], so you hereby agree that you will abide by Sections 317 and 507 of the Communications Act of 1934. [*317 is the "payola" statute. 507 is the "quiz show" statute. See REALITY for more.*] If you don't, we have the right to kick you off the label and cancel the portions of this contract where we agree to do stuff for you, but we will still be able to ask you to do stuff for us. We'll let you know by sending you a letter. No calls, thank you.

REALITY: For those who don't have their pocket guide to FCC regulations handy, section 317 is the "payola" section, which says that the playing of a certain song on the air for money must be disclosed to the public. This makes sense for recording artists. But Section 507 is the "quiz show" section. It prohibits giving answers to quiz show contestants.[3] I guess record companies are concerned that they may be held liable if artists are being fed answers to questions when they go on MTV.

What's so messed up about this is that I know labels that will privately encourage you to break this very clause. They will do this through your manager and producer, who will not be interested in taking you on unless you are "committed to doing everything to get a hit." To add insult to injury, if you do hire someone to bribe station directors and then get caught, the label can hold you in limbo, because it states expressly in the contract that if you are involved in any crime, they can terminate or "suspend" an Option Period,[4] during which time you are still bound exclusively to the contract. This is intended to apply mostly to things like drug charges, which, on rare occasions, pop stars have been known to be busted on. In the past few years, however, this has spread to gun possession, trafficking, extortion, prostitution, and, as in the case of the subject of this particular chapter, racketeering, which is what paying a radio station manager a bribe to play your record is considered to be by the law.[5]

NEGOTIATE

It doesn't seem reasonable to me that while under contract to a company, you trash them without regard for protecting that company's investment in you. But I have known labels that encourage artists to break this clause and then claim that they don't have to fulfill their obligations to that artist, though the artist is still obligated to make records for them. (Even if they're in jail.) This is unfair and should go, go, go. I would try to insert a clause saying that if the label doesn't support you in any situation where you are not actually found guilty of something, then you should be released from any obligation to them.

Following the above left to the jaw is this right uppercut:

2) In the event that Pacific, in its sole and exclusive discretion, elects to expend any monies in connection with third-party promotion or marketing of any record embodying Master Recordings hereunder, Pacific shall have the right to charge fifty percent (50%) of such costs against and recoup same at any time from any and all royalties (excluding mechanical royalties) accruing to your credit hereunder. Pacific will consult with you regarding Pacific's marketing plans (including, without limitation, Pacific's plans to utilize independent promoters).

2) Should we decide to finance this [*potentially illegal*] activity (which we call "third-party promotion"), we will recoup 50% of whatever we spend from—guess where? Yep! Your "royalties."

We will tell you about the marketing plan and if we decide to hire an independent promoter. If you don't fully object [*in writing, in triplicate, through a notarized attorney*], we'll assume it's okay with you.

REALITY: Hiring an independent promoter can add up to many hundreds of thousands of bucks. Promotion of one Single can cost anywhere up to and over $1,000,000, with the aim of getting heavy rotation in all four major regions of the US on top radio stations. You will not likely see a dime of "royalties" if they do this too much.

Put a limit on how much can be spent in this regard. Say, $100,000. That way you have a fighting chance. The label will counter with some BS about getting written consent from you to spend this money. They will make it sound as if this is a good thing, as now they need your permission to spend the money. Don't fall for this. They want written permission so that they can say that you authorized it. This gets the Feds off their back. If they insist on exposing you to potentially criminal behavior in exchange for this money, then the least they can do is give you the $100,000 and let you hire your *own* independent promoter. (They already thought of this. See "Advances," page 17.) One thing, though—don't let your manager commission this money. It's earmarked for your promoter. Oh, and save a little in a bank account—for bail. So regarding Singles:

The relative probability of you choosing your own single is directly proportionate to how similar your choice is to that of the label.

Videos

There will likely not be a subheading called "Music Videos" in your contract. The labels call this MARKETING, or an AUDIO VISUAL WORK. A look there will reveal the following on the subject.

   Note: "Covered Video," sometimes called a "Videogram," is a fancy word for "music video."

Pre-Production

[6] Why "about" five months? Well, because it's impossible to say the exact length of "Option Periods." Usually they are around 10 to 14 months. The above says that they will produce a video within the Option Period, but after the Album is released. This usually means about five months into the "Period."

Pacific will produce or cause to be produced at least one (1) Covered Video for the Commitment Album released during the initial Contract Period hereof and for the Commitment Album released during each Option Period hereof, provided that you have fully complied with your material obligations to Pacific hereunder. With respect to all

We will produce or make someone else produce at least one music video for each Album you make for us, within about five months of the Album's release.[6] But only if you have been a good artist and done everything in this contract.

Covered Videos, the following shall be applicable:

a) With respect to Covered Videos made in connection with the initial release of a Commitment Album, the selection(s) to be embodied in each Covered Video shall be **mutually designated** by you and Pacific, provided that you shall be deemed to have approved any selection that has been or will be embodied on a Single.

b) Each Covered Video shall be shot on a date or dates and at a location or locations to be **mutually designated by you and Pacific**, subject to the Artist's reasonable prior professional commitments.

If we make a video, the following shall apply:

a) For videos that are made for the promotional campaign for your new Album, we're gonna **decide together** what song will be made into a video, as long as it's the same song we already decided together will be the Single.

b) We'll decide where and when to shoot the video. Of course, we'll try to work around your schedule. If you don't like our choice of times and dates and locations, you have five days to object.

REALITY: Production schedules for film crews are generally so tight that canceling the shoot, if you objected, would cost thousands, which you would have to pay for. So, once again, they are giving you no real choice in this matter.

3) The producer and director of each Covered Video, and the concept or script for each Covered Video, **shall be approved by both you and Pacific.** Pacific shall engage the producer, director and other production personnel for each Covered Video, and shall be responsible for and shall pay the production costs of each Covered Video in an amount not in excess of a budget to be established in advance by Pacific (the "Production

3) You can submit suggestions for videos which we might even use. But we will choose the producer, director, and the concept for the video. We'll **give you five days to object to it if you don't like it**. We'll hire everyone, and pay all the production costs up to the amount on the "mutually decided-upon budget" [*which we decided for you*] (called the "Production Budget").

Budget"). **You shall be responsible for and shall pay the production costs for each Covered Video which is in excess of the Production Budget.** In the event that Pacific shall pay any production costs for which you are responsible pursuant to the foregoing sentence (which Pacific is in no way obligated to do so), you shall promptly reimburse Pacific upon Pacific's request, **and all such costs not reimbursed may be recouped** by Pacific from any monies otherwise payable by Pacific to you hereunder.

You pay for anything over that amount. If you don't have the money, we might lay it out for you, but you're going to have to quickly pay it back.

Anything you can't pay back right now will come out of your next Advance or "royalties" due to you.

LOOPHOLE ALERT!!!

EXPLANATION: Although the label just said they would "reimburse you money and take it out of your Advance," that's not really the same as "Advancing you money." The difference is that by structuring it as a pay-us-back-right-now plan, it could be considered a "loan," and if it is a loan, then the label can lawfully charge you interest. This is very bad. By the time you build up enough money in your "royalty" account to pay back the $50,000 or so that you went over budget, you could end up owing double.

NEGOTIATE

Although this is a rarely enforced interpretation, get this thrown out. If they agreed to call the music video budget an Advance, then why not call the overage an Advance as well? The label's lawyer will argue that the word "loan" is not used and therefore you're being paranoid. Don't buy this crap. The clause is deliberately ambiguous. If it's no big deal, as they will claim, then there should be no problem tossing it out.

Your Performance in the Video

The Artist's compensation for performing in such Covered Videos (as opposed to your compensation with respect to the exploitation of such Videos which is provided elsewhere in this Agreement) shall be limited to any minimum amounts required to be paid for such Performances pursuant to any collective bargaining agreements pertaining thereto; provided, however, that the Artist hereby waives any right to receive such compensation to the extent such right may be waived.

You must be paid as an actor for your performance in the music video because of an agreement we have with several unions. This is not the same as the money you will earn from the sale of the video (which is in "Royalties," page 80). The amount will be the minimum union scale [*about $250 a day*].

But you waive your rights to receive this money if the union will let you.

REALITY: $250 a day might seem like good money to you right now, but if you're a big star, you should be able to set your day rates just like any other star. As to the second part, the unions will not let you waive your payment, because they make their money by getting you paid, so that you, in turn, can pay dues to them. However, major labels have a "relationship" with unions and have been known to get them to "excuse" a performer in certain situations.

NEGOTIATE

Get rid of this entire clause. It does nothing for you. You shouldn't have to be obliged for the next 10 years to appear anytime or anywhere the label wants you, for only $250 a day. It's absurd.

1) Each Covered Video shall be deemed an item of "Materials" covered by your warranties, representations and indemnification obligations hereunder. Pacific will have the right to reject any Covered Video or any element contained in a Covered Video which in Pacific's

1) As far as this contract is concerned, videos are no different than Master Recordings [*because they are all "recordings" of you*]. As such, all the same bullshit applies, including all the requirements for "delivery." It also includes your promise to pay us back for legal fees if anyone sues

reasonable, good faith opinion is patently offensive, constitutes an obscenity, violates any law, infringes or violates the rights of any Person, or which might subject Pacific to liability or unfavorable regulatory action.

us because your video pissed them off, or infringed on their copyright (see "Indemnification and Warranties," page 263).

We have the right to reject anything in a video that in our sole opinion is uncool, fucked-up, or that could bring Big Brother down on us.

REALITY: Well, this is interesting: labels will reject anything they think is distasteful in your video. Makes you wonder how some of these videos ever get made.

There is a more important issue here, which is this concept that videos are the same as any other type of recording that you do for them. Sounds okay, except for the fact that you have virtually no control over the video. The Album was an entirely different story—the budget came out of a specific Advance (see "Advances," page 23), you went over it with the producer before handing it in, and you had several months to look it over. You were there when the money was being spent and you were actively involved in the creative process. The video is a whole other universe: you will not likely be in the editing room, the budget will be created by the video production company's little elves (whom you will probably never meet), and the content will be storyboarded without you being present.[7] Yet the above says you are responsible for all of it.

NEGOTIATE

When you're a famous artist, it won't be hard to get all costs related to the video to be *not* recoupable, including lawsuit-related things. If your deal is a 360, this will be moot as well, because all these monies will come off the top to create "Net Profits." The video is a tool designed to promote their product—the Album. And since you had no real control over the content of the video, you should not be liable. Let the label pay for it. If you sense that you have some leverage in the negotiations, even if you are not a hot property right now, *always, always, always* ask for this. All they can say is no, and they won't be offended that you asked. In most cases they will agree to half being recoupable as a starting point. If that doesn't work, then ask for a separate fund, structured the same way that the Advances are structured (a sliding scale that is paid to you) so that *you* can pick the production company. In other words, have the money flow from you to the video production company. It's more work for you, but at least you have some control over your rapidly climbing debt to the label.

Recoupable Video Costs

Far removed from all other clauses regarding videos, buried deep in the myriad of clauses about ROYALTIES, the following paragraph about the recoupable costs and liabilities of the video can be found.

7) Pacific shall charge **all Production Costs** to the Video Account and, at its election, may at any time transfer and charge to the Audio Account (excluding mechanical royalties) up to one-half (1/2) of such Production Costs and may recoup the transferred Production Costs from any and all royalties accruing to the Audio Account.

7) We'll charge all the costs for making this video to a special account we set up for you called the Video Account. However, anytime we feel like it, we can also charge up to half of these costs to your Audio Account[8] (but we won't touch your mechanical royalties).

[8] The "Audio Account" is the account that all royalties go into from the sale of Albums. It goes by similar names in all Big Four contracts.

REALITY: This is very bad for you. Video costs are not within your control, even if they say they are your responsibility. Now they will come out of your "Audio Account," by which they mean, of course, your "royalties." The label knows that there will be little to no money from the sales of videos. This is their way of passing this promotional expense off on you.

NEGOTIATE

Try like hell to get rid of this. Remove all language that relates to the "Audio Account." Keep the video costs recoupable only from *video*-related sales.

8) You shall be solely responsible for and shall pay any and all monies payable to the Producers and directors of the visual portion of the Audiovisual Records or

8) You are responsible for paying the people that will work on the video (such as the producers and directors) and anyone else who can or should get a royalty from selling

Covered Videos, and to any other Persons (except publishers of non-Controlled Compositions or of Independent Interests in Controlled Compositions which are embodied in the Audiovisual Records or Covered Videos and any unions or guilds or their funds) who are entitled to a royalty or any other payment in respect of the exploitation of the Audiovisual Records (each such person being herein referred to as a "Royalty Participant"). **Notwithstanding the foregoing**, if Pacific shall pay or be required to pay any such monies directly to any Royalty Participant, then Pacific shall have the right to deduct same from any and all royalties payable to you hereunder.

the video (which we call a "Royalty Participant").

The two exceptions to this are 1) your music publishing company (if any), which will collect any money due from the sale of the video; and 2) any union dues that are created from the work you are giving people in the cast and crew.

Only kidding; if we have to pay anyone but you a royalty, it gets tacked onto your debt to us.

REALITY: In fact, there will likely always be someone who will want to be paid from the constant airing of the video. Why? Well, one reason that I've seen many times is that video producers are sometimes sloppy. They forget to get a *release* from the people on the street, like the artist's girlfriend who begged to be in one shot. (A release is the one-page contract that allows a video producer to use the "performance" of the people in the video without paying them a "royalty." If you've ever been an extra in a movie you were probably asked to sign one of these.)

Without a signed release, a person could always claim that by having their image used in a video, they are being unfairly exploited, and/or that their privacy has been violated. This causes problems for the label, which is why they make it your responsibility. Some believe that a major label will step in and deal with this, if it comes up. The label may even forget to charge you for it, because they may not know exactly *how* to charge you for it. So this is not a big concern. Still, you should always hold your video producer liable for any claims that arise from people who never signed a release.

In fact, here's your axiom for the day on video:

The label makes you completely responsible for the costs
and liabilities for your video.

Touring

It is almost impossible to make money and become famous without touring. Yet most first-time record deals don't offer much in this respect. The hope for most new acts is that they get to open for a headline act and thus get recognition. This has been the standard formula for decades, but how much does it cost the artist? Let's see …

Under the subheading of PERSONAL APPEARANCE or TOUR ARRANGEMENTS or PERFORMANCE OBLIGATIONS you will find something like this:

If the Artist undertakes a personal appearance tour of at least (15) major Phonograph Record markets in the United States in connection with the initial release of the first Commitment Album of the initial Contract Period, then:

If you decide, during the first six months after the Album is released, to tour 15 major cities in the US to promote your first Album, then:

a) Within a reasonable time before the plans for the tour are completed, you will notify Pacific of a complete itinerary, specifying the details of each engagement (including the time and place of each appearance). The itinerary (and each item thereof) will be **subject to Pacific's reasonable approval**.

a) Before you book each city and date for your tour you will give us a complete intended schedule, including all the details of the tour, **in plenty of time for us to voice any objections.**

b) Only if **Pacific approves** of the tour and each item of the itinerary (and thereafter there is no substantial change of any element thereof without Pacific's prior written consent), then, provided the tour is completed in accordance with the approved itinerary, Pacific will pay you that amount, if any, by which your direct expenses actually incurred in connection with the tour exceed your revenues for such tour, but not more than Seventy Five Thousand Dollars ($75,000) for the first Commitment Album of the initial Contract Period. **Said payment will constitute an Advance** and will be one hundred percent (100%) recoupable from all royalties (except Mechanical Royalties) becoming payable by Pacific to you and will be made upon Pacific's receipt of documentation of the tour expenses and revenues satisfactory to Pacific.

b) **Only if we approve** of each and every item and stop of the tour (and you don't go changing anything on us at the last minute, without our approval), then, assuming you stay on schedule, we will pay off any remaining out-of-pocket expenses (after we subtract the money you make from this tour, of course). We'll only cover actual touring costs, though [*not your trip to Disney World while in Florida*], and no more than $75,000 for the first tour after we release your first Album.

This money will, of course, be **100% recoupable from your "royalties"** (though, once again, we won't touch your mechanicals).

See the footnote at left.[9]

In order to get us to pay you this Advance you must keep very accurate receipts of every little expense that you want reimbursement for. Otherwise, forget it.

If we approve your decision to bail on the tour, we will cut into the 75 Gs mentioned above by one-fifteenth (1/15) for each city (or region) you didn't get to play.

[9] Though they say they won't take your mechanicals out of this fund, they do have the right to do so. See "Offset Right," page 113.

If Pacific approved the shortening of any such tour, the amount set forth in the first sentence of this subparagraph will be reduced by one-fifteenth (1/15) for each market deleted from the itinerary.

REALITY: Was that what the deal memo said? Go back to page 10 and read it carefully. It said "up to $75,000." Not "$75,000," or "at least $75,000." This means that $75,000 is the *max* they will pay. The rest comes out of your pocket, and they can make deductions to this as well.

Where's the clause about how the label will pay for the hotel rooms you smash up, or bail money for paternity suits? Didn't see it, did ya? Here's the skinny: The label approves of everything beforehand (no surprise there), and they will make up the difference between what you make and what you spend, but only if you don't change the tour schedule. Of course, this is a near impossibility, as schedules are changing constantly, and you'll only have about four months from the time you "deliver" your record to the time the Contract Period ends.[10] Labels know how impossible this is, so they usually don't enforce this clause very much as long as the band or group is really working hard and not getting into trouble.[11]

The reality is that on a first tour, most artists have to arrange everything themselves, with little help from the label. The label will bankroll it up a point ($75K in this case), but that money goes pretty fast. It's a fairly generous figure, too—I've seen much lower numbers: around $25,000 and worse on a first deal with a major, and around $5,000 to $10,000 on an indie. This is about enough to buy a van and sleep in fleabag motels with room service by Denny's. Naturally, the hope is that you can reach superstar status and be able to force your absurd demands on concert promoters—such as the now-famous Van Halen request of segregating M&Ms by color, or the insistence of a particular pop diva that Evian be served to her dog.

One more kicker here is that while you were making your first Album you probably held down a day job. But now that you're on the road promoting your first Album, where is your income coming from? The label has nothing to say on this issue. For this reason, many bands pad the budget and arrange kickbacks with their road crew. Labels are not stupid. They know this occurs. But this "accepted level of theft" gets the label out of claiming that the artist is an "employee" of the label while touring.

NEGOTIATE

Until you prove yourself, this will be a tough battle. What you should try to negotiate is the *aggregate*. That is the *total* amount that the label agrees to reimburse you for tour costs. Try to get it to be *not* recoupable. (Hey, it's worth

[10] See page 280 for the exact lengths of "Contract Periods."

[11] "Trouble" is a relative term. If you get into "trouble" but the publicity results in the sales of more records, the label won't mind, even though they will recoup any money they spent on getting you out of "trouble."

a try.) Indie labels will budge more on this than majors, in my experience. Fifty percent recoupable for a new act is not unheard of.

Other points: Throw out all this "schedule" language. Almost all new acts start off by opening for bigger acts, following the big band's mammoth tour bus around the country in their little VW microbus. The label knows this, so have them agree to "best efforts" language regarding the schedule, since it will not really be up to you anyway.

Touring 360 Style

In 360 land the label is like the Mob—they get a little piece of everything.

During the Option Period following the release of the Album from the previous Option Period hereunder, Pacific will be entitled to 7.5% of gross revenues from Artist's touring proceeds payable on the same gross revenue basis as Artist's then-current management company commission and payable for the same touring events that Artist's then-current management company commission is payable.

For the tour you do to promote the Album you just recorded for us, we, the record company, will be entitled to 7.5% of the total amount of cash from your proceeds, and you're gonna pay us at the same time and in the same way as you pay your manager.

REALITY: So now you have two managers. Except only one of them is doing any actual work for your tour. That's the one who sweated it out with you all the months before you were signed. Now the label wants a cut of your tour to offset the losses they claim they're having because of a downturn in the economy, or the fact that they haven't found a way to keep music as cool as video games, or the fact that they pay some of their executives way too much. You need to help them.

NEGOTIATE

This is well worth your time to haggle over. First, none of the tour proceeds or advances should be part of "Net Profits." Make it a separate enterprise entirely. In other words, tour advances should be recoupable only from tour proceeds.

Second, make them do some actual work. If you're new, get them to get you a slot on a great tour. They can do that with a phone call. Get them to get you a golden sponsor to offset costs. You can not talk them out of getting a piece of your tour, but you can shame them into doing a little bit of work in exchange for the money.

> Conclusions

What price fame? An age-old question. Our new words for the day are "consent," "mutually agreed," and "reasonable."

The label makes decisions for you
and gives you an extremely narrow window wherein to object.

They make it impossible to really object due to the firm hold they have over your career. But unless you negotiate otherwise, you will be financially responsible for all these decisions. Whenever these new words are used in quotes from now on, they will mean everything that's been covered in this chapter.

Now you know what "reasonable" really means. In the next chapter, "Merchandising," we'll see more of what you will be asked to be "reasonable" about.

Turn the page.

CHAPTER 6

Merchandising and Rights in Recording

or "How much of me do they own?"

"On Dec. 31, 1999, my publishing contract with Warner-Chappell expired, thus emancipating the name I was given before birth—Prince—from all long-term restrictive documents. I will now go back to using my name instead of the symbol I adopted to free myself from all undesirable relationships."
—Prince

T-shirts, posters, dolls—the works. It's been said that merchandising is where an artist really makes his or her money. And it's true. Or it was, at least until 360 Deals came along.

Many artists I have spoken to over the years find it depressing that they made more money licensing their name and face to some toy company than off "royalties" on a million seller.

As you become more famous, your face (called a "likeness" in LabelSpeak) will exponentially increase in value year after year, at the same time that your "royalties" are diminishing from declining sales.

A good negotiator will try to keep as much of these rights intact as possible so that you have the ability to market them down the line. The label, on the other hand, wants to own as much of these rights as you are willing to let them.

Why This Clause Exists

A label's ability to make money rests solely on its ability to exploit the artist in every known way. This means they will have control over the right to make copies of your work, commonly known as a *copyright*. When you sign a recording contract, you are in essence signing a transfer of the ownership and title of your work so that another party (the record company) can duplicate it and sell the duplication.

Obviously, this right has to be granted *exclusively*, meaning that you can't give the right to copy your work to more than one company; otherwise you would have competing companies trying to "sell" the same records and merchandise to the same market. Believe it or not, doing so would be legal—there's nothing in the law that stops you from granting the rights to your recordings, your name, or your face to more than one entity, causing several companies to compete with each other to sell you. To this day, I still hear of artists from foreign countries flying into town and making cheap deals with one label, then going down the street to another and making the same deal. They do this 10 or 12 times, each time leaving with a $5,000 check for selling *all of their merchandising*, and smiling. Each label thinks it got the better end of the deal. By the time they figure it out, it's months later and the artist has flown the jurisdiction.

Labels don't like to make their job any harder than they have to, and so they will include a series of clauses that grant rights for your name, music, and face to them *exclusively*. This plugs that gap and makes it *fraud* for you to grant those rights to anyone else. This makes sense, but in a typical label pattern, while they are asking for something reasonable, they will stretch the limits and stick their hand deep into your pocket. And when it comes to merchandising and other so-called 360 rights, even though they may never actually make good use of them, labels want to be in the driver's seat.

⊳ The Standard

The first step taken by the label to control your work is getting you to agree that they "own" the work, since it was created specifically for them. This is typically done with the clause below, called "Work for Hire."

Work for Hire, or "The Old Plantation"

Surrounded by confusing passages in the Copyright Act of 1976 is the phrase "Work for Hire." If you plan on making money with your creations, this is a concept you should learn. It's a deceptively simple phrase that seems to mean that you're hired to do something, but is, in truth, a convoluted legal argument about what an employer can rightfully take from his employee. This is boring legal stuff but important. So I'm going to attempt to make it interesting:

Imagine you're a scientist working in a lab owned by a detergent company. They manufacture "Miracle Glow," the floor polish that makes your floor look like the hood of a brand-new Corvette.

Your job is to mix the secret formula for Miracle Glow with a diluting agent so that all the toxic particles are filtered out, and all that will remain is a sweet-smelling liquid. The company plans to market that new liquid as an air freshener. This process is called R&D in the industrial world, which stands for "Research and Development."

Now a funny thing happens when you're experimenting with this stuff. You discover that if you mix Miracle Glow with sugar and add a bit of guar gum, you get an amazing cream that, if spread on top of bread or cake, makes an awesome dessert topping. You're understandably excited. And since the detergent company you work for isn't in the food business, you figure that you can now take this invention and go market it for yourself. Right?

Not so fast. In your employment contract it specifies that any work you do for the company using *company* equipment and in the *company* lab is *company* property.[1] Even ideas in your head are considered company property. This is "Work for Hire," and it's no joke. It means that while under contract, anything you do or think about doing is owned by the company.

But how does this apply to you? You wrote most of your masterpiece songs long before you signed a recording contract. Right?

Wrong. You thought you did. It may have seemed as if you created those songs months, maybe even years earlier. But this was just an illusion. In actuality, you never had an interesting thought before you signed this major-label contract. How do I know? It says so in the contract, in these clauses lifted from MASTER RECORDINGS, sometimes called RIGHTS IN RECORDINGS (this is a long one, but it's broken up into sections):

[1] The Sharp Rule made it so that you don't even need a contract. Just employment.

The Cheesy Sell-Out Scam

Under no circumstance shall Pacific be deemed to have waived its right to any Master Recording hereunder, except by a written instrument signed by a duly authorized signatory on behalf of Pacific expressly waiving such right. Therefore:

All Master Recordings made or furnished to Pacific hereunder or made during the Term (including all duplicates and derivatives thereof) and all Records made therefrom (including the copyright in such Master Recordings for the full term of copyright and any renewal and/or extension of such copyright), together with the performances embodied therein, shall, from the inception of recording, be exclusively and perpetually Pacific's property, free of any claim whatsoever by you, Artist or Producer or any Person deriving any rights from you, Artist or Producer. All such Master Recordings, from the inception of recording, shall be deemed **works made for hire** within the meaning of the United States Copyright Act.

Pacific owns everything you record while under this agreement, unless we specifically say otherwise in writing. Therefore:

All master recordings made by you and given to us while under this contract (including dubs and alternate versions) and future versions (and their copyrights for the next 95 years) will belong to us from the time they are recorded, and only to us; no one else.

Everything you record, from the time you record, will be **considered things that we directly asked you to do that you did for us and only for us.**

[*Even if they are spontaneously created in the studio and not part of the songs we approved of. So even though we don't approve of the songs, we still own them. Cool, huh?*]

Without limiting the generality of the foregoing, you and Producer hereby assign to Pacific all of your, Artist's and Producer's right and title to the copyrights in perpetuity in and to such master Recordings, and all Records made therefrom and all renewals and extensions of said copyrights, and Pacific and its subsidiaries, affiliates, licensees and assigns shall have the sole, exclusive and unlimited right throughout the universe to manufacture Records, by any methods now or hereafter known embodying any portions or all of the performances embodied in Master Recordings recorded during the Term;

In every way that this could possibly benefit us, you and your Producer assign to us all of your rights and ownership to the copyrights forever, for all recordings you make while under this contract.

We can assign these rights to our sister companies for them to exploit anywhere in the known universe.

REALITY: You just gave this label the right to sell your recordings to anyone, anywhere. Including advertisers for cigarettes, booze, and the Army. (They're just looking for a few good songs.)

You know you don't want to give them this. But there's a serious problem: if the label has to get your permission each time it wants to license a master, you'd probably make them beg. Maybe never even give it to them. Why should you? The label doesn't generally share any of the licensing money with you. And even if they did share, say, half of it (a common compromise), there is still little incentive to give in, because if you're sitting there with $100,000 unrecouped, why should you care if the label gets to make an additional 25 or 50 grand? You're not actually getting any of it in your pocket. It just goes toward recoupment. So to make sure you don't get snippy, the label starts off by asking you for everything in The Thick and waiting to see if you object. Which you will—through your lawyer or manager.

NEGOTIATE

The label will say, "Okay, okay, what *specifically* don't you want us to use your music for?"

You will respond with the usual: "Tobacco, the military, and anything overtly corporate." Whatever you ask for they will put in, but *only* what you ask for. So be sure to ask for every single thing you can possibly think of that you don't want them to consider as a licensing avenue. Because anything you leave out is fair game. The key Loophole Creator here is "Without limiting the generality of the foregoing."

JESUS SAVES THROUGH BEER

As discussed in the main text, unless you state specifically in The Thick that you don't want the label to license your recording to certain types of vendors, they will try to sell you to everyone and anyone they can.

The Apostles, a Christian rock band, were victims of this. They hailed from conservative religious families. The lead singer's father was a renowned AA sponsor in their home town. (Ironically, the label they were signed to was Interscope, now owned by Seagram's, makers of vodka.) So naturally when it came time to negotiate their licensing clause, the band had some restrictions they wanted the label to observe.

Their language specifically read like this: "No masters recorded hereunder will be used to promote the sale of alcohol." Seems specific enough, right?

When "The Choice He Made," their spiritual song about the sacrifice of Jesus, was licensed for a radio spot depicting a factory worker choosing Coors over Heineken, they hit the roof. "How could the label do this?" they cried.

After several months of runaround, they were finally informed (via a letter) that the marketing department at the label thought the clause in The Thick meant the sale of *cleaning alcohol*, not booze.

"Alcoholic beverages" was never specified.

The spot ran many times a day on Top 40 stations around the country. And so, when the Apostles toured the Midwest, they found themselves unable to listen to the radio. Instead of serving the Lord, they were served a healthy dose of their melody selling blue-collar hops. The Lord works in mysterious ways. So do record companies.

BE SPECIFIC!!!

The Guaranteed Release Scam

The clause above continues:

...to perform publicly and to permit public performance of such Records; to repackage, sell, transfer, deal in, exploit or otherwise dispose of such Master Recordings and Records at such times and places, in any and all media and manner, and under any trademarks, trade names or labels (except with respect to initial releases, in which case such releases shall be under the Pacific (or "Pacific") trademark, trade-name or label), as shall be determined by Pacific in its sole and exclusive discretion; or, **notwithstanding any provisions hereof**, Pacific and/or its subsidiaries, affiliates, licensees and assigns may, at their election, delay or refrain from doing any of the foregoing.

You also grant the rights to all live gigs and any recordings of them to be exploited in any possible way now or in the future, and under any label name we choose (except for the initial release, which will definitely be under the "Pacific" name and label). We can do all this without getting your permission, and,

Forget about what it may say elsewhere in the contract: neither us nor our sister companies have to do anything we just said if we don't want to.

LOOPHOLE ALERT!!!

EXPLANATION: This says they can exploit your record anywhere, or choose not to. If they choose not to, that's the same as *not releasing the record at all.* But they promised to release your record in about five other places in this contract. They get away with it by using the Loophole Creator "Notwithstanding any provisions hereof." Keep in mind that if they don't release your record, you are not entitled to any mechanical royalties, either (see "Controlled Compositions," page 155).

NEGOTIATE

Just ask them to be "reasonable." They won't argue with this, except for the part about not having to release your record. They will keep that in, and in all fairness, they should have that right.

With respect to the exploitation by Pacific of any Master Recordings recorded during the Term other than in satisfaction of any Minimum Recording Obligation, Pacific's sole obligation shall be to accrue royalties hereunder at the applicable rates set forth herein. Pacific may use Master Recordings hereunder for synchronization in motion picture, television and other audiovisual soundtracks, background music and any other purposes.

As far as your outtakes go, the only thing we owe you on those are the same "royalties" promised in this contract. We may use these recordings in films, TV shows, or anywhere else that we choose.

LOOPHOLE ALERT AGAIN!!!

EXPLANATION: The definition of "Master Recordings" includes any outtakes. Your contract specifies that you are to be paid "royalties" on *anything* you "deliver." But you can *only* earn a "royalty" if the material makes it *on to a record*. They own your outtakes, but they don't have to pay you for them. If they do sell an outtake for usage in a film, they only have to pay you "royalties" from the sales of the soundtrack, and not any licensing fees.

NEGOTIATE

Get this thrown out completely. The label should either accept or reject the new recordings, and all copyrights for rejected work should revert back to you. Also, a portion of the licensing fee should go to you directly, bypassing the recoupment account. (This is very hard to get.)

REALITY: I expressed most of my grievances about this clause in the Loophole Alert above. But there is some good news here. The clause, as written above, does not appear in many major-label contracts any more. I give it to you here because many contracts on smaller indie labels are hand-me-downs from older contracts on larger labels. In fact, if you see this type of "work for hire" language in your agreement, it's a tell-tale sign that your label's legal department has not been keeping up with the latest trends. This would be good for you and, if you see it, keep your mouth shut. DO NOT NEGOTIATE.

The reason this clause has been updated is because labels have been beat on this in court. Like the example given at the beginning of the chapter about the scientist working for the detergent company, the label wants to create the impression that the demos they fell in love with and which inspired them to sign you did not exist until after you signed this contract and thus are "works for hire." For years they got away with this, until several judges decided that this stretched the limits of "work for hire" too far. Now what you will find in the vanguard contracts is something like this, added to the bottom of the clause:

To the extent, if any, that you and/or the Artist may be deemed an "author" of any such Master Recordings, Covered Videos or Artwork, you and/or the Artist hereby grant to Pacific a power of attorney, irrevocable and coupled with an interest, for you and/or the Artist and in your and/or the Artist's names, to apply for and obtain, and on obtaining same, to assign to Pacific all such copyrights and renewals and extensions thereof.

If a judge says we were wrong in claiming that this is a "work for hire" and it turns out you really are the author/owner of these recordings or videos or cover artwork, then you will grant to us the right to sign your name without prior approval in matters relating to the selling or marketing of all this stuff. This includes our right to apply for an extension of the copyrights, renewals, and extensions.

REALITY: These lawyers get smarter every day. Now, "It's still a 'work for hire' [which means that it was created for the label] unless a judge says it's not." (Which will cost you big $$$ to find out.) "And if a judge says it's not, then you are the owner, but you grant us the right to have control over it." This is the same as saying, "I'm going to drive your car every day. I can sell it, chop it up, and give the parts away, change the color, the style, anything I want. But it's still your car because you are holding the Title." This is lame, but until a judge says that this is just another way of getting around the "work for hire" provisions, it will remain the standard.

TV and Movie Licensing

Having your single used as the title song of a hit summer movie is the dream of many a songwriter/artist. The labels license recordings to film producers every day of the week. The license to do this is called a "Master Use" license. Here are the clauses that govern this.

If Pacific receives income from the use of Master Recordings hereunder in synchronization with motion picture or television soundtracks or in Videograms (as hereinafter defined) or if Pacific licenses the use of any Master Recording hereunder on a flat fee or cent-rate basis, Pacific shall accrue a royalty hereunder of Your Fraction of fifty percent (50%) of the net amount of such income so received by Pacific. For purposes of this subparagraph, "net amount" shall mean the gross amounts received by Pacific in connection with the subject matter hereof, less duplication and less Pacific's out-of-pocket costs and any amounts which Pacific agreed to pay to third parties

If we get a flat fee lump sum of money in exchange for getting your track in a movie or TV show or a music video, we'll keep most of that money, but will apply a small part of it (the "net amount") to your account.

"Net amount" here means the total amount of money we get, minus any costs for making copies and any expenses [*some of which we'll make up later*], and for union payments, for paying an agent for making the deal, for paying a music

(such as, without limitation, mechanical copyright payments, AFM and other union fund payments). supervisor, and for paying any other freeloaders.

REALITY: More and more, song placement in motion pictures is becoming a bigger source of revenue for artists than physical sales like CDs. Naturally, labels look for ways to keep the money from leaving their bank. It used to be that in older recording contracts, artists got *no money* from the licensing of their song to a film. Labels considered this their exclusive territory, and the Master their property to peddle. That's when an artist could actually make money on LP and CD sales alone. This concept has changed, thank god. Unfortunately, labels still won't define what the actual percentage is that the artist receives for licensing, unless you make them.

To give you an idea of the numbers: Songs in a big Hollywood film typically are licensed for about $15,000 for background use and anywhere from $50,000 to $100,000 for featured use (which is when a song gets played over the opening or closing titles, or is prominent in the mix elsewhere in the movie). If the song is used in connection with an advertising campaign for the movie, then the label receives more fees. Out of this money, only about 20% will end up being applied to your debt.

NEGOTIATE

This is a tough area, and might not be a battle worth fighting. Many labels will yield on this point and go to 50% if pushed. Try to have them establish a separate fund for these monies. Have that fund paid out as soon as the money is collected, rather than put into the bottomless pit of recoupable royalties.

Your Face and Name

The next step in the process requires the label to gain control over how your likeness and professional name are used. (And you thought you owned those cute little cheeks.)

Take a moment to examine the quote from Prince at the beginning of this chapter. You may recall that for several years, in place of his name, he used an unpronounceable symbol. Though many people never understood his motivation, it was, in fact, an effective protest that demonstrated just how important these clauses can be. If this clause is poorly negotiated, you can easily find yourself, as did Prince, in a battle with a label over the use of your most sacrosanct birthright—your own name.

These clauses are lifted from a subheading called NAMES, VOICES, LIKENESSES, AND BIOGRAPHIES (also, MARKETING or, in Warner contracts, GRANT OF RIGHTS).

a) You warrant and represent that Pacific shall have the perpetual right, without any liability to any Person, to use and to authorize other Persons to use your name and biographical material, and the names (including any professional names now or hereafter used by you), facsimile signatures, voices, any likenesses and biographical material of Artist and Producer for purposes of exploitation of Master Recordings and Records hereunder. You warrant and represent that you own the exclusive respective rights to use your Artist name in connection with the manufacture and exploitation of Master Recordings and Records. You, Artist and Producer shall cooperate with Pacific's promotional and publicity efforts relating to the exploitation of Master Recordings and Records.

a) We can let anyone use your name, face, and facts about your past, without fear that someone may get offended and sue us. [*So make sure you told us the truth, because the label is not responsible if they print it and it's a lie. (Artists rarely lie about their past anyway.)*]

You assure us that you own the rights to your name and image and can grant them to us so that we can [*own them completely and*] "sell" your record.

So that we can make money on your recordings, you will agree with everything in our PR campaign.

(b) If any Person challenges Artist's right to use a professional name, Pacific shall, promptly after its receipt of notice of such challenge, notify you thereof in writing. Furthermore, during the Term, Artist will not change the name

(b) If someone contacts us to say they have the rights to use your name, we'll send you a letter informing you about this. Also, you can't change your name while promoting an Album for us without our permission.

```
by which Artist is professionally
known without the prior written
consent of Pacific.
```

REALITY: This one clause has been the subject of more lawsuits than any other in The Thick. Who owns the name of a group or artist? If you want out of your contract, and you spend the thousands of dollars it will take to get out of the contract, does that mean you *can't* perform under the name you just spent years building up? Usually, yes, that's exactly what it means.

Courts have found that if a group or artist can prove that they've performed under a specific name for a substantial period of time, then they get to keep the name in about 75% of cases. However, if the name of the group was created when the signing took place—such as Menudo, New Kids on the Block, or Expose (three prime examples of 1990s groups with replaceable members)—the label or production company who created the name gets to keep it.

If the label innocently suggests that you change your name as a condition of signing the contract, *watch out!* If this happens, make sure you have a clause in The Thick that states *emphatically* and *specifically* that *you own your name*.

But this is not enough. You must make sure that you also own the license to *use* your name, or you'll end up in the same situation as the "work for hire" bullshit above, where you own it, but don't have the right to use it.

Understanding the distinction between *ownership* and *administration* is the key to all the points in this chapter. If you come away with an understanding of this distinction, you'll be more knowledgeable than 90% of the artists out there.

NEGOTIATE

Be specific. Have a definite clause in the contract that states that if you leave the label, you take your name with you. ***Don't* give in on this one without a fight.**

Endorsements

Extra cash often comes from product endorsements. You've seen them: your favorite musician standing proudly next to his instrument in an ad. You get paid big bucks for those. Well, if they let you.

(c) During the Term, neither you nor Artist shall authorize any Person other than Pacific to use your name, or **likenesses** in connection with the advertising, marketing or sale of any item related to the making of records.

(c) While promoting a record for us, you can not let anyone else use your name or **image** (other than us) for selling tape or music-related equipment [*in other words, no endorsements are allowed*].

(d) (i) If you receive one or more offers ("Third Party Offer") from one or more third parties to enter into an agreement granting a third party the right to use any name, portrait, picture or likeness of Artist or other identification of Artist in connection with the manufacture, advertising, sale and/or distribution of non-Record products ("Merchandising Rights") you will

(d)(i) But if you get an offer to appear in an ad or endorse something, you will…

(A) immediately furnish Pacific with a written proposal ("Proposal") setting forth the deal points of such Third Party Offer; and

(A) immediately give us the offer in writing ("Proposal"), stating exactly what the offer is; and

(B) offer to enter into an agreement with Pacific on the same material terms as the Third Party Offer (except Pacific shall not be required, as a condition of accepting any Third Party Offer, to agree to any terms or conditions which cannot be fulfilled by Pacific as readily as by any other Person or to waive any of its rights hereunder).

(B) give us the chance to match the offer (but if we do, we're not required to match the terms of the offer if what they are going to do for you is something really simple and stupid that we could do for you ourselves. If we do allow you to take this offer, it's strictly a courtesy).

(ii) If Pacific does not accept the terms of the Third Party Offer within thirty (30) days after its receipt of the Proposal, you may then accept the Third Party Offer, provided that such agreement shall be on terms the same or more favorable to you as the terms set forth in the Third Party Offer.

(ii) If we don't give you an answer for 30 days, you're free to accept the offer as long as they don't change their offer and pay you less. [*In plain English, no sandbagging here. They can't offer you something ridiculous just to push us out of the picture and then lower it after we give up our option.*]

REALITY: What's all this really about? It's about the label not wanting to give up any rights so that others can exploit you, after they've invested so much in making you a star. (Even though you are paying them back all the money they invested.)

Let's say that Roland wants you to appear in an ad with their newest sampler. You can't do this unless the label has the chance to match the offer. Since selling keyboards is not their gig, they will probably say okay. But what about if you get an offer from a company doing something the label does do? What if, for example, the label is doing a bad job of selling your T-shirts and along comes a merchandising company that will pay you gobs of money to put your picture on thousands of shirts in stores across the country? The label might get a bit jealous and want to consider taking you more seriously. But what if the offer was a game just to get the label to wake up? The language above puts a whammy on this strategy. It makes sure that the offer is legit. This means you can't get your cousin to offer you a ton of money just for show, and then back out after the label can't match the offer. It would be a great trick, though. Believe it or not, artists have tried it. An important workaround for the labels is the common 360 provision that grants labels the rights to be the artist's merchandise broker. Here's what a typical 360 merch clause looks like:

Pacific has created a full-service merchandise division, and so we have the ability to design and manufacture merchandise for all purposes, including tour, music and apparel retail and online.

We've hired a couple of people who used to sell stuff and put together a "full-service merchandise division." This gives us the ability to design and manufacture merchandise for all purposes, including tour, music, and apparel, retail and online.

a) For all merchandise sales by Pacific to consumers and retailers, Pacific will bear all costs (including manufacturing and distribution costs) and will pay the Artist the same royalty rate as the Artist's Top Line album royalty rate. By way of example, if the publisher's price to dealers ("PPD") (after discounts) of a T-shirt is $10, the Artist will receive $1.40 per T-shirt (i.e., $10 x 14% royalty). This royalty shall not be collateralized with any other royalties due hereunder.

a) We'll pay for the costs (including manufacturing and distribution costs) of all the merch and will pay the Artist the same royalty rate as the Artist's Top Line album royalty rate. By way of example, if the publisher's price to dealers ("PPD") (after discounts) of a T-shirt is $10, the Artist will receive $1.40 per T-shirt (i.e., $10 × 14% royalty). This royalty shall not be collateralized with any other royalties due hereunder.

b) Notwithstanding the above, for those shows and personal appearances secured by the Artist, the Artist will have the right to sell merchandise off-stage and keep all proceeds therefrom. The Artist will purchase such merchandise from Pacific at an amount equal to 75% of the PPD of such merchandise (plus shipping costs). By way of example, if the PPD of a T-shirt is $10, the Artist will pay Pacific $7.50 for such T-shirt and the Artist is free to sell such T-shirt for a price in their discretion and keep all proceeds from such sale.

b) But, for those shows and personal appearances that you book yourself, you can sell the merch offstage and keep all the cash.

But you're gonna have to first buy the stuff from us. We'll give you a good price, however: 75% of the PPD of such merchandise (plus shipping costs). By way of example, if the PPD of a T-shirt is $10, the Artist will pay Pacific $7.50 for such T-shirt and the Artist is free to sell such T-shirt for a price in their discretion and keep all proceeds from such sale.

Objections to Use

What if you hate what they come up with for the marketing campaign? As was covered in the last chapter, you have five days to object. But then there's this paragraph that creates a huge **loophole** in that.

You and the Artist will cooperate with Pacific, as it reasonably requests, in making photographs and preparing other materials for use in promoting and publicizing the Artist, the Recordings and Covered Videos made under this Agreement, at Pacific's expense and subject to the Artist's prior professional commitments.

You're going to be "reasonable" when we tell you to do a photo shoot or personal appearances in relation to promoting the record. We'll pay for certain things [*like travel and hotel*] and try to work around your schedule. [*But we don't really have to, as you'll read in a minute.*]

Pacific will make available to you for your approval, at its offices, any pictures of the Artist or biographical material about the Artist which it proposes to use for packaging, advertising or publicity in the United States during the term of this Agreement. Pacific will not use any such material which you disapprove in writing, provided you furnish substitute material, satisfactory to Pacific in its sole discretion, in time for Pacific's use within its production and release schedules. If you object to any previously approved likeness (other than any likeness embodied in Covered Videos or on the packaging for any Record hereunder) or biographical material and provide Pacific with replacements therefrom

If you schlep down to our office, we'll show you all the artwork, photos, and other promo materials we plan to plaster everywhere.

If you hate it, we'll bag it. But only within the five-day limit,[2] and only if you give us phat replacements [*nothing shabby*] in time for our release schedules [*which is not really possible, if you consider the five-day rule*].

If you change your mind about stuff that you had already approved [*either because you neglected to object or because you changed your mind since*] and you've given us replacements that we think are cool, we will not use the old ones (with

[2] See "Promotion," page 170.

which are approved by Pacific, Pacific shall not make any new use of those likenesses and biographical material to which you have objected. No inadvertent failure to comply with this paragraph will constitute **a breach of this Agreement,** and neither you nor the Artist will be entitled to injunctive relief to restrain the continuing use of any material used in contravention[3] of this paragraph.

a couple of exceptions: the video, if it's already shot, the album cover art, or any bio material).

But if we go ahead and use stuff you hate, this doesn't mean that **we stabbed you in the back.** You or your producer can not sue us for money you may have lost, or money that you are entitled to, just because some judge thinks we're mean sons-of-bitches. Even if he does, you cannot prevent us from using the pictures we think will sell the record.

[3] **Contravention:** A fancy word for when the label breaks their word and doesn't care about it.

Notwithstanding the foregoing, upon receipt by Pacific of notice from you specifying its failure to comply with the provisions of this subparagraph, Pacific will use its reasonable efforts to prospectively cure such failure, it being understood that Pacific shall have no obligation to recall any material used in contravention of this subparagraph.

Regardless of what it says above, if and when we receive a letter from your attorney telling us that you are pissed that we ignored you, we may be "reasonable" and try to comply, but we don't have to recall anything that we already sent out.

REALITY: In my experience, unless you negotiate a specific amount of time during which they can comply, it will always be too late to do anything.

The Internet and
Fan Club 360 Provisions

Ah yes, everybody's favorite whipping boy. The hot topic at seminars and entertainment conferences has been this issue of who has the right to make a website using the artist's name. Essentially this comes down to an issue of who controls the artist's virtual identity. How will this clause deal with that? Under the section marked GRANT OF RIGHTS,[4] you'll find this little beatch:

(A) Artist hereby licenses to Pacific the exclusive right throughout the Territory during the term hereof, free from any claims whatsoever by Artist, to utilize Artist's professional name (1) in connection with the establishment or maintenance of a site or sites on the Internet having the URL "[Artist].com," or such other single URL based on or containing Artist's professional name as Pacific may select; provided, that Pacific may register such URL in any and all territories and top-level domains (e.g., .com, .net, .uk, .tv, etc. and including, without limitation, the URL "yourname.com"), (together, the "Artist URL"), and (2) in connection with a site (a "Successor Site") on each system which succeeds or is similar to the Internet (a "New System"); provided, however, that

(i)Artist shall have the right to create and maintain its own "unofficial" site(s) (the "Artist-Controlled Site") using a URL other

(A) You give us the exclusive right throughout the known universe and for as long as you're under contract to us to use your name so we can...

(1) make and keep a site on the Internet having the domain name "[your name].com," or any other name we can think of; and we may register that domain name in any and all forms (e.g., .com, .net, .uk, .tv, etc., which we will call the "Artist URL"), and...

(2) use your name for any other type of New System site which might be developed after the Internet but which is similar to the Internet (a "Successor Site"). But we'll give you the right to:

(i) create and maintain your own "unofficial" site(s) (the "Artist-Controlled Site"), but you can't use your name as part of the address,

[4] WEA had been at the vanguard of these types of clauses, no doubt due to their alliance with Internet giant AOL.

than that used on Pacific's site so long as no such site is referred to as an "official" site relating to Artist unless Pacific agrees otherwise in writing, and

like we can, and you can't refer to it as the "official" site for yourself, unless we say you can specifically in writing. [*Don't hold your breath.*]

(ii) Pacific agrees that, during the Web Site Term, Artist shall have the right to establish a link to and from any of the Artist Sites (as herein defined) with the Artist-Controlled Site, and Pacific shall coordinate with Artist with respect to the establishment of such links. **Without limiting the foregoing**, during the Term, Pacific shall have the exclusive right to register in Artist's favor the Artist URL, and to register similar names selected by Pacific in connection with any Successor Site, and to secure any and all renewals and extensions thereof on Artist's behalf, and Artist hereby appoints Pacific as Artist's attorney-in-fact for such purpose. Artist further agrees that the operation and contents of the Sites bearing the Artist URL and any Successor Sites (together, "Artist Sites") shall be controlled by Pacific during the Web Site Term; provided that the creative approach utilized in connection with the initial development of any Artist Site shall be subject to the **mutual approval** of Artist and Pacific; provided that Pacific's

(ii) have a link from your "unofficial" site to and from our cool site, as long as you let us know about the link and it doesn't interfere with ours.

There are no limits to what was just said. During the entire length of this contract, Pacific has the exclusive right to register and control all URLs with your name and names sounding like yours [*for those sneaky people who think they can beat us at this game by using different spellings that sound like your name*] and all renewals and extensions for these names. You agree that we can sign your name and handle anything related to these sites including all legal matters. You also agree that we can say anything about you that we want to on the sites, as long as it syncs with the image we want you to project.

Naturally, we'll ask you what you think, as long as you agree that inadvertent failure to so consult with Artist shall not constitute a breach of this agreement. During the Web Site Term, Pacific shall have the exclusive right to refer to a site on the Internet or on any New System as the "official" site relating to Artist.

(B) Pacific shall have the right to establish links to and from Pacific's Internet and New System sites with all other sites relating to Artist that Artist controls, in which Artist has an interest or with respect to which Artist has granted any third party the right to operate or administer, including fan club sites and sites relating to Artist's merchandising and touring activities. Artist shall coordinate with Pacific with respect to the establishment of such links.

(C) Fan Club Provisions: Pacific shall have the exclusive right to the "Official" Artist Fan Club (the "Fan Club"). Pacific shall host and maintain a Fan Club website (the "Fan Club Site") which shall, for example, include a home page and message boards and provisions for order fulfillment with respect to goods and services made available on the Fan Club Site, and shall be the sole and exclusive owner of the

if we "accidentally" forget to get your consent, it doesn't mean that we've broken our word. During both the time you're under contract with us and the period of time after, called the "Exploitation Period," we have the exclusive right to refer to our sites on the Internet as your "official" sites.

(B) Pacific shall have the right to establish links to and from Pacific's Internet and New System sites with all other sites relating to Artist that Artist controls, in which Artist has an interest or with respect to which Artist has granted any third party the right to operate or administer, including fan club sites and sites relating to Artist's merchandising and touring activities. Artist shall coordinate with Pacific with respect to the establishment of such links.

(C) Fan Club Provisions: We're your "Official" Artist Fan Club and shall host and maintain a Fan Club website that will include pages and message boards to buy your swag. We'll ask you what you think [*once*] before we design it for you, choosing all the fonts, graphics, etc., and you shall have access to the Fan Club Site database so you can offer VIP tickets to your fans as well as:

Fan Club Site during the Merch/Fan Club Term. Artist shall have the right to approve the content of the Fan Club Site and shall have access to the Fan Club Site database. On behalf of the Fan Club, Artist shall use Artist's best efforts to obtain from tour promoters presale and VIP ticket opportunities.

(i). Fan Club Benefits/ Membership Costs: To be mutually agreed upon by Artist and Pacific.

(ii). Fan Club Profit Split: Artist and Pacific shall split on a 50/50 basis **net profits** (after deduction of direct out-of-pocket costs and a 5% administrative fee) in connection with all Fan Club income, subject to recoupment of the Merch/Fan Club Advance set forth above.

(i). Fan Club Benefits/Membership Costs: To be mutually agreed upon by you and us.

(ii). We'll split all the cash the site generates with you 50/50 **after we deduct absolutely everything we can think of first** and a 5% administrative fee in connection with all Fan Club income, subject to recoupment of the special Merch/Fan Club Advance we paid you (see page 330 for what that is).

[5] The WIPO is an ad hoc policing organization that includes its own court in which complainants can state their case for trademark and copyright infringement.

[6] In a related fictitious story, Volkswagen is being sued by Paul McCartney for possible infringement due to confusion with the Beetle automobile. It's apparently easy these days to mistake a popular car for the former Beatle's recent string of popular hits. In an interview with himself, McCartney said, "I just don't want people to think I'm an imported fad from Germany." Sorry Paul, still love ya.

MADONNA DECLARED MORE POPULAR THAN JESUS WHILE STING GETS STUNG IN CYBERSPACE

In 2000, the World Intellectual Property Organization (WIPO) concluded that the domain name Madonna.com was rightly owned by the one and only Material Girl, and promptly ordered a porn distributor, who had originally squatted on the name, to relinquish it.[5]

Madonna, the "singer" (who has appeared in *Penthouse* and published a book of explicit photography), apparently felt that this rogue site and its "trashy material" might tarnish her image and confuse people about her message.[6] The WIPO's decision was in direct contrast to one made earlier that same year in the case regarding the domain name Sting.com. British pop star Sting was unsuccessful in convincing the WIPO to enforce the transfer of the domain name under the same argument used successfully by Madonna. (Probably due to the fact that Madonna's testimony was more compelling to the all-male panel of lawyers.) The WIPO stated that they denied Sting's request because the word "sting" is "a common English word." Whereas "Madonna" could only mean the performer. (Apparently these guys have never been to Italy.)

After the decision, Madonna was seen making a note in her Palm Pilot to register the domain names "God.com" and "Christ.com." (I made that part up.)

But according to an industry watchdog group, in the calendar years 2000–2001, Sting was the most bootlegged artist on the Net; with some 11,580 plagiarized Police sites plus an additional 3,797 sites selling his solo music. Where is the justice?

Meanwhile, up in Canada, it seems that Céline Dion has had more success in this area. The WIPO awarded her the rights to the Internet domain name Celinedion.com, copping it from an enthusiast who ran an unauthorized fan site. He had been usurped by the WIPO previously for the rights to Juliebrown.com and Brucespringsteen.com. Sting remains.

How does this affect you?

Recent developments in recording contracts have put the onus on artists to assign exclusive rights to their domain name to the record company. The practice has been met with much criticism from artists and their management, as it puts the artist's entire virtual identity in the hands of the label. What if the label decides not to sue as aggressively as Madonna, Sting, or Céline Dion, because you're just not "selling" enough records? One could find their web identity in the hands of crazed fans.

Also, there is the flip side of the issue; if your *real* name is something like Bowie, Prince, Bono, etc., you will have to change it if you want to have a domain name that matches your own, lest you incur the wrath of major-label lawyers.

Sting is lobbying for reform in this area, but his efforts have received mixed reviews. It seems lawmakers are taking him about as seriously on this issue as Hollywood took his acting career.

(C) After the expiration or termination of the term hereof, Artist hereby grants to Pacific the non-exclusive, perpetual right to establish a site on the Internet and any New System utilizing Artist's professional name in connection with

(C) When this contract is over, we will still have the right to establish and maintain an Internet presence in your name.

```
Pacific's  distribution  of  Masters
and  other  recordings  subject  to
this  agreement.
```

REALITY: So the artist now has put his *virtual identity* in the hands of the label. Many experts feel this is overreaching. As the Internet's importance blossoms, it's my opinion that artists will regret any ground-giving precedent they agree to here. Labels want this right for a very good reason; many artists get pissed at their labels, and subvert their marketing strategy by buying boxes of their own records (at the artist's wholesale discount price) and then reselling them on their site. Labels understandably needed to put a stop to this. Thus the stringent clauses above.

But let's say that you've changed labels in your career. You went from Universal Music Group (UNI) to Warner Music Group (WMG). You can't give exclusive rights now and forever to two companies. This will create a serious problem down the line as one record company continues to promote the record you made on that label via the web, while the new label does the same with the new recording you made for them.

What will happen? Well, no one knows yet. It's still too new. But I would think that the original label would have a claim against both the artist and the new label for creating a new website that they designate as the "official" one.

➤ Conclusions

Now you've "delivered" your record, complied with all the "material terms" of this contract, signed over your name, your likeness, and everything else you thought no one would ever take away. Now it's up to the label to do their job and distribute the damn thing and make you a fortune. But who says they have to?

We'll find out in "Distribution."

Turn the page.

CHAPTER 7

⦿Release and Distribution

or "How do I know if and when they will release the CD?"

In my first book, *Confessions of a Record Producer,* the chapter "Understanding Distribution" shows how signing with a small label is often the same as signing with a major in regard to how records get to the stores. So why not just sign with the indie and not have to put up with a one-sided contract?

First we need to understand exactly what a record company means by the word "distribute." A common confusion among new artists is to substitute in their head the word "distribute" for the word "sold." A label may tell an artist in the courting stage that they intend to "distribute" over a million records. The artist will instantly start the cash register in their head rolling until it tilts. But, in truth, "distribute" simply means "to part with permanently." Many companies "distribute" thousands of records each day. But artists are rarely paid for them. Record companies give away many records for promotional purposes. These are also "distributed," but artists are not paid for these either.

Clearly, this word requires some looking into.

Why This Clause Exists

Why indeed? To make sure that the label actually spends the money to get your record out there. Why would you need a clause to guarantee that? I mean, the label won't make money if they don't "sell" the records, right?

Well, maybe. Sometimes in business it's better to *not* release something than to release something. For instance, if a small company was more interested in being taken over by a large conglomerate Big Four label than they were in releasing and promoting new artists, they might outbid all the other labels on the block and hoard new artists, even buying up old contracts on other labels, and then not releasing anything. Why? So that their catalogs get real fat. Then they sell the whole thing to a Big Four who will cherry-pick through the catalog and decide what to keep and what to throw to the dogs. Another scenario is to keep a competing band that sounds similar to a band on their own label from releasing a record first.

This is all great business strategy for the label, but you didn't get into this deal to be part of some corporate merger. You want screaming fans and in-store signings? You want the record out there making cash. None of this can happen if the label doesn't release.

Think this is far-fetched? Chew on this fact: *Most major labels only release records for about 10% of the artists they sign.* This means that the odds are less than one in 10 that your record will be released if you sign with a major. This is not a criticism of them; they give more shots to new acts than small indies because they have more development cash. But the other edge of that sword is that they also create more "limbo acts" (my vernacular for an act that never gets released and remains on the roster for years) than any one else in the biz.

So there is an inherent conflict of interest between the label's goals and the artist's. Labels want to trim the fat, while artists want to be thought of as the prime rib. Who will win? If an artist can't convince the label that she is worthy of a release, what then? Can she distribute her own record? Can she take her Master Recordings to another company? Well, that all depends on how cleverly the clauses regarding Distribution were negotiated.

Interested now?

Here we go.

⬤>The Standard
Who Says We Have to Release Your Record?

Study these clauses often found in RELEASE OBLIGATIONS.
  Eat lunch first.

Provided you have fulfilled all of your material obligations in a **timely manner** under this agreement:

Only if you've done everything we've asked you to do and complied with all the loopholes and hidden traps in this contract **in an amount of time that we, at our sole discretion, think is "reasonable"**:

(a) (i) Pacific hereby guarantees to commercially release the First and Second LP in the United States and Canada within five (5) months after the date of delivery in accordance with the provisions herein of the respective LP. If Pacific fails to so release the First and Second LPs, Pacific shall be deemed in breach of this Agreement.

(a) (i) We promise to release your first and second Album in the United States and Canada within five months after the date that you've "delivered" it.[1] If we don't release your first and second Albums, consider us official liars [*called a "breach of contract" or "breach"*].

[1] See "Master Quality," page 122, for exactly what this means.

(ii) Except as specifically set forth in (a) (i) above with respect to the First and Second LPs, Pacific shall commercially release each Product LP[2] in the United States as Top Line LPs and within five (5) months after the date of delivery in accordance with the provisions hereof. If Pacific fails to

(ii) Except for what's said above in (a) (i) we'll release your first two Albums in high-end music stores in the US and Canada [*such as HMV, Best Buy, Borders, Virgin Megastores, etc.*] within five months from the date you "delivered" it. If we forget to release the record or refuse to release the record, you have 30 days after the five-month period to tell us that you want out

[2] "Product LP" is the same as LP, which is the same as Album.

do so you may notify Pacific, within thirty (30) days after the end of such five (5) month period, that you intend to terminate the Term unless Pacific releases such Product LP within sixty (60) days (the "Cure Period") after Pacific's receipt of your notice. If Pacific fails to release such Product LP before the end of the Cure Period, you shall have the right, by giving Pacific notice (the "Termination Notice") within forty-five (45) days after the end of the Cure Period, to terminate the Term. On receipt by Pacific of your Termination Notice, the Term will end and all parties will be deemed to have fulfilled all of their obligations under the agreement except those obligations which survive the Term (e.g., warranties, audit rights, re-recording restrictions and obligation to pay royalties or any advance which had become due and payable prior to such termination and was not theretofore paid). **Except with respect to the First and Second LPs**, your only remedy for failure by Pacific to release a Product LP in the United States will be termination in accordance with this subparagraph.

of this deal. We then have 60 days to decide if we want to release the record. (The 60 days is called the "Cure Period.")

If we fail to release this record within the 60-day Cure Period, you can tell us 45 days later that you are ending this bullshit (which we call a "Termination Notice") [*but you're still under contract, mind you*].

When we get your Dear John letter to end this contract, we'll both agree that we did our jobs and it just didn't work out. [*You can't go screaming to the press that you were dissed.*] (You still get the right to audit us,[3] and we still have to pay you "royalties" and any Advances that you're still due,[4] but you still agree not to record this material—that we refuse to release— for anyone else.)[5]

That's for the first two Albums. For Albums 3 through 7:

[3] See "Auditing," page 254.

[4] See "Royalties," page 92, and "Advances," page 21.

[5] See "Merchandising," page 197.

If you fail to give Pacific either of those notices within the period specified, your right to terminate will lapse. Except as specifically set forth in (a)(i) above with respect to the First and Second LPs, your only remedy for failure by Pacific to release a Product LP in Canada will be as set forth in subparagraph (b)(ii) below.

If you miss the first 30-day window or the second 45-day window for any of the other Albums, then you're locked into this contract and all its obligations forever (or another five years; whichever comes first). Except for what was mentioned regarding the letter and termination of the contract, your only other course of action, if we fail to release you, will be what's in subparagraph (b)(ii) below.

REALITY: Typically, Albums Three through Seven take approximately five years to complete. This is a small window and can easily be missed. Usually you will have forgotten about it by the time it comes around. See the chart on page 285. My advice is this: The minute you sign this contract, create 10 years' worth of calendar pages in your app of choice, and mark off the intervals mentioned above.

Time ———————————————————————————————————→ 9½ months later

Album "delivered"	Five months later: Release Date. If label fails to release, then …	a 30-day window in which to notify them. Then…	Label has a 60-day "Cure Period" wherein they can decide to release. If they don't, then…	45 days later you can send them a Termination Notice and the deal is off

CURE REQUIRES A LEAP OF FAITH

In 1983, Long Island hair-band Renegade, after playing the club circuit for years, finally scored a Top 10 hit. Renegade hated their five-Album deal on Chronologic Records, which only paid them 9% of the SRLP, substandard even then. Renegade tried to renegotiate, but Chronologic stopped returning their calls and sent them a demand letter stating that the group was required to "deliver" their next Album in five months.

Hoping to pry free of Chronologic, Renegade hired a top music attorney to find a loophole in The Thick. Although the lawer could not find one, Father Time provided a solution.

When Renegade finally did "deliver" their next Album in June of 1985, the label, hoping to put the fear of God into the arrogant group, took their sweet time deciding if they would even release it. In December, Renegade's lawyer sent Chronologic a "reminder." The label decided to wait until the last possible moment to respond, taking full advantage of their "Cure Period." They waited until the "29th, 30th, or 31st of the second month from when the Cure Period begins," as the contract stipulated, before issuing their decision.

But someone at the label was not looking closely at their calendar. If they had, they would have seen that the Cure Period's last day would fall on February 29, 1986. Except that no such date exists, because 1986 was not a *leap year*.

Chronologic missed their window, and Renegade was free.

The label sued, but dropped the complaint two days before they were scheduled to appear in front of a judge.

Renegade signed with another label and put out the Master they recorded for Chronologic. It went gold. They put out two more Albums before splitting up in 1988. Chronologic was absorbed in the corporate mergers of the early 1990s. Everyone was fired.

(ii) **Except as set forth in** subparagraph (a)(i) above with respect to the First LP and Second LP, if Pacific fails to comply with subparagraph (b)(i) above with respect to any particular Product LP in any Release Territory, you may notify Pacific within thirty

(ii) **Apart from** the First and Second Album being released in Canada within five months after you "deliver" them, and all the other foreign releases, if we don't release your Third through Seventh Album in Canada or any of the foreign countries within five

(30) days after the end of the applicable period, that you intend to invoke this subparagraph (b) (ii) if Pacific does not release that Product LP in that Release Territory within sixty (60) days after Pacific's receipt of your notice ("License Cure Period"). If Pacific fails to do so, you will have the right ("Outside License Option") to require Pacific to enter into an agreement ("License Agreement") with a licensee ("Licensee") solely and exclusively designated by you who is actually engaged in the business of manufacturing and distributing Records in that Release Territory, authorizing the Licensee to manufacture and distribute the Records derived from the Master Recordings contained in that Product LP in that Release Territory. You may exercise your Outside License Option by giving Pacific notice within forty-five (45) days after the end of the License Cure Period.

Your only remedy for failure by Pacific to release will be exercise of your Outside License Option in accordance with this subparagraph (b)(ii). If you fail to give Pacific either of those notices within the period specified, your rights under this subparagraph (b)(ii) will lapse.

months after you "deliver" them [*mentioned above*], you get only 30 days to send us a "Screw You" letter and tell us that you intend to get someone else to do our job in those countries. Then we get 60 days to decide if we're going to allow that. If we don't object within that 60 days ("License Cure Period"), you will have the right to force us to let any company you want to reproduce and release your first or second Album in those countries. This has to be a legit record company [*not your cousin Carmine who takes records to swap meets in his pickup truck*] that distributes records in that country. But you must first give us 45 days notice after the end of the 60-day period.

The only thing you can do if we diss you or screw up is to shop for another distribution deal. [*You can't sue us for loss of income or anything else.*] And you can only do that for this one Album that we refuse to release, and only in the territory that we refuse to release it in. And guess what—if you fail to give us either of those notices, then you're outta luck, pal.

NEGOTIATE

Insert a sentence in this clause that requires the label to inform you in writing 30 days before each release in each territory. They will hem and haw and say that this is too much paperwork for them. Screw them. It's *no* big deal for them to send you a letter. Especially when you (or your lawyer) point out how unenforceable the above clause is without a notice.

And Who Says We'll Let Anyone Else Release Your Record?

As you might guess, since you owe the label money, they want to make sure that if you fly the coop, that you fly to another company that they can reach and one that has enough cash to buy out your account.

Pacific shall direct such Licensee to pay Pacific all revenues payable under such licenses. Pacific shall credit fifty percent (50%) of such revenues (less fifty percent (50%) of payments, if any, Pacific may be required to make pursuant to subparagraph (b)(ii)(A) below) to your account hereunder and shall retain the balance of such revenues. Each License Agreement will set forth the compensation for the license as you negotiate with

We're gonna tell this other company to pay us all the new money you earn from "royalties" on their "sales." Then we'll credit half of all the cash they give us toward your debt to us. (Don't forget about the reserves.[6]) We'll also deduct any payments we have to make to any unions (as it says below).

[6] See page 238 for what a "reserve" is. The *Confessions* chapter "Returns, Reserves, and Cutouts" provides a more thorough analysis.

the Licensee, and you will use your best efforts to ensure that each License Agreement will contain such other provisions as Pacific shall require, including but not limited to the following:

You will negotiate each Royalty and license fee on your own [*just do a good job, because we get half, remember*], but there are a few things that we require before we grant you this right:

REALITY: Let's breathe for a second before we get into what the label will require of your next plantation owner. After holding you in limbo for about a year or more, the label now expects you to find and sign with another company. You'll have to go through the negotiating process again. Remember that if you accept a lower Royalty than what you were already getting, you will still owe people (like the producer) a fixed percentage (usually 3%–5%). In the original deal on Pacific, this translated to about 25% of your "royalties." This seemed fair at the time, but if you accept a lower percentage from the new company, you'll be in bad shape. And you can be almost certain it will be lower, since the new label will sense your desperation. If you had a 14% Royalty, they'll now give you 10% or 9%. Since you will still owe 3% of this to the producer, very little will be left for you. Remember—your original label gets half of the "royalties" you earn, which will go to pay back what you owe them.

So You Want to Change Labels?

This next series of clauses deals with the conditions that your first label requires of your new label, as outlined in the last section above.

(A) The Licensee will be required to obtain and deliver to Pacific, in advance: (I) all consents by persons which may reasonably be required (including but not limited to recording artists); and (II) all agreements by other persons which Pacific may reasonably require to look to the Licensee, and not to Pacific for the fulfillment of any obligations arising in connection with the manufacture or

(A) The other company that we may let do our job [*since you think we suck*] will be required to obtain and deliver to us, in advance: (I) permission to do this release from everyone who worked on the record (singers, musicians, the producer), and (II) all agreements from anyone who might still think we owe them money from your Albums and will come knocking on our door after you leave us (including unions,

[7] In case you're scratching your head wondering what this is about, it's referring mostly to the AFM's pension fund that major labels pay into for the sale of each record they sell. (See page 86 in the chapter on Royalties, or the *Confessions* chapter "The Major Label Deal from the Record Company's Point of View" for more on this.) Smaller labels don't contribute to this fund.

[8] This is a 7% per record sold surcharge that Big Fours pay to the union, and which allegedly goes to the side players who play on recordings but give up their rights to receive royalties.

[9] Many people skip this step, hoping the new label won't take the time to make sure the artist actually did all this paperwork. This usually works. Labels don't have the personnel to track down every person to ask them if they signed this thing or not. I know of more than one situation where an artist signed all the releases himself, and didn't even try to disguise his signature. The label never noticed.

distribution of Records under the license (including such agreements by unions and funds established under union agreements).

You will use your best efforts to cause Licensee to become a first party to the Phonograph Record Manufacturers Special Payments Fund Agreement dated November 1979, entered into by Pacific with the American Federation of Musicians, or the successor agreement then in effect, and if Licensee does not so become such first party, then any payments required to be made by Pacific in connection therewith shall be deducted from royalties accruable hereunder. The license will not become effective until the Licensee has complied with all the provisions of this subparagraph(b)(ii)(A)above.

contracts, and their retirement funds).[7]

If they're not already part of our Big Four cartel, that's okay as long as they give some of their money to the union's pension fund and musicians Royalty Compensation Fund[8] [*which we've been begrudgingly contributing to since 1979 so that our delivery trucks don't "disappear"*]. If they refuse to pay up, and the union requires us to pay up for them, the money we pay for them will be deducted from your "royalties" [*what a shock*]. And furthermore, we're not gonna approve this deal with this other company until they do everything in this paragraph.

REALITY: Aside from the union crap, this is Pacific's way of making sure that after giving the rights to your Master to another company, that the producers and musicians (whom the label may still owe money to) don't keep pounding on their door for money they were supposed to make on "royalties." The label wants to see, in writing, that these people will now go banging on the *new* label's door. Getting all this paperwork together will be challenging. When the new label sees these IOUs, they may think twice about buying your Master unless they are a sophisticated enough label to deal with all this.[9]

Let's continue, because you're not off the hook yet.

(B) The Licensee will make all payments required in connection with the manufacture, sale or distribution in that Release Territory of Records made from those Master Recordings after the effective date of the license, including, without limitation, all royalties and other payments to performing artists, producers, owners of copyrights in musical compositions, the Music Performance Trust Fund and Special Payments Fund, and any other unions and union funds. The Licensee will comply with the applicable rules and regulations of the American Federation of Musicians and any other union having jurisdiction and any other applicable laws, rules and regulations covering any use of such Master Recordings by the Licensee or any Person deriving rights from the Licensee, in the manufacture and sale of Phonograph Records or otherwise.

(B) Your new record company will make all payments required for the manufacture, sale, and distribution of your record in their territory, including payments to artists, producers, writers, the Music Performance Trust Fund and Special Payments Fund, and any other unions and union funds. They will completely cooperate with the Musician's Union (the AFM) and any other unions. They will follow all the laws, rules, and regulations covering any use of your music by them or anyone who is in their pipeline of payment [*including pressing plants, delivery services, plastic recycling companies, promotion companies, and any other vendors*].

REALITY: This just about clinches it for you. It's not enough that the new label waltzes with the union—everyone they do business with must do the same dance, or they don't qualify under this clause. To comply with the above you are limited to about four companies in the world. Can you guess which ones? They are the only companies for whom it does not pay to ruffle any feathers. The Big Four, as they are called. (See the *Confessions* chapter "The Big Four").[10] And, as it should not surprise you to learn, none of these companies will likely be willing to distribute you, because they probably already passed on you once when you were shopping for a deal. Remember? And even if they didn't, they're gonna

[10] The Big Six, in older editions of *Confessions*.

have to wonder why Pacific doesn't want to distribute you. If Pacific no longer wants you, why should they?

The band plays on…

(C) No warranty or representation express or implied will be made by Pacific in connection with such Master Recordings, the license, or otherwise. You and the Licensee will indemnify and hold harmless Pacific and its licensees against all claims, damages, liabilities, costs and expenses, including reasonable counsel fees, arising out of any use of the Master Recordings or exercise of such rights by the Licensee or any person deriving rights from the Licensee; provided, however, that if such claims, damages, liabilities, costs and expenses arise out of actions attributable to the fault of Pacific, then Pacific and you shall share same in equal proportion.

(C) We don't guarantee anything regarding the Master Recordings or the license. You and your new company will cover the costs of any lawsuits, including attorney's fees and damages awarded, if any, and hold us and our affiliates completely blameless in the event you get sued or we get sued because this other label screwed up somehow;

but if the action arose out of something we did, then we will share both the cost and the blame with you.

(D) Upon execution of the Licensing Agreement, Pacific will instruct its licensees in that Release Territory not to manufacture Records derived from those Master Recordings for sale there. But, **Pacific and its Licensees will have the continuing right at all times to manufacture and sell Recompilation Albums** which may contain those Master Recordings in that Release Territory.

D) As soon as you sign an agreement with a new label, we'll tell our affiliates in the country(s) where this new label has distribution to stop producing the old records that you made for our label. The only **exception is for compilation records or Greatest Hits records, which we, and the new label, will always be allowed to produce and distribute.**

(E) Each Record made under the license will bear a sound recording copyright notice identical to the notice used by Pacific for its initial United States release of the Master Recording concerned, or such other notice as Pacific shall require.

(E) Each new copy of our old records made by your new label will bear a copyright notice (and possibly a logo placement) that has the same year as the ones that we were using. [*Which means Pacific gets to promote their name on the new label's liner notes.*]

(F) Pacific shall have the right to examine the books and Records of the Licensee and all others authorized by the Licensee to manufacture or distribute Records under the license. The Licensee will not have the right to authorize any other Person to exercise any rights without Pacific's prior written consent.

(F) We have the right to look at the books of your new label any time we choose to make sure they're not ripping us off. This goes for their vendors and affiliates as well. But they will not have the right to let anyone else "sell" your record. That's final.

REALITY: So if you want to get your masters away from your first label and license them to another label, because of Pacific's confining requirements for how they define another label, you have no choice but to license these masters to another major label. Got that? Call me crazy, but I don't see one major label allowing another to come in and audit their books. So this clause will be the one that will make it impossible for you to sign with a new *major* label. Every major-label contract has this clause in it, and therefore, every label knows it's a condition of licensing your masters.

NEGOTIATE

There is no way you will be able to license your masters unless this clause is taken out or modified in some way. You might try to arrive at a mutual agreement between both labels on the rights to audit the other label. But even better would be to remove "royalties" as a contingent, and agree to pay the first label a percentage of the income you receive from this revenue stream. That way, all you have to do is show them your tax return. If they don't like this idea, then it's a sure sign that they intend for you to stay with them for a long, long time.

Buying Back the Masters

Don't wanna shop for a new deal? What about just buying the masters back from the label and putting the record out yourself? Wouldn't that solve all this crap? Yeah. Good idea. But wait… they thought of that too. *Voilà!*

(G) In the event that Pacific elects not to distribute Master Recordings made under the Term hereof, then during the Cure Period you may make known to us in writing of an offer to purchase the rights to Master Recordings made during the Term thereof for the purposes of distribution of Master Recordings by parties other than Pacific, then a price no lower than $100,000 and no higher than the aggregate amount under Artist's account with Pacific shall be attached to the releasing of Master Records hereunder this paragraph, and a check in the full amount of the Purchase Price, delivered within thirty (30) days following the expiration of the Cure Period referred to above, and, upon your complete exercise of such right of purchase, the Term shall be deemed terminated.

In the event Pacific cures such failure to release within the Cure Period, or in the event you fail to timely exercise your right to so purchase such Master Recordings, then Pacific's rights with respect to such Master Recordings shall remain in full force and effect.

(G) If we don't release your first or second Album, then during that 60-day period (y'know, the one mentioned above, where you let us know that we're about to try and shake you), you can send us a letter stating that you intend to buy back your own masters so that you can put the record on the street yourself.

If you do want to buy your own masters from us, we can sell them to you for any price we want to, but we'll tell you now it's gonna be at least 100 grand. We might want much more, though, but we won't ask for more than the total amount of money you owe us [*which could be millions by now*]. If you agree to this price, then you have a month after the time you notified us to get us a check for that full amount. If that check clears, then we will consider this contract to be over.

If we decide to release the record anyway while you're getting the money together (now that we know you're serious) or if you fail to get us the money in time, then we get to keep the masters and the rights to them forever. *Ha-ha!*

REALITY: I've seen this dance many times. The label informs the artist that it doesn't intend to release the album he's been investing all his heart and soul into for the last several months. The artist goes scrambling to scrounge together the hundred grand or more required to buy the rights to this record. If it's an artist's debut Album, labels will usually resell the masters without a fuss. But if it's the second or third album after a first Album that was a hit, it becomes almost impossible to get those files.

Remember that the amount of money that the label can ask for is the total amount of cash they've spent to date. How do you know what that amount is? You will have to take their word for it, or pay out of your pocket, for an audit. (And remember—you only have 30 days to make this claim or you lose this right.) And even if you do opt for this ghastly decision, an audit can take months, maybe even years.

Since labels release fewer albums than they make, as stated earlier, it pays to have this clause well negotiated. Notice that there's no mention of when the label is required to give you your masters once they've received your money. I've seen several situations where it took six months or more to get the files.

NEGOTIATE

First of all, there must be a limit on the amount you have to come up with to buy your own masters. The label gives you a floor amount in the contract—but the ceiling is as high as they can calculate. Even though the label claims that they have a formula for the ceiling, it's based entirely on their records. Which means that if the artist wants to challenge it, he must pay for an audit before he and the label can even agree on the price of the masters. The costs of this are so prohibitively high that it's tantamount to the label having the absolute power to say whatever they want about how much the artist owes.

You could easily get away with agreeing to pay no more than $200,000 per master. That's the easy part. The hard part will be getting them to keep each album separate. In other words, if you're buying out your third album, there's no reason for you to pay them back for the debt left over from the other two, since the debt is manufactured, and not real out-of-pocket debt. The label should only be entitled to out-of-pocket debt for the actual cost of that particular recording.

And while we're on the subject, I also don't see anything in the above clause about the outtakes to which the labels claimed ownership back in the chapter on "Master Quality." You should get those thrown in as well as part of your "buy-out." Take it all. If you're leaving, take everything you think belongs to you.

Otherwise you could work your butt off to get a deal with a new label, and your old label could cash in by releasing those "basement tapes" of yours that they still "own."

Also, set a "delivery" date for *them* to give *you* the files. Talk about turning the tables! Specify that the company has 10 days from when they receive and cash your check to "deliver" your masters, after which time you can charge them interest or a penalty. They may laugh in your face at this request, but try for it anyway.

❯ Conclusions

So the company doesn't even have to release your record if they don't want to. You can leave the label with your masters and get another deal. The only problem is that there's nowhere you can go and still be in compliance with the label's qualifications for "another label." Plus, there is little chance of you being able to afford to buy back the masters from them anyway, due to all the Double-Dips and loopholes created earlier. In essence, if you get out of this deal, it's for one reason: the label has no further use for you, and since you've been a good camper, they take pity on you and let you go.

So, since you're stuck with them, you'd better get in the business of knowing if they're adding up all those nickels and dimes correctly. How? The next chapter, "Auditing," will show you where all the hidden accounting schemes are, and how to catch the label when they claim they don't owe you any more money; or, if you're going to buy them out, will show you how much you're going to owe.

Turn the page.

CHAPTER 8

Auditing

or "How can I catch the label in a lie?"

"Not everything that can be counted counts,
and not everything that counts can be counted."

—Albert Einstein

Here's your big problem. You're gonna get a "royalty" statement and go, "What the hell *is* this? *Where's all my money?*"

Your first impulse will be to reach for the phone and call your manager or lawyer to begin instituting an audit. Your manager or lawyer will try to talk you out of it. This is not a conspiracy.

Before you spend gobs of money on accountants and lawyers, you have to take a close look at what you actually agreed to in the contract.

The natural inclination for many musicians and artists out there will be to skip past this chapter. If you're like every other artist I ever worked with, then your philosophy is something along the lines of: "Thinking my record company ripped me off should be my biggest problem." Or the other requisite attitude: "It won't happen to me."

Well, it's this author's opinion that if more artists paid a little more attention to the clauses involved with auditing, then they would not end up in a situation that is all too familiar to artists such as TLC, Toni Braxton, and the Back Street Boys. These artists all "sold" millions of records, but only earned minor royalties, because they were unable to gain access to the label's books for a long time. And when they did, the clauses in their contracts limited their methods of catching the label in a lie. Both of these problems were the result of a poorly negotiated set of auditing rights.

So if you want to follow in their footsteps, skip this chapter. For those who haven't flipped yet, let's get to work.

Why This Clause Exists

An "audit," according to *Webster's Dictionary*, means "an official examination and verification of accounts." Record contracts rarely have a subheading called "Auditing." Usually it is either called ROYALTY ACCOUNTING or ROYALTY PAYMENTS. But the loopholes are hiding elsewhere, often in the usual places like DEFINITIONS and MISCELLANEOUS. Below all is revealed, maybe for the first time in a major publication.

A common oversight on the part of artists and their attorneys is this: While fighting the good fight over the percentage of the "royalty," they often overlook the second most important step in the process of making money off a major label deal—finding out when these "royalties" will actually be paid, and what rights you have to object to how they are being added up. As you will see, there are some nasty and devilishly clever loopholes and double-dips surgically implanted in the contract that could make it impossible for you to ever get paid, even if you had a "royalty" that was 25% of SRLP.[1]

[1] SRLP: Suggested Retail List Price. See page 350 for details.

Over the years, as artists began to see that the percentage of their "royalty" was meaningless if they could never collect it, lawyers got "smarter" and began asking for more and more in this area of auditing.

Auditing Primer

To really get what's going on, you will need to know the key primers "Net Sales," "Net Profits" (covered in Chapter 2: Royalties and/or Revenue Share, on page 37), "reserve,"[2] and "SoundScan."

[2] "Returns" and "reserves" are discussed in more in the chapter on Royalties.

Net Sales

You may remember back in the chapters on Royalties and Revenue Share and Advances that only "Net Profits" are paid to the artist after the Advances are recouped and only "net sales" are used to pay royalties and calculate your next Advance. Here's a more detailed analysis of the contract's definition of "net sales."

"**Net Sales**" – Gross sales, less returns, credits and reserves against anticipated returns and credits.

"**Net Sales**" – the total amount of money we get from sales of records, minus the amount of units that stores [*and dishonest people who sell promo copies*] return to us, and the money we credit back to them in exchange for the returned unit,

Returns will be apportioned between Records sold and "free goods" in the same ratio in which Pacific's customer's account is credited.

[*But to be "reasonable" about the returns account*] the total amount shall be figured as an equal amount between the number of records you "sold" and the amount we give away for "free."

Confused? Even with my translation? Don't worry. You're not supposed to be able to figure out what this means. In fact, if you ask the label's lawyer to explain it, and he happens to be new to the biz, he'll have no idea what it really means either. It seems like it's saying, "records sold minus records returned for a credit." But if that's what it's saying, then why not just say that? And if that is what it's saying, you might not ever get any money. Say you shipped 100 records and "sold" 50, and 50 shipped back. Fifty (records "sold") minus 50 (records returned) = 0. Add to that the credit for the return, and you sink deeper into a deficit position for each record you "sell." Sounds crazy.

It's abundantly clear that the strategy of the label here is to be intentionally unclear. How can you have a reserve against "anticipated returns and credits"? Does that mean that the label, knowing the Album sucks, gave credits to the store *before* the store decided to ship back the record? That's awfully generous of them. Ask any attorney to explain this clause to you and he will tell you that it simply means "the amount of units that were *shipped* minus the amount the label actually got paid for." But most will also agree that the lawyer who wrote this clause probably had Asperger's.[3]

Maybe it's called "net sales" because all your money is caught in a proverbial net, like flapping mackerel gasping for their last breaths before they meet their maker. Can you imagine a huge, swinging net full of all your money, flapping and gasping for life as it's held in the clutches of a mammoth crane dangling over the deep blue ocean? That's a good image to work with for this chapter.

Okay, enough flowery rhetoric. **This is what it really means:**

[3] This particular version of the definition of "Net Sales" comes from a UNI/Interscope contract. But most of these clauses in all label contracts are written with virtually identical language.

Let's say that your label shipped 100 records. Fifty were "sold," 25 were returned, and there are still 25 of them floating around out there. Here's how it works:

---

100 Records Shipped

---

50 "sold"

25 "returned"

25 might return

[4] Records return due to the consignment system in which they are distributed. If this one standard changed, then the entire recording contract would undergo serious reform. Many believe the "instant sales" model of the Internet could be the answer.

Based on meetings with a psychic medium (often called a "financial analyst" who uses a crystal ball called a "marketing report"), the label estimates that 10 of those 25 units out there will likely return. Here's the equation:

Records "Sold"
50

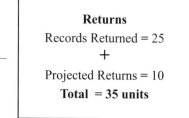

Returns
Records Returned = 25
+
Projected Returns = 10
Total = 35 units

Net Sales
15 units

The example above is the basis for creating a "reasonable reserve" of 35% (35 records out of 100 "shipped"). Since no one knows exactly how many records will return, the label picks a mean average, which is called "the reserve."

[5] Let's face it, if they paid you the full amount, would you really have the discipline to put it in the bank and not touch it for two years while waiting to see if any records shipped back? I know I'd be spending that shit so friggin' fast that if the label came knocking at my door wanting some back, I'd laugh so hard that my wind would knock them down the stairs.

The Reserve

A *reserve*, as I've explained previously, is an amount of money the label holds back in case a whole bunch of records return.[4] A common reserve is 35%, meaning that only 65% of the total amount of records "shipped" will be eligible for the "sales" calculated in that accounting period. The balance is held for between six months and two years. This is common, but is it "fair"?[5]

Let's construct an example. Let's say a Top Line CD sale is calculated through the Meat Grinder at $1.25 per unit. Say one million CDs "shipped" and 300,000 CDs "returned." That's 700,000 CD "sales." But, as you saw above and will also see in ensuing clauses in this chapter, the "reserve" will be 35% of the 1,000,000 units "shipped." So…

"Sales" (units shipped minus units given "free") 700,000 @ $1.25 each = **$875,000**	−	"Reserve" (based on 1,000,000 units "shipped") 350,000 units @ $1.25 cents each = **$437,500**	=	Net Sales **$437,500**

In these numbers (which are typical), a 35% "reserve" means you'll get about 50% of your money in this pay period. You'll get the rest after they "liquidate" the Reserve sometime the following year. This is obviously unfair. **Especially when you consider that your sliding scale royalty and the qualifications for the Maximum/Ceiling amount of your next Advance are based on Net Sales.**[6] When you add the complexity of the "Net Profits," as in a 360 Deal, it gets even more complicated and even more unfair to the artist. (Please review the definition of "Net Profits" on page 23. You'll need to be aware of how it interacts with "net sales.")

So to be "reasonable," the label has to try to "apportion" the amount of records "shipped" to the amount that they anticipate will be returned. How do these mystical psychic financial analysts know how many records will sell in the next six months? How can *you*? Technology provides an answer.

[6] "Sliding Scale Royalty": see "Royalties," page 37. "Maximum/ Ceiling Advance": see "Advances," page 17.

SoundScan

To appear impartial, most major-label contracts suggest the employment of an independent bean counter to input some hard data into the "figuring" of "anticipated returns." Enter SoundScan, the messiah of the retail record sales business. It scans the bar code on the actual unit at the point of purchase. This system has been in use since 1991. It's been a huge asset in revealing how many records are actually selling. Artists love it because now they don't have to rely on the honesty of their record company telling them how many records are "selling" or the "projections" of their analysts. They can find out on their own just by subscribing. Anyone can subscribe. You don't even need to be in the music industry.

And now, with full understanding of the key primers, let's see if we can catch the label in a lie.

▶The Standard Royalty Accounting

The first thing you are hit over the head with in the contract, under the subheading "Audit Rights" or "Accounting," is this mind-numbingly long and wordy paragraph that, in my belief, is designed to mentally exhaust you beyond the average human's ability to reason. In this chapter, the clause to which I refer is broken into four parts in order to really put it under the microscope. Take a moment and read it intact to get an idea of what I'm talking about. Keep some aspirin handy.

Pacific will compute your royalties and shares of Net Profits as of each June 30th and December 31st (or such other semi-annual periods as Pacific may elect in its sole discretion) for the prior six (6) months, in respect of each such six-month period in which there are sales or returns of Records or any other transactions on which royalties or shares are payable to you, or liquidations of reserves established previously. Within three (3) months following the end of each such semi-annual period, Pacific will send you a statement covering those monies due and will pay you any royalties or shares of Net Profits which are due after deducting unrecouped Advances and chargeable costs under this Agreement and such amount, if any, which Pacific may be required to withhold pursuant to the California Revenue and Taxation Code, the U.S. Tax Regulations or any other applicable statute, regulations, treaty or law. After the term, no statements shall be required for periods during which no additional monies due accrue unless you give Pacific a written request therefore before the expiration of the semi-annual accounting period to which the desired royalty statement relates. In computing the number of Records sold, as well as merchandise items, revenue from publishing, touring, personal appearance, endorsements, etc, only monies for which Pacific has been paid shall be deemed applicable, and Pacific shall have the right to deduct returns and credits of any nature and to withhold reasonable reserves therefore from payments otherwise due you. For purposes herein, the "reasonableness" of such reserves shall be determined for sound recordings by SoundScan sales figures. Each royalty reserve against anticipated returns and credits will be liquidated not later than the end of the fourth semi-annual accounting period following the accounting period during which it is established. If Pacific makes any overpayment to you, you will reimburse Pacific for it; Pacific also may deduct it from any payments due or becoming due to you. If Pacific pays you any royalties on Records which are returned later, those royalties will be considered overpayments. Pacific may at any time elect to utilize a different method of computing royalties so long as such method does not decrease the net monies received by or credited to you hereunder.

How's that headache? Now we'll break it apart and see what it really says, in slow motion.

Accounting "Periods"

The first few lines establish the times of the year that the accounting department actually does the work. But there's a loophole even there. See if you can catch it.

1) Pacific will compute your royalties and shares of Net Profits as of each June 30th and December 31st (or such other semi-annual periods as Pacific may elect in its sole discretion) for the prior six (6) months, in respect of each such six-month period in which there are sales or returns of Records or any other transactions on which royalties or shares are payable to you, or liquidations of reserves established previously.

1) We will check the scoreboard every six months and see if we owe you any money. We'll do this on June 30 and then again on December 31 (or any other increment of six months that we decide) and calculate for the last six (6) months. We'll figure out "sales" and returns, and any other transaction for which you might earn money, and any money you've actually earned that we've been holding back in reserves.

LOOPHOLE ALERT!!!

EXPLANATION: This is actually a self-created loophole. First the label says that they will do accounting every six months—once in June and then again in December. But then they say that they could change that period to whenever they choose. So let's say that you're expecting a "royalty" calculation on January 1, which would be right after their December accounting period. But the label decides in the middle of December to change their accounting periods to April and October. And then in April they decide to switch back to June and December. When exactly do you get paid? This is why I call this a "floating accounting period."

NEGOTIATE

For majors this is not a big deal, because they rarely alter their pay schedules, as that would screw up the finely tuned quarterly and annual reports they are required to file. But indies have a lot more flexibility to play musical pay-schedule. A simple solution, and one that's not too hard to get, is this: A specific clause should be added here that guarantees that no payment period will be more than six months after the last one, regardless of whether or not the company changes their policy. Get it in there. Without a specific clause that says this, the label can forever be floating the accounting period on you and every other artist on the label.

Let's continue. It gets better.

Deducting Your Advance from Your "Royalties"

Within three (3) months following the end of each such semi-annual period, Pacific will send you a statement covering those monies due and will pay you any royalties or shares of Net Profits which are due after deducting unrecouped Advances and chargeable costs under this

Within three (3) months after each six-month accounting period, we'll send you an accounting statement showing you how much you've earned after we deduct all the Advances we've given you. After that deduction, we'll pay you the balance, if any. We'll also deduct any taxes that the law requires.

Agreement and such amount, if any, which Pacific may be required to withhold pursuant to the California Revenue and Taxation Code, the U.S. Tax Regulations or any other applicable statute, regulations, treaty or law.

After the term, no statements shall be required for periods during which no additional monies due accrue unless you give Pacific a written request therefore before the expiration of the semi-annual accounting period to which the desired royalty statement relates.

After you stop making records and pimping swag for us, we're not gong to send you any more "royalty" statements, unless somehow you manage to "sell" your merch even though we stopped promoting you. If you want us to send you a statement anyway [*so you can see for yourself*], then you'll have to bug us for it with a certified letter before that accounting period ends, and then we'll send you a statement for that exact accounting period *only*.

LOOPHOLE ALERT!!!

EXPLANATION: How are you supposed to keep track of where the accounting periods begin and end, and how many records you've sold, if they stop sending you statements?

You can't.

NEGOTIATE

Ask for a statement regardless. Just like having to file a tax return even if you didn't earn anything, the label is required to send a statement to you even if you didn't earn anything.

The Reserve

Now comes the hammer. Here Pacific establishes the structure of the statement.

(18)

In computing the number of Records sold, as well as merchandise items, revenue from publishing, touring, personal appearance, endorsements, etc, only monies for which Pacific has been paid shall be deemed applicable, and Pacific shall have the right to deduct returns and credits of any nature and to withhold reasonable reserves therefore from payments otherwise due you.

Regardless of how many records we ship to stores [*and are sold under the table, off the truck, etc.*], songs we've helped place, merch we've helped push, or tours we've financed and booked, only the product for which we have received actual cash shall be deemed "sold" [*except for all the exceptions that we inserted, which includes cutouts, record clubs, scrap, and military and scholastic records. About 60% of the places we "sell" records to won't be considered*]. We have the right to deduct the amount of records returned to us as well as any store credits we had to issue from payments that are due to you. We will hold a "reasonable" amount of money back from your "royalty" payments as a "reserve," in case there are many returns.

For purposes herein, the "reason-ableness" of such reserves shall be determined for sound recordings by SoundScan sales figures.

What we call "reasonableness" regarding your reserves will be determined by the SoundScan sales figures.[7]

[7] SoundScan: A computerized bar-code system, like the one used at a supermarket checkout, for keeping track of record sales in the major chain record stores. Some smaller stores are starting to use this system. The numbers are available to anyone who wants to pay a monthly subscription and are accepted as an approximate number (about 75-80%) of US sales.

DOUBLE-DIP DETECTOR

EXPLANATION: If you look at the Master Chart on pages 352–353, you'll see that reserves are figured on records shipped, but above it says they will be deducted from records "sold." This is a clear Double-Dip, as these numbers are bound to have a good 20%–60% differential.

NEGOTIATE

Reserves should, in a fair world, be based on records "sold." Get this if you can. It won't be easy, but it's worth far more than a higher "royalty." In digital sales there should be NO reserve. Some majors are cognizant of this. Other are cognizant, but act like Luddites when it suits them.

REALITY: So here's the structure of a "royalty" statement. Set up as above, "royalties"[8] for sound recordings will be figured out like this:

Money received by the label for records "sold" (not records shipped).[9]	−	35% of records "shipped."	=	"net sales" on which they will calculate your "royalties."[10]	−	Any Advances you have not recouped from "net sales" if it's a standard deal, and if it's a 360 Deal, applied to the matrix of deductions to arrive at "Net Profits."

You may have noticed the SoundScan name in the clause above. As stated in the introduction to this chapter, the record company decided that since artists trust SoundScan, they might be able to use it to get you to be more "reasonable." And on the surface it seems reasonable. Doesn't it make sense to base a "reserve" off of sales reports, rather than an arbitrary percentage of "anticipated returns" based on how many records were "shipped"? Sure it does.

Here's the problem. If they base the reserve on this system, then the amount of units they withhold from calculating your "royalty" will not be based on 65% of all records "shipped" or even all records sold. It will only be based on 65% of records sold *that are tracked by SoundScan.*

[8] A "royalty" in this contract means: A percentage based on a configuration. The configuration is a combination of: 1) the type of record; 2) at what price it sold in the territory it sold in; and 3) the type of packaging it came in. See page 48 in "Royalties" for a complete explanation.

[9] When in quotes, "sold" in this book refers to the definition of "records sold" in the contract, which means different things for different types of records. With LPs, it's 85% of actual sales. With tapes, CDs, and the Internet, it's 80% (see "Royalties," page 45).

[10] An interesting aside: Gold and platinum record awards are based on records shipped, not sold. In this way an artist can have one or two platinum records and still not get paid due to major-label accounting practices.

This is a ruse.

For starters, SoundScan will only include US "sales," and will only include the major record store chains. Most Mom & Pop stores are out of the loop, because they do not report to SoundScan. Also, forget about the thousands of records that slip through the cracks via cutouts, scrap, record clubs, etc. They won't count either. These omissions will have a radical effect on certain types of music, such as rap, that have higher "sales" through small stores versus larger ones. The quick math in the sidebar "Soundscam" will reveal the "reasonableness" of this.

[11] Master Pee is not his real name. My apologies to any act really using this name. I am truly sorry.

[12] Wonder is a fake name. You probably figured it out, but my sneaky lawyer says I have to tell you anyway.

SOUNDSCAM

This is the true story of a rapper named Master Pee.[11] He was signed to a Big Four imprint called Wonder Records (where, if your record earns royalties, it's a Wonder).[12]

Because Pee is a rap artist and rap typically sells more records through smaller stores, for the Master's first Album, *Pee Is Number One,* Wonder shipped only 100,000 units to major chains, but shipped 400,000 to Mom & Pop stores. That's a total of 500,000 records shipped.

Pee then did a tour in several small towns and shopping centers and had his video played a little on MTV.

The small Mom & Pops sold all but 150,000 units of *Pee Is Number One*. The major chains sold 50,000, returning the other 50,000 records.

Pee's label uses SoundScan as a yardstick for predicting how many records might return. Even though they "sold" 300,000 records in total, SoundScan only tracks the 50,000 units that sold at places like Tower and Sam Goody's. (These stores are now defunct, but you can substitute Best Buy and Wal-Mart. The examples still hold up.) This made Pee's reserve of 35% only 17,500 units, and the statement for that accounting "period" paid him on 282,500 units. (He'll get the rest in about a year or two.)

Major chain: 50,000 sold	+	Mom & Pops 250,000 sold	=	Total "sold" 300,000	−	35% reserve of major chain: 17,500 units	=	Pee paid on **282,500** units this "period"

Now these are great problems to have, especially if you're Master Pee making dope ducats on touring and have your own line of hip-hop apparel. But Pee was determined to get a Top 40 crossover hit the next time around. And he did. He came up with a hot single called "Pee Is in D'House" and put it on his second Album, *Pee Is Not Number Two*.

It worked.

The major chains sold 350,000 records and the Mom & Pops sold 50,000 for a total of 400,000 units of *Pee Is Not Number Two*. Did the Master do better now that he was getting props from the big chains? Let's see.

Major chain: 350,000 sold	+	Mom & Pops 50,000 sold	=	Total "sold" 400,000	−	35% reserve of major chain: 122,500 units	=	Pee paid on **277,500** units this "period"

Even though Pee "sold" a total of 400,000 records with no returns on his second Album, the 35% reserve was only figured against the 350,000 units sold through major chains (or 277,500 records—65% of 350,000). Pee had a hit, but in his next royalty check he only got paid on "sales" of 277,500 units. He had to wait until they "liquidated" the reserves to get the rest. "That's *wack*," cried Pee. "I got paid *more* by selling *less* records with my first Album. *What up*?"

What up is that because SoundScan only tracks the big stores as of this writing, it can be used as something of a decoy for the anxious artist.

Something here is very, very, wrong. But Wonder Records calls this "reasonable." Is it any Wonder?!

Reserves: Length

Next, they tell how long they intend to hold on to this "reserve."

Each royalty reserve against anticipated returns and credits

We'll liquidate the reserves for each individual record no later than two

will be liquidated not later than the end of the fourth semi-annual accounting period following the accounting period during which it is established. If Pacific makes any overpayment to you, you will reimburse Pacific for it; Pacific also may deduct it from any payments due or becoming due to you. If Pacific pays you any royalties on Records which are returned later, those royalties will be considered overpayments. Pacific may at any time elect to utilize a different method of computing royalties so long as such method does not decrease the net monies received by or credited to you hereunder.

years and six months after the release of each record.

If we accidentally overpay you before that time, you'll give us the money back or we'll take it out of the next payment we make to you [*six months later*]. If we pay you, and after two years and six months more records come back to us, those "royalties" previously paid will be considered overpayments, and you will give them back. If we get tired of computing your "royalties" the way we normally do, we can change the method without telling you, as long as the amount we owe you isn't affected.

LOOPHOLE ALERT!!!

HALF-ASSED EXPLANATION: The interesting part is the last bit about using a "different method of computing 'royalties'" as long as it doesn't affect the amount they owe you. How's that even possible? And even more to the point, if there is no change in the result, why change the method? Let's be honest: the only reason to change the method is to affect the result. This will be explained later in this chapter. Look for it. It's amazing.

REALITY: This *sucks*. They hold the money as long as they have returns in their warehouse. How do you know they will ever actually dump, or "liquidate," the returned records? What if they take this massive deduction and then keep the records and sell them years later? (Okay, this is a bit paranoid on my part.) They will eventually have to make room for the next poor artist's records in their warehouse. But do they actually have to wait this long—two-and-a-half years—to do this? Usually no. In many situations in which an artist is selling well, the label will liquidate the reserve within the first year. And even though it says that the artist has to pay back any money that is overpaid to them, I know of no situation in which an artist was asked to cut a check two years after liquidation.

NEGOTIATE

Most of this will be obsolete in about five years anyway. Digital sales need no reserves and have no returns. But as long as CDs still make up the majority of music sales, you need to trim the fat off this clause. You must persuade the record company to reduce the amount of time they can hold the reserve. What's fair? In my opinion, considering the scam of record sales outlined on page 102, six months is an appropriate period of time. But you'll have a hard time getting this until you've proven yourself worthy. It's an important issue and even more worth pushing for, in my opinion, than getting a higher "royalty." My experts tell me that getting a 50% liquidation in nine months, and 50% in 18 months, for a new artist should be a breeze. Go for it.

Also, the amount of the reserve should be reduced as low as you can go. This is definitely far more important that the amount of the "royalty," and a common scam in major-label negotiations is to "give in" to the artist's lawyer on a higher "royalty," but to raise the reserve percentage at the same time. Managers and lawyers, in order to seem cool, will often report only the raised "royalty" to their clients, downplaying the increased reserve as "nothing they should concern themselves with," since it doesn't affect them for two years. (I've actually heard this rationalization verbatim many, many times from lawyers.) It sounds like you will get more money now and less later, but it's actually the reverse. The scam is that there rarely *is* a later, and so the record company acts like an insurance company and plays the odds that most people won't last long enough or have the stamina to audit and collect.

I've seen reserves as high as 40% and I've seen them as low as 20% on some new artist deals. A common split is to allow the label to use a sliding scale—40% for the first Album, 30% for the second, and so on. Labels will often say that on the seventh album the reserve will be 10%, "liquidate-able" within six months. There has never been an artist or a band signed to a major since 1991 that has had more than seven albums on any one major label. Guns & Roses was the last.[13]

Another compromise is to insist that the reserve be automatically liquidated after a certain "sales" marker: 350,000 units seems fair for a major, 10,000 for an indie.

[13] Artists such as Bob Dylan have been making records for the same label for many years; he's been with Columbia since 1962. Many stars from the '60s and '70s made five to eight albums on the same label. But these days there are very few. The times they be a-changin.'

Summary

This brings us to the end of the first headache clause regarding auditing. So let's review before we go on.

This clause says:

1. The label calculates your earnings every six months and pays you three months after that (except that the six-month period can float around a bit).

2. You will receive an accounting statement three months after they figure out your earnings.

   a. The accounting reflected in that statement will show the amount of records that shipped back and didn't "sell," as well as any Advances against "Net Profits" that are not recouped at that time.

   b. It also says that after you stop "selling" records, swag, and booking tours, they will stop sending statements unless you bug them with letters.

3. The structure of the accounting will show actual "sales" minus "reasonable" reserves, based on SoundScan's estimations (for sound recordings). All this equals "net sales" against which the various royalty configurations in the Meat Grinder will be applied (see page 59 for configurations). The final number will be applied to "Net Profits" to determine if there are any.

4. And finally the length of time they can hold this reserve is six months to two-and-a-half years before they "liquidate" and pay you the back "royalties," or splits of "Net Profits," if any. If they overpaid you, you must now pay them back.

Now go back and read the version at the beginning of the chapter and see if you are more comfortable decoding it, or if you'd like, just throw up instead.

Free Goods (RFGs)

In a galaxy far, far away from the "royalty" clauses or the payment clauses will be this little thing stuck in the MISCELLANEOUS section. It's the definition and establishment of the "Free Goods" clause. This is another bit of record industry linguistics reeducation. This term of art is clever, in that it paints an image of something that is given benevolently. But this is not the truth. Just because something is given to someone and no money changes hands doesn't mean that there is nothing earned by the giver. If I give you my favorite CD for free, I get no money, but you may feel obliged to do me a favor in return. Maybe give me one of your old CDs. No artist is ever paid on this personal transaction, yet we both feel that we benefited.

The real definition of "Free Goods" might as well be: *Records and merch given away for which you receive no "royalty," or which are applied as a deduction to "Net Profits."* They are in effect "royalty-free goods," or RFGs, as I call them. In the clause below the label specifies that the percentage of RFGs (15%) will be based off *Top Line* records, which means using sound recordings as the basis for our examples—remember sound recordings? It's a contract to create sound recordings; CD Albums that sell in major record chains for $16 and up. If you look in the preceding subchapter you can see where that math leads you—right into the toilet.

As benign as the name sounds, "Free Goods" (RFGs) is a killer Double-Dip and loophole, because CDs given away as "free" are often returned to the record company for a credit if they don't sell. And these days fewer and fewer of them do. The record store and the label both receive a benefit, but the Artist doesn't get a dime.[14] Furthermore, your label may decide to deduct from your account an RFG from another artist's account. "How can they get away with that?" you cry. Let's have a look.

Pacific shall have the right to distribute Free Goods not in excess of its then current Distributor's standard policy ("Standard Free Goods"), which, for Albums currently is fifteen percent (15%) of the aggregate units of all Top Line Albums distributed under this Agreement. In addition, from time to time, Pacific or its Distributor, jointly or separately, shall have the right to conduct special sales programs of limited duration which include the distribution of Free Goods in excess of the limitation

We have the right to give away your records ("Free Goods") in large numbers, consistent with the amount of records we give away normally. We call this "Standard Free Goods," which for Albums is currently fifteen percent (15%) of all units shipped to major record retail chains. Plus, from time to time, we or our Distributor [*which is another branch of our company, so it's still really us*] can put on these little garage sales where we give away lots of units far in excess of the 15% we just agreed to above.

14 "How Normal Retail Sales Allegedly Work," on page 98, explains this in detail and is required reading for those who own this book.

set forth in the preceding sentence ("Special Free Goods"). If Pacific distributes Free Goods in excess of the foregoing limitations, Pacific will not be in breach hereof, but Pacific will pay you your normal royalty on such excess.

We call these "*Special* Free Goods" [*and special they are*]. If we give away more CDs than that, then we won't be liars as far as this contract is concerned—we'll just pay you some extra "royalties" for the "mistake."

REALITY: It really doesn't matter what the label agrees to base the percentage on, because it clearly states above that they can give away as many records as they want, whenever they want. If they go over the 15% marker, they have to pay you a "royalty," but how do you know when they did that? You don't, because it's never sectioned off that way in your quarterly accounting statement. They just make a 15% RFG deduction regardless of whether they've actually only given away 5% or 30%. A-*ha*!

Also, if the label has given the record away to a movie company or radio station for promotional purposes, that's cool, but what about RFGs given as sales incentives?

Record companies don't like to discount the wholesale price of records because they think it makes them look weak. Instead they will give a "free" box of CDs to a store that buys a certain quantity. What is that number? Well, we can't actually ever know, but we can guess, based on the number that they want to deduct from your "royalties," which is 15%. In reality it's probably 10%. So what I'm saying is that they will tell a record store, "Hey, buy 10 boxes of this new artist and we'll give you a 'free' box on the side; you can then keep all the profit." You get no "royalties" from this "free" box.

Labels say that they must give records away to promote a new artist. It's hard to argue. When it comes to "selling" records, they are the experts, but they are also experts in overcharging the artist for these sorts of things. There is no way that I know of to ensure that the label is giving away *exactly* 15% of your records and not 10% or 5%. Since this doesn't appear on your statement, you're SOL.

But there's more.

What about when the label has these little "garage sales," as I call them, in which they give away boxes of many different artists? Let's say they only give away one box of your record, but 10 boxes of some other new act that isn't selling well. The label still charges *both* artists a 15% deduction. *That's a* huge

Double-Dip. You are being charged for subsidizing another artist's promotion. This happens every day in major-label land.

So, to recap: "Free goods" are not really free to you. They are a Double-Dip because:

1. There is no way of knowing whether the label is keeping their word and only giving away the amount they agree to. Even if they give away less than 15%, they still deduct the full 15%.

2. Because they give away the records of many artists in a sales program (or "garage sale," as I call it), you are then being charged for the RFGs of another artist.

Here's your axiom for the day:

> **Free Goods may imply records "given away for free,"**
> **but they are, in fact, records that are royalty-free to the label.**
> **They should really be called "Royalty-Free Goods."**

Now go back to everywhere in the contract where "Free Goods" are mentioned. There will be many places, especially in the areas where "royalties" are discussed. You will see that "royalty" calculations don't begin until after the label deducts their "free goods" percentages. (See the definition of "Records Sold," page 39.)

NEGOTIATE

All you can do is get this number down as far as you can. This is far more worthy of a battle, in my opinion, than fighting over the raising of your "royalty." This clause will drain you dry, believe me. When you are a hotshot, you can have the "free goods" clause thrown out completely.

You should also try to get the label to promise that they won't combine their "garage sales" of your records with any other artists. It's possible they can agree to this, but it is a sword that cuts both ways. If you are a new artist hoping to ride the publicity of another artist on your label, you may not want the label to be restricted in how they promote you in relation to other artists. It's a tough call. In the end I think you want your records separated, but each artist is different.

Additionally there is the issue of Mechanical Royalties, the money you get for licensing your songs to the label. The law says that you should be paid for these records whether the label gives them away or sells them, but in the Controlled Composition clause (page 155) you agreed to only get paid on records "sold."

Ask for any Free Goods over the 15% threshold to be excluded from nonpayment of mechanicals. You'll probably get it.

Also, what about downloads? Why should there be RFGs in downloads? The labels will argue that they are losing so much money through illegal P2P that they want to apply the RFG deduction even to a configuration that does not *ever* have any "giveaways." You'll have to decide if the battle is worth fighting based on how many other concessions they are making in the overall negotiation of the deal.

Now that you have a full understanding of the tools used by the label's accounting software, it's time to begin...

Auditing Your Record Company

There's just a few rules you'll need to know.

As you can see from the above sections, you need to determine if the label is actually "cheating" you before you decide to spend any money on an audit. Because if you do, there are some provisions that restrict you. Here they are, pulled right from the subheading ROYALTY ACCOUNTING in your contract.

Suing the Label: When You Can and When You Can't

(ii) If you have any objections to a royalty statement, you will give Pacific specific notice of that objection and your reasons for it within two (2) years after the date that Pacific is deemed to have sent you that statement. Each royalty statement will become conclusively binding on you at the end of that two-year period, and you will no longer have any right to make any other objections to it. You will

(ii) If you think we screwed up on a "royalty" statement, you need to tell us in writing about it within two years after we sent it to you, or you're outta luck forever.

If you wait any longer than that, you lose the right to sue us. [*We, of course, reserve our right to sue you forever.*] If you don't file a suit against us within six months after the end of this period, you lost your chance.

not have the right to sue Pacific in connection with any royalty accounting, or to sue Pacific for royalties on Records sold or receipts derived by Pacific during the period a royalty accounting covers, unless you commence the suit within six (6) months after the end of that two-year period. If you commence suit on any controversy or claim concerning royalty accountings rendered to you under this Agreement, the scope of the proceeding will be limited to determination of the amount of the royalties due for the accounting periods concerned, and the court will have no authority to consider any other issues or award any relief except recovery of any royalties found owing. Your recovery of any such royalties will be the sole remedy available to you or the Artist by reason of any claim related to Pacific's royalty accountings.

If you sue us for any of this "royalty" accounting bullshit, you can *only* sue for the money you think we owe you for that one period. *Nothing* else. And if a court finds that we have cheated you, they can't punish us in any way—such as having us pay you an extra amount to make up for our dishonesty. They can only force us to pay you the amount we should have already paid.

REALITY: This is the label's way of limiting their debt to you. If you can only sue for a single accounting "period" and the label has been ripping you off for several years, then according to the above clause, you will have to initiate several lawsuits, one for each "period." In addition, because of 360 Deals, labels want the right to audit the Artist to make sure they are getting their fair splits from touring, merchandise, sponsors, etc.

NEGOTIATE

Goes without saying: Get rid of it. But beware—when a label sees you spending time and money to change this around, it's a red flag to them that you might be a potentially litigious artist. However, you have an opportunity to turn the tables here. Insist on reciprocal audit provisions. That means that when the label wants to audit you, they have to follow the same nasty and ridiculous guidelines they make you adhere to. To see what I'm talking about, read on.

The Person You Hire to Catch Them

You think you can get your Uncle Ernie to do this audit? Think again. Some contracts have a series of clauses that say that the "auditor" must have experience auditing other labels. This is a very short list. They also say that he or she can't presently be auditing the label on behalf of another artist on that label, or auditing another label, while doing your audit. That narrows it down to about a dozen people. And here's a few more parameters:

(iii) Pacific agrees that you may, not more than once during any calendar year, with respect to any statement rendered hereunder, audit its books and records for the purpose of determining the accuracy of Pacific's statements to you. Without limitation of any of Pacific's rights hereunder, during any given audit, you shall have the right **to audit statements rendered during the three (3) consecutive years** immediately preceding the date of the audit, provided such statements have not previously been audited by you.

If you wish to perform any such audit, you will be required to notify Pacific at least thirty (30) days before the date when you plan to begin it.

Pacific may postpone (not unreasonably) the commencement of your audit by notice given to you not later than ten (10) days before the

(iii) You can only check out our books once a year.

Just because we let you do this doesn't mean that we're waiving any rights that we've established in the contract, or admitting to any wrongdoing on our part. You can only inspect statements **going back three years** from when you first ask us to do this audit. And you only get to audit us once. If you ask to see a statement that you've already seen, we don't have to show it to you.

You have to let us know 30 days before you want to do an audit.

We can string you along [*and the accountant and lawyer that you're paying by the hour*] and postpone your audit [*for an amount of time*

commencement date specified in your notice; if Pacific does so postpone, the running of the time within which the audit may be made will be suspended during the postponement. Provided Pacific has made its books and records available to you for the purposes set forth herein,

if your audit has not been completed within one (1) month from the time you begin it, Pacific may require you to terminate it on seven (7) days' notice to you at any time; Pacific will not be required to permit you to continue the examination after the end of that seven (7) day period.

You shall not be entitled to examine any manufacturing records or any other records which do not specifically report sales of Records or calculations of net receipts on which royalties are accruable hereunder. All audits shall be made during regular business hours upon reasonable notice, and shall be conducted on your behalf by an independent Certified Public Accountant. Audits conducted hereunder may not commence unless all prior audits, if any, have been settled. Further, such examination shall be conditioned upon the CPA's written agreement to Pacific that the CPA will not voluntarily disclose any findings to any Person other than you, the Artist, your Attorney or other advisers.

not mentioned] as long as we give you 10 days' notice before we let you near our books again.

If we do postpone, the amount of time that you are allowed to request this audit (three years, as mentioned above) will be extended [*'cause we're reasonable guys*].

You get one month to audit us during which we will have to make our books "available" to you. If you're not done in a month, we can tell you it's all over—as long as we give you a week's notice to clear out.

You only get to look at the "sales" records. Don't think we're gonna let you see any of our other records, such as our costs for manufacturing [*which is where the packaging deduction comes from. See page 53*]. Those are all our secrets. You don't get to see them.

All audits shall be done during regular business hours [*that's between 9 to 5 Monday to Friday in case you've never held a normal job*]. You have to hire and pay an independent Certified Public Accountant (CPA) to do the actual auditing, and he won't be allowed to examine anything until any previous disputes between us have been settled. Any other audits will only happen if your CPA finds something fishy [*which he won't, because we're very careful. I mean, thorough. Very thorough*]. If he wants more time or he needs additional records to audit, he's got to tell us that in writing, and he's gotta promise that he won't show or tell anything he learns about us to anyone other than you or your attorney.

All this is on your dime and will take place in one location in the US where we keep the books.

```
Each examination shall be made at
your own expense at one single
regular place of business in the
United States where the books and
records are maintained.
```

REALITY: Let's break this up a bit and take it slow. Here's what the clause above says:

1. You can only see the books once a year

2. You can only go back three years[15]

3. You can only audit the royalty statements of any one "period" at a time

4. You can only audit the company once in your lifetime

5. You have to give them 30 days' notice, but they can cancel for indefinite lengths of time and then only give you 10 days' notice as to when you may resume

6. Your audit can't take more than 30 days as long as they make the books "available" to you

7. If you take longer than 30 days, they can cut you off *forever* with only seven days' notice

8. You can only examine "royalty" statements, and nothing else, such as manufacturing records

9. You have to do this during regular business hours and with a CPA that you hire[16]

[15] If fraud is found, you can go back as far as you need. But fraud is harder to prove than you might think.

[16] CPA stands for Certified Public Accountant, but can at times also stand for Cleaning, Pressing, and Alterations, or Constant Pain in the Ass (depending on who hires the CPA).

10. If there are any other disputes between you and the label, the label won't allow your audit until those disputes are settled

11. The CPA cannot show his finding to anyone except the label and your attorney

12. You pay for the entire audit, even if it turns out that the label ripped you off

Many artists labor under the delusion that if they catch the label in a lie, that the label will 'fess up, hang their head in shame, and pay them off. This is a very optimistic assumption. The likelihood is that if you find an "error" in their accounting, they will circle the wagons and challenge your CPA's findings. Typically, many contracts require the CPA to "discuss" his findings with the label before he makes his final report. You can imagine what goes on in those discussions.

But, if there is a discrepancy, you have to first ask for money from the label and get turned down before you sue. The very day your CPA claims that there might be something fishy, the business affairs department of the label (that's the room full of bulldog lawyers who do nothing all day but think of new ways to protect the label's booty) will begin drafting a breach of contract suit. This will be done as a knee-jerk defense to the fact that you're about to sue them. It's a you-can't-break-up-with-me-cause-I'm-breaking-up-with-you-first kind of strategy.

While you're busy answering the breach of contract suit, you will not be allowed to view their books any further, as this would now be considered revealing privileged information to a litigant against the company.

You will have to settle any claims against the label. This will likely take months but could take several years. When it's over, you will have to re-retain the same CPA (so as not to change horses in midstream) so that he can finish the job he started months ago. The label does not have to show the same records twice, so you'd better hope that the CPA took careful notes and doesn't need to compare any new documents to any old ones.

NEGOTIATE

Try to get rid of everything. Ask for expanded time periods. Thirty days is not a reasonable amount of time to do an audit of three to five years of paperwork and file a report, especially while they're throwing all these curveballs at you. There will probably be statements they "forgot" to give you. You'll have to have the CPA request these, and it could take weeks to "find" them. Ask for six months.

Set aside any litigation. The contract should specify that they do not have the option to withhold any financial records at any time. Spell out exactly what "available" means. It's kept vague in the standard form above.

Also, ask for reimbursement of the cost of the audit, if a discrepancy of more than 10% is revealed. Be prepared to accept 20% as a compromise.

You Got 'Em—Now What?

So you nailed them. They were skimming off the top, inaccurately reporting foreign "sales," taking too many "free goods," not figuring the correct amount on records "sold" through record clubs, taking too large a deduction for packaging, and neglecting to calculate the money they owe you from download "sales" at the correct configuration. Combined, all of these things cost you about $100,000 in money that would have recouped into your account. Had they added correctly and not made a mistake, you would have recouped and been paid about another $50,000 in "royalties" over a five-year period. This 50 grand was the difference between being in the black and making your quota to get to the next plateau on your Sliding Scale "royalty."[17] Aside from the interest that you would have accrued had it been in your bank, not being paid this 50 grand also potentially cost you many thousands more, because of the extra half point you would have made in "royalties" off your other records.

Do you get any of this money? No.

You are only entitled to the money they mistakenly calculated off those exact "royalty" statements. Nothing more. At least that's what it says. Go back and read it if you don't believe me.

[17] See "Sliding Scale Royalty," page 64.

NEGOTIATE

Ask for and insist on payment within 30 days of all money found and a retail-based royalty of 2% for all records still sitting around their warehouse that they plan to sell to rack jobbers and scrap dealers. Also ask for an extra point on the records "sold" for which they forgot to pay you.

If they say "no," what are your alternatives? Here's one:

Severability

Severability. This is a $20 word for separating yourself from the company you are contracted to. The last part of the auditing-related clause has something that addresses this. It has a long history that goes to the heart of some of the more famous lawsuits by artists against their record companies. This list includes George Michael, Toni Braxton, TLC, and a gaggle of others.

They all learned the hard way that:

Just because you caught your label in a lie
doesn't mean that you get to walk out of the contract.

Below is another huge misconception under which many artists labor. Check it out:

Without limiting the generality of the preceding sentence, neither you nor the Artist will have any right to seek termination of this Agreement or avoid the performance of your obligations under it by reason of any such claim. The preceding three sentences will not apply to any item in a royalty accounting if you establish that the item was fraudulently misstated.

In every possible way that this can work against you, and at the same time, without limiting any of our rights, you're not allowed to ask a judge to release you from this contract, or to give you permission to stop working for us just because we tried to cheat you and you caught us. [*After all, it was just business, nothing personal. We still love you.*] This doesn't apply to "royalty" statements, though, if it turns out that we cheated you deliberately, and not by accident. [*Good luck proving that one!*]

REALITY: Entire legal careers have been built on the two sentences above. The truth is that it's not likely you'll *ever* be able to prove that the label cheated you deliberately. A judge will, in all likelihood, decide that you don't have to keep making records for this label if it's clear that they're not going to pay you. But you are still not free to make records for anyone else, because this contract is *exclusive*.

◗ Conclusions

Figuring out how many records you "sold" wouldn't be so hard if the label was more precise about how many records they gave away for "free." You are going to make millions for this company, but finding out exactly how much you are truly entitled to might cost you most of what you've earned. It could also cost you your relationship with the label.

So by now you should have a pretty good idea of what you're getting into. You are responsible for borrowing a ton of money, most of which you never get to actually touch. All this is hard enough, but what about a monkey wrench being thrown into the mix: What if you, or one of your bandmates, gets arrested? What about the kooks who claim you ripped them off? How will the label protect you from all this? Do they even have to? Well, not surprisingly, it's you who must assure the label that none of this will happen, not the reverse. In the next chapter, "Indemnification and Warranties," we'll learn exactly what the label expects you to be responsible for.

Turn the page.

CHAPTER 9

Indemnification and Warranties
or "What happens if I get in trouble with the law?"

*"Music oft hath such a charm
To make bad good, and good provoke to harm."*

—**William Shakespeare**, *Measure for Measure*

Many a newspaper story has been written about the irreverent artist who trashes his hotel room, punches out paparazzi, and snubs his own label. What about all that stuff? Would it burst your balloon substantially to learn that most of that stuff is orchestrated by publicists? Hopefully not. Yes, in the old days (the '70s is the "old days" for me, BTW), these things did go on organically. But the stakes are much higher now than they were then, and clauses in recording agreements are quite specific. In this short chapter we will learn exactly when the label will cover your bill and when they won't. This coverage—or lack thereof—applies not only to your trashing of hotel rooms, but also applies to stealing songs, use of samples, and anything that you do that would cost money.

Why These Clauses Exist

Unlike every other chapter in this book, there *is* a subheading in the contract that's called "Indemnification." At least it comes pretty close: WARRANTIES;

REPRESENTATIONS; RESTRICTIONS; INDEMNITIES. This is a postcard way of saying, "You're not gonna do anything to embarrass us, *right*? Here's how we make sure."

Over the past 50 years, labels have had to pay the bill for many an artist's responsibilities. Insurance companies do a lot of business with large labels, insuring them against new lawsuits every day. I would guess that over 1,000 suits are filed each month against various labels and their affiliates. It's a legal mess. The public never hears about most of these because they get settled out of court. The kind of insurance policies needed to absorb the risks of the music business cost big bucks, naturally, because recording artists notoriously are *big* risks. And since labels appear to have deep pockets, this makes them a likely target for those trying to get rich suing them.

In their pitch to you at the deal memo stage, the label comes on like a fatherly figure who will take care of you. In exchange for this protective Big Brother philosophy, you give up a large percentage of your income.

Unfortunately, all this promised protectionism is as tenuous as the promise of "royalties." You, the artist, are responsible for *everything*. You are required to carry your *own* insurance, and if the label is sued, even though the insurance company might cover their loss, you have to reimburse them. So they have turned a simple procedure, designed to limit risk, into yet another profit center.

Much like a doctor who is afraid to help an injured person he finds on the street lest he be sued, so too have artists begun to practice a form of defensive (or prophylactic) producing. And, over time, the lawyers for labels have made sure that this process is as anal as it can be, with a series of obnoxious clauses that turn an artist into a lawyer.

I guess misery loves company.

Here we go.

❯ The Standard Indemnification

This long word simply refers to the act of repaying someone money that you cost them. *Webster's* puts it this way: "to compensate for or guarantee against damage, loss, or expenses incurred."

This sounds straightforward in theory, but it gets complex because people and companies tend to try to deflect responsibility in these matters.

(a) **You will at all times indemnify and hold harmless Pacific and any of its Licensees** (collectively the "Indemnitee") from and against any and all claims, damages, liabilities, costs and expenses, including legal expenses and reasonable counsel fees, arising out of any breach or alleged breach of any warranty or representation made by you in this Agreement or any other act or omission by you or the Artist, provided the claim concerned has been settled, subject to the provisions of subparagraph (b) below, or has resulted in a judgment against any Indemnitee. Pacific will notify you of any action commenced on such a claim. You may participate in the defense of any such claim through counsel of your selection at your own expense, but Pacific will have the right at all times, in its sole discretion, to retain or resume control of the conduct of the defense.

If any claim involving such subject matter has not been resolved, or has been resolved by a judgment or other disposition which is not adverse to any Indemnitee, **you will reimburse Pacific** for fifty percent (50%) of the expenses actually incurred by Indemnitee in connection with that claim.

For the whole time you're in this deal, you will agree to never blame us or our "fake" indie labels and sister companies for any claims against you. If we get sued, you have to pay for everything, including lawyers' fees, damages, and anything we can think of. You will agree that we did nothing wrong and were not involved [*even if we were*]. You can protect yourself a little bit by hiring your own lawyer. But we don't want to see you in court [*unless we need you to testify*]. We're the quarterbacks here. You're allowed to observe as a courtesy, and we might even listen to your lawyer, but we don't have to do what he says.

Now if we lose the lawsuit and a judge or jury has insisted that we need to pay off some amount of money that we think is ridiculous, **you will pay us back** (or our sister companies, bless their hearts) fifty percent (50%) of *everything*—the award, our lawyer's fees, *everything*.

Pending the resolution of any such claim Pacific will have the right to withhold monies which would otherwise be payable to you under this Agreement in an amount not exceeding your potential liability to Pacific under this paragraph; provided, however, Pacific will not withhold monies which otherwise would be payable to you under this Agreement if you make satisfactory bonding arrangements in accordance with subparagraph (b) below.

If someone files a claim against you or us, and we were about to pay you some money, we will now hang on to your cash until this whole matter is resolved. But we'll only hold on to the amount that they are asking for in their suit. The only exceptions are the stuff mentioned in (b) below.

REALITY: So if the label has to come up with a financial settlement, you pay half. How is this a recording expense? It's not. It's a legal expense. The tricky part is that their lawyers work on salary, and would receive the same pay whether they're working on your behalf or not. So what does this mean when the label says you are obliged to pay half their legal bills? That you have to pay half the salaries of their legal department? Naturally you should not. This is yet another Double-Dip.

One could infer that the clause means the label will hire outside counsel to defend against the suit, but that's not what it says. And if we've learned anything in this book it's:

If it ain't written, it ain't so.

The label also says that they will hold only the amount that they are being sued for. Of course, most people sue for 10 times the amount they would settle for. So for a million-dollar lawsuit, even though the damages might actually only equal about $100,000, the label will have to hold the full amount of a million dollars in reserve.

Insert a sentence that specifies that this clause can *only* apply to the label's necessity to hire outside counsel. If they use in-house counsel to defend the suit, you shouldn't have to pay anything. It's business as usual. And even though it says so above, you should have the right to retain your own counsel and not be dependent on the label to "protect" your rights. Put in a clause about that as well.

As to the amount they hold, there is no reason for this, unless the amount they're being sued for is enormously excessive (for example, if it's tens of millions of dollars). It's absurd for a label to hold 10 times the amount for which they're being sued, especially considering that the label will most likely settle for less than $100,000. Put a limit on this. Remember, the label wanted to be the quarterback—they can't then also drag it out at your expense. Let it be at their expense.

But all is not lost here. Check out this next twist:

(b) If Pacific pays more than $10,000 in settlement of any such claim, you will not be obligated to reimburse Pacific for the excess unless you have consented to the settlement, except as provided in the next sentence. If you do not consent to any settlement proposed by Pacific for an amount exceeding $10,000 you will nevertheless be required to reimburse Pacific for the full amount paid unless you make bonding arrangements, satisfactory to Pacific in its reasonable discretion, to assure Pacific of reimbursement for all damages, liabilities, costs and expenses (including legal expenses and reasonable counsel fees) which Indemnitee may incur as a result of that claim. If no action or other

(b) If we shell out more than $10,000 in settlement of any claim, you don't have to pay us back for anything over that amount, unless you have agreed to the settlement [*which you will, believe me—see REALITY below*]. But if you do not agree to the amount we want to settle for, even if it's over $10,000, then you *do* have to pay us back for the full amount anyway. The only way out of this one for you is to agree in writing to put up some collateral (like your house). Or you can agree to do something else for us that satisfies us in our "reasonable" discretion, and which makes us comfortable that we'll get the money back from you one way or another. [*For example,* proceeding for recovery on such a claim has been commenced within one (1) year after its assertion, Pacific will not continue to withhold monies in connection with it under this paragraph.

you could record an extra album, make a personal appearance, tell people how cool we are in your next interview, bring us another artist to suck dry, or something along these lines.]

If there is a settlement, but the guy suing us never manages to collect his money from us and within a year just stops trying, we won't continue to hold your money in reserve.

REALITY: I have never seen a lawsuit against a major label that was settled for less than $10,000. So forget that part. The lawyer's fees alone will come out to that much. So can you "not agree" to the settlement and thus escape having to pay for half? For example, the label comes back to you and says they want to settle for $100,000. This means $50,000 will be your share. You hold out and say no. Will it work?

Sure, but you're now in "breach of contract," as per this clause and several others that we've reviewed already.[1] The general concept is that any time money is involved, the label holds the strings. If they, in their sole "reasonable" discretion, believe that you owe them money and you refuse to pay, they can suspend the length of the contract until you come to your senses. They can do this without paying you any additional money, and you're not allowed to work for anyone else during the time that you're under suspension.[2]

What will likely happen, in reality, is that the label will either ask you for another album, or to do something else that will compensate for this disaster. You'll do it.

[1] See "Merchandising," page 212, "Terms and Exclusivity," page 314, and "Release and Distribution," page 225.

[2] See "Terms and Exclusivity," page 310, and "Merchandising," page 197.

NEGOTIATE

You can try to get rid of this, but I'm not sure it's worth it. It certainly isn't a high priority, in my opinion. If you've already achieved all the other points on your Christmas list and there's room in your legal budget, then try to get this modified. Get it to be a fixed number, and make sure that the compensation is something specific. Always be *very* specific.

Song Stealing and Defamation

Plagiarism is among the most common reasons people sue other people in the music biz. Another one is libel—if someone feels you are talking shit about them in one of your songs. Here's how both of these are dealt with in your recording contract:

No Materials, as hereinafter defined, or any use thereof, will violate any law or infringe upon or violate the rights of any Person. "Materials", as used in this Article, means: (1) the Master Recordings made or furnished under this Agreement, (2) all Controlled Compositions, (3) each name used by the Artist, individually or as a group, in connection with Recordings made hereunder, and (4) all other musical, dramatic, artistic and literary materials, ideas, and other intellectual properties, furnished or selected by you, the Artist or any Producer and contained in or used in connection with any Recordings made hereunder or their packaging, sale, distribution, advertising, publicizing or other exploitation, including, without limitation, all label copy and liner note information provided by you or the Artist.

Nothing you create under this contract will upset anyone enough to sue us. This includes:

(1) the recording you make;

(2) the songs you've written:
(3) what you call yourself in the public eye and:

(4) any performances you do in movies, TV, videos, ads for the record, books you write, T-shirts, merch, or ideas that you have. [*How you're supposed to manage that, when you can't control the editing, scripts, etc., is not our concern.*]

REALITY: In case you didn't read the fine print, this one will be impossible for you to follow, and just as impossible for the label to enforce. Actors in movies and TV rarely have say over these things in most entertainment-oriented contracts. Producers usually assume that role. Only in the record industry are artists held to this level of responsibility. This would be like suing Tom Cruise because a character he plays in a movie is a racist. Absurd.

But what the label is more concerned about is if a person claims that you stole their song. This happens daily, and the contract is worded the way it is above to make sure you're responsible for any disputes that arise in this matter.

NEGOTIATE

Get rid of this. They will use the argument above, that they can't be responsible for you stealing material. If they claim that, then add a line that makes this paragraph specific to allegations of plagiarism, nothing else.

You Da Man

To ensure that everything in this contract also applies to the people in your group or entourage, the label has concocted this little ditty.

³ See page 197 for more on "Work for Hire."

Each and every vocalist, musician, Producer and other individual whose services you furnish in connection with the preparation of a Master Recording or Covered Video under this Agreement either will have done so as an employee within the scope of his or her employment or will have expressly agreed in a written instrument signed by him or her and by the party commissioning the services that the Recording or Covered Video, as applicable, will be considered a "work made for hire." A copy of any and all such instruments will be furnished to Pacific upon the request of Pacific.

We consider anyone who works on your record to be your employee, and they will sign a piece of paper that says so, and that states that any service they provide on the record or video will be considered a "work made for hire."[3] [*You are responsible for everything they say to the media, do, or break, while they are working for you.*] A copy of all these agreements will be given to us.

REALITY: What this is about is making sure that the blonde wiggling her way into the camera's attention does not later come back and sue you for using her "image" without permission. Producers get everyone in a video or record to sign a "release" that gives them permission to exploit their image and/or a recording of their voice. This clause just makes you, the artist, personally responsible for doing their job. It's another version of the clause before it. But the wiggling blonde isn't the only thing you have to worry about. Read the sidebar "Screwed by the Pooch."

SCREWED BY THE POOCH

In 1987, metal headbangers Hammer Head had an eight-Album deal on Pacific Records and wanted to include a screaming guitar solo in their Single "Body Rock." Despite the fact that each member of the band was a competent lead guitarist (even the drummer), they opted to bring in one of their idols, Steve (Mad Dog) Vivante.

Steve was partnered with another national rock act at the time, but with permission from his record company, he did his up-and-coming friends Hammer Head a solid, and laid a wicked kick-ass solo over the bridge of "Body Rock." The riff was so cool that in the final mix it was featured in the intro and outro of the song.

When the Album was released, "Body Rock" became an instant radio hit. Mad Dog's solo was the obsession of every wannabe rock guitarist's late-night practice sessions. It was infectious. It was the hook of the year. It was also someone else's song.

Yep. Mad Dog didn't realize that the solo he played matched the melody of another song that was an R&B hit only 10 years earlier, called "Sweet Sugar." Not only did he not realize it, no one at Pacific Records caught it, either.

Needless to say, lawyers for "Sweet Sugar" filed a complaint in a California court, not against Mad Dog, nor against Pacific, but against Hammer Head themselves. Since Mad Dog was operating as their employee when he did the solo, Hammer Head became solely responsible for the plagiarism.

Hammer Head settled out of court by handing over 50% of their hit song's publishing. Mad Dog Vivante is wildly accepted as one of the most influential rock guitarists of the 1980s. The episode didn't cost Pacific a dime. The record sold over 3,000,000 copies.

You Are Special

You probably already knew that, but did you know just *how* special you were? Here the label tells you, in a heartwarming way:

The services of the Artist are unique and extraordinary, and **the loss thereof cannot be adequately compensated in damages,** and Pacific shall be **entitled to seek injunctive relief** to enforce the provisions of this Agreement.

(The preceding sentence will not be construed to preclude you or the Artist from opposing any application for such relief based upon contest of the other facts alleged by Pacific in support of the application.)

You are one of a kind. If we lose you it's not like losing an accountant or a lawyer. There are thousands of those, but you are an *Artist,* and **your loss to us cannot be measured in dollars.** But since money is the only remedy we have, **we are entitled to sue anyone we want,** to make sure that no one tries to take you away from us, and to make sure that you don't decide to leave us on your own. We love you and we're very possessive. We will sue them and we will sue you, for your own good, to make sure that you do everything you agreed to in this contract. (This is called "injunctive relief" and it should prove to you just how fortunate you are to have people like us to protect you.) However, you're still allowed to object if we try to sue the bastard that's trying to seduce you away from us, and you can come up with evidence that shows that he wasn't trying to do that at all [*which you won't, because proving a negative is nearly impossible*].

REALITY: The legalese for this is "tortuous interference." In English, that means that if anyone, even your mother, tries to get you to breach your contract with the label, or even talks in a way that makes you feel like leaving your label, the label has the right to sue their pants off. If you are schizophrenic, and you are talking yourself into breaching this contract, then the label can force you to sue yourself. Just kidding. (I think.)

Suits are filed each year on this basis alone. Often they're filed against a competing label that is trying to lure you away with a better offer. If your label finds out that you have been approached by another company and that you entertained the offer, even for a second, they will not be pleased. When it comes time to ask a favor of them (which you will be doing constantly throughout this contract), don't count on their cooperation.

Forget it. They won't take it out. Honestly, I can't blame them.

Your Group Name and Who Can Join

Anyone who's spent time with a rock, R&B, or rap group will share a similar experience of personnel changes. People leave and new players come in, sometimes every month or so. When they do, do you change the name of the group? Who owns the name exactly? How does that affect your record deal? These clauses come from the section often labeled GROUP ARTIST.

Your Name

(i) As used herein, the term "Name" shall mean the name "Pacific" and every other name (if any) by which Artist as a group may hereafter be professionally known.

(i) In this contract the word "Name" [*with a capital "N"*] means any name that you are known by to the public.

(ii) You **warrant and represent** that you are the sole and exclusive owner of all rights in and to the Name.

(ii) You **assure us that you have taken all legal steps** to make sure that no one else is using this Name and that no one will be offended by you using it. If you're wrong, you pay.

REALITY: These two simple lines can hang you more than you know. (For an eye-opening rationalization of this, see *Confessions,* "Name Blockage"). Group Names are more common than most people think, and they are worth more money than most people assume. People will spend big bucks to protect a Name, because it carries with it a recognition of a certain level of quality.

So You Want to Join Our Group, Now That We're Signed?

After a group is signed, personnel changes are quite common. This can happen after entire albums are recorded and a member takes sick, or has a fight with the rest of the group. At this point, all of his or her tracks have to be redone by someone else before the record can be released. I've seen this happen even with lead singers.

It's not uncommon for band members to leave a group after one or two Albums for family reasons (or maybe to finish college). Maybe they've had enough of the road, the low pay, or are tired of always losing girls to the lead singer.

Unfortunately, getting replacements won't be as easy as when you were not signed to a label and you simply placed an ad in the local downtown paper. Now there's a bureaucracy to deal with. Here's the clause that deals with that. After reading this you may want to jump ahead to "Terms and Exclusivity" and see what happens when you want to leave the group. Also at the end of the last chapter there is a clause that deals with this.

No Person shall become a Member (whether as an additional member or in replacement of a Member who has left Artist) unless you forthwith deliver to Pacific a ratification of this agreement (in the form set forth in subparagraph below) signed by you and such Person. Upon the countersignature of such ratification by Pacific such Person shall be deemed to have become a Member.

Nobody's allowed to join the group (whether as an additional member or as a replacement for a member who left you) unless you immediately give us written and signed notice and receive our approval. (The form directly below is our recommendation.) We don't have to agree to it, and nobody can be added to your group without our okay.

So, let's see what they have to sign…

(ii) The form of ratification referred to in subparagraph above is as follows:

(ii) The form referred to above is as follows:

"Pacific" Music, etc. –
Gentlemen:

"Pacific-Affiliated Labels" –
Label Dudes:

I acknowledge that I have read all of the terms and conditions of that certain recording agreement (the "Agreement") dated _____ between you and _____ regarding (specify

I've read all of the outrageous terms and conditions of this recording agreement dated _____ between you and my buddy, _____. I can live with it.

the Name), and all of the terms and conditions of the assent and agreement to be bound, **guarantee and indemnity** executed by the members of (specify the Name) in connection with the Agreement.

I promise I'll pay back the label for money that I cost them in lawsuits filed against our group or any of its members.

DOUBLE-DIP DETECTOR

EXPLANATION: This is the label's way of spreading out their liability. If there are four people in your group and you break up, the label will still have exclusive contracts with each of you.[4] Therefore, their liability for the clause above, where the artist agrees to "indemnify" the label, will be spread out among four new contracts with each group member on their own. In this way the label creates a reverse pyramid scheme, increasing their ability to recover money from the artist many times with each new signing. One lawsuit could then be collected against each member of the band. It's brilliant, but probably unenforceable in a court of law.

[4] See "Terms and Exclusivity," page 279.

The letter continues...

In consideration of your acceptance of me as an additional or substitute member, as the case may be, of (specify the Name), I agree that I shall be bound by each provision of the Agreement and each provision of said assent and agreement to be bound, guarantee and indemnity as if I were an original signatory thereto, except that the effective date of my becoming so bound shall, when countersigned by you, be the earlier of the date hereof

As a condition to you accepting me as an additional or substitute member, I agree that I'll obey every clause of the Agreement as if I were the original member whom I am replacing. The difference is that I am only bound by this contract as of the date of the signing of this letter once you co-sign this, or the date upon which I first did anything for the Artist [*i.e., rehearse, perform, sing on a demo, or anything else*].

```
Very truly yours,                        Props. Peace out,

_____/           _____,
date: _____."            date: _____."
```

REALITY: So you're already a member of this group and you didn't even know it. That's what it says. If you participated in even one rehearsal (prior to signing the form), you may be bound by the terms of the Thick. This is not a likely matter in reality, but it's interesting to know.

Say you were rehearsing with a signed band for several months as sort of an audition, and during that time you did something which could be considered wrong by the terms above. You might already be in trouble. This *does* happen quite a lot. Just as artists rarely read their entire contract, new members read it even less frequently.

An example of the kind of thing that is considered "wrong" would include playing on friend's demos, or that weekend wedding gig that made you an extra $300 in cash, etc. Kiss it goodbye. You're now part of the plantation. Grab a shovel, dig in, and make music! How many of your friends would you be able to enlist if they knew exactly what they were getting into? Maybe none. But if they are true friends, you owe it to them to share all the facts before you get them into something they may later regret.

As the artist, you must remember that each of these people who join are *your* responsibility. If they screw up, you have to *indemnify* the label. (Notice how I try to use our new words in sentences!)

NEGOTIATE

Few people ever bother to negotiate this clause, because it's a far bridge that most never cross. If you do negotiate this point, there are a few things you could ask for that could save a few of your friendships. For starters, you can make the co-signing of the agreement by the label mandatory within 10 days of the presentation of your intent to add this particular member. Also, you can try to get the retroactivity bit thrown out. Once the label co-signs the form, the actions of your new member from the time he began auditioning for the band months back no longer are relevant.

⊘ Conclusions

No matter what business you are in, whether you're a toy manufacturer, limo driver, or restaurant owner, if you are an independent contractor, you are required to warranty your product. If you drive a car, you must carry insurance—it's a form of warranty. If you're a chef, you must guarantee the restaurant that your recipes do not contain poison. Even I have to promise the publisher of this book that everything I've written is accurate. Songwriting is no different.

The scary part is that as long as you are under contract, all of the provisions that you've read above will follow you around, wherever you go, whatever business you go into, even after you're finished being a big pop star.

Exactly how long would that be? I've saved that question until the end, and now you'll see why in the last chapter, "Terms and Exclusivity."

Turn the page.

CHAPTER 10

➤Terms and "Exclusivity"

or "How long do I have to put up with this shit?"

"Marriage is the prime cause of divorce."

—Alfred E. Newman

T his is a very long chapter, but (like every other chapter in this book), this one is the most important. No, it's not as sexy as royalties or Advances, but how long you're trapped in a deal, good or bad, is essential if you plan to live past 30. I'm guessing that you do, so pour a tall cup of Joe and get comfortable.

Albert Einstein, creator of the Theory of Relativity, said, "Time is relative to the point of view of the observer."[1] He meant that what seems like a long amount of time from one point of view might be perceived as a short amount of time from another point of view. He was speaking of large distances in the trillions of miles, and what happens to light when it travels this distance. Regardless, with this logic he would have made an excellent recording contract drafter. What seems like a large amount of time to you (since your career will likely be about five years) is to the label a short amount of time, since they are an immortal machine, replacing personnel like the master computer in *The Matrix* replaced its "Agents." This "immortality" makes them a bit insensitive to your desires regarding the contract's length.

[1] Einstein actually said, "The world line of every object is a geodesic in the continuum." I changed it a little bit.

Why This Clause Exists

"Terms," as used in most conversations, mean the conditions under which we do business. *What are your terms?* is the most commonly asked question in deal making. If you have a credit card, then you know the terms are something like: pay it off in increments, one month at a time. For every month that the credit card company carries your debt, they charge you interest. If you don't pay, they cut you off and your credit goes bad. Fairly simple. If you want a credit card, then you must accept these terms.

But in a recording contract, the "Term" subheading simply refers to the length of time you'll be in business with the label. Even though the "terms" are all in the first few pages of the contract, there are many other *real* terms about the conditions under which you will be making records on the plantation, scattered throughout the Thick.

❯ The Standard
How Long Is This Deal?

Of all the inequities in the recording contract, the very worst, in my opinion, is the label's total lack of commitment as to how long your actual engagement will last. In the past this was never vague—some contracts were five terms long, with each term equaling one year. The artist would make a record a year, with a total of five records for each of the five terms. Pretty simple stuff.[2]

These days that type of "term" is only present in little indie deals, or ones in which the lawyers are not up to date on the vanguard of recording contract trickery. Most contracts these days span a nebulous length of time that starts when the artist signs The Thick (or even before) and keeps going until the label says they're no longer interested in them, and then a bit after that.

This is not an easy thing to design in LabelSpeak, because the law requires a contract to have a specific beginning and ending (either based on time or delivery of services). Without a specific beginning and end to a service agreement, courts routinely decide that the contract is unfair.

Keeping people forever guessing about their fate or employment status, unable to pursue other ventures in life, is called "indentured servitude" (or "slavery," as it used to be known), and was the basis of George Michael's legal campaign to disconnect himself from his label, Sony Music. It didn't work.

[2] Refer to "The Decoding of an Actual Warner Bros. Recording Contract," in *Confessions*, to see how this was done in the 1970s and early 1980s.

So how do they do it? Since the law requires that a contract have a specific length, how do these sneaky lawyers manage to skirt around it, and keep you on the plantation forever?

The entire technique revolves around the totally absurd way that contracts define the words "Term" and "Contract Period."

But before we get to that, I want you to do something. Flip back to the first page of this book and read the first item in the deal memo. Go ahead. I'll wait.

Okay. Show of hands, who thinks that what they just read means that this is a seven-Album deal? Who thinks it's a deal that should last six or seven years? It sort of sounds like that, doesn't it? But, as you'll see in a moment, it doesn't say anything like that. In fact, when you see the final contract, that one line in the deal memo will be radically expanded to what you are about to read.

The clauses below come from the subheading TERM, and are usually found toward the front of The Thick:

The "Term" hereof shall commence on the date hereof and shall consist of the Initial Period and each Option Period, if any.

The total amount of time you will be exclusively engaged (called the "Term") starts on the date you sign this and is made up of two things: a span of time called the "Initial Period" followed by several other amounts of time called "Option Periods."

The "Initial Period" of the Term, unless terminated as otherwise provided herein, **shall end eight (8) months following the initial commercial release in the United States and Canada of the Second LP** or, if the Second LP is not released (but without limitation of any of Artist's rights hereunder with respect to such failure to release) twelve (12) months after delivery of the Second LP.

The "Initial Period" portion of this deal will start when you sign this contract and **go until eight months after we decide to release your second record in the United States and Canada.** If we decide not to release the second record, then the "Initial Period" will end 12 months after you "deliver" your second album.

Pause a second and review: A "Term" is the total amount of time that you are under contract and is composed of two things: 1) A first span of time that starts when you sign and ends eight months after you "deliver" your second Album—unless the label decides that they don't like your second Album and won't release it, in which case the terms ends one year after you "deliver" that ill-fated second Album; and 2) a second span of time that has not yet been defined, called an "Option Period." Which we're going to learn about now. Got it? Don't go ahead unless you are crystal clear on this. Because it's about to get more confusing. See the sidebar "Initial Period" table for clarification.

Initial Period

<table>
<tr>
<td>Recording and "delivering" first Album

+

Eight months after "release" of second Album</td>
<td>or</td>
<td>Recording and "delivering" first album
+
Period of first Album's "release"
(about five months)
+
Recording and "delivering"
second Album
+
Period of second Album's "release"
(about eight months)</td>
</tr>
</table>

"Initial Period"

The Initial Period and each Option Period of the Term are each sometimes herein referred to as a "Contract Period" or a "Period."

"Initial Period" and "Option Period" [*still undefined*] are all interchangeable in this contract with the phrase "Contract Period" or just plain vanilla "Period."

Each "Option Period" shall commence upon expiration of the immediately preceding Contract Period and, unless terminated as otherwise provided herein, shall end eight

An "Option Period" starts right after the previous "Period" ends. Unless we drop you, it will go for eight months after we release your Album (in the United States and Canada). If we don't release

(8) months following the initial commercial release in the United States and Canada of the prior Product LP or, if such prior Product LP is not so released (but without limitation of any of Artist's rights hereunder with respect to such failure to release), twelve (12) months after delivery of such applicable prior Product LP.

it, the Option Period ends 12 months after you "delivered" the Album.

Pause again. An "Option Period" starts the minute the last "period" ends. If they don't release the Album, then the "Option Period" ends one year after you "deliver" it to them. One more thang: "Period," "Contract Period," and "Option Period" all mean the same thing.

And now here's the hammer:

You hereby grant to Pacific seven (7) separate and consecutive options to extend the Term for Option Periods on the same terms and conditions applicable to the Initial Period.

You agree that we will have the right to extend the total amount of time that you are exclusively bound to us ("the Term") seven separate times, one after the next. Each extension will be considered an Option Period, and is tied to the same conditions, loopholes, Double-Dips, and trap doors as the Initial Period.

LOOPHOLE ALERT!!!

EXPLANATION: Ninety attorneys out of 100 will read that and think it means that you are giving the label a seven-year contract. This is because, in the real world, a "term" is a specific length of time. But here the "Term" is LabelSpeak for an undetermined length of time that can be truncated or extended at the whim of the label. Only attorneys familiar with Big Four contracts will catch this Mobius

REALITY: Most Albums take about four months to produce. The label will then tinker with it for several more months until they decide that it's "delivered." Then the marketing department will throw it around a bit, until they decide when to release it. (Either right before Christmas, right after the start of the New Year, Spring, or in September, when school begins.) *When* it's released will be based on what else the label is releasing at certain times and, more important, what competing labels are releasing at those same times.

So to estimate the length of an "Option Period," figure a minimum of about 14 months to a maximum of two-and-a-half years. Then *multiply by seven*. Then factor in the "Restriction Period" (see page 312) of two years, during which you can't record these songs for anybody else. Then figure out how old you will be when this contract's "Term" is over.

The following is optimistic:

Initial Period
- Recording of first album (4–6 months)
- "Delivering" of first Album
- "Period" of first "release" (5–10 months)
- Recording of second Album (4–6 months)
- "Delivering" of second Album
- "Period" of second "release" (5–10 months)

Total: 18–32 months
(Provided that the label doesn't send you back to record more, and that the marketing goes smoothly)

First Option Period
- Recording of third album (4–6 months)
- "Delivering" of third Album
- "Period" of third "release" (5–10 months)

Total: 9–16 months

Multiply by *seven*. And you get:

Jan 2011	Jan 2012	Jan 2013	Jan 2014	Jan 2015	Jan 2016	Jan 2017	Jan 2018	Jan 2019	Jan 2020
1st Option Period (a.k.a. "Initial Period")			2nd Option Period		3rd Option Period		4th Option Period		5th Option Period

Jan 2021	Jan 2022	Jan 2023	Jan 2024	Jan 2025	Jan 2026	Jan 2027	Jan 2028	Jan 2029	Jan 2030
6th Option Period		7th Option Period		Exploitation Period (Sunset Period)					

Timetable of a Typical Eight-Album Deal

NEGOTIATE

First of all, investigate how long it takes the label to get a record on the street from the time it's "delivered." Ask them this at the courting stage. When they give you the answer, write it down *in front of them*. Then when it comes to negotiating time, make them live up to it in the contract. Show them what they said. Catch them in this lie; it's important. Without this, try to always insert a sentence that creates a "drop dead" date in the above clause. That's a date by which the label must release the record or the Option Period ends promptly. If you notice, they only give you this for the Initial Period (12 months) and not the Option Periods. If you can, make it so that if the Option Period ends *prematurely*, then the Term also terminates. You should understand by now the difference between "Period" and "Term."

Another thing: The Initial Period has two Albums. I know you think it's better for you if the label commits to as many records as possible. You probably optimistically think this translates into a form of "job security." But it doesn't. Get one Album per "period."

Finally, I fail to see why one can't simply add a sentence like, "notwithstanding anything herein contained to the contrary, no Option Period will be longer than one calendar year." If you're feeling aggressive, try instead to make it eight to 10 months. Some indies will give it to you.

And there is some really good news. In California, any service contract that is over seven years long is invalid.[3]

[3] It's unclear whether this means terms extending beyond seven years are invalid, or that the entire contract is invalid.

Exploitation Period

Even when it's over, it's not really over. Most contracts have a "period" that starts when the last Option Period ends. It's sometimes called a "Sunset Period" or an "Exploitation Period."

As defined herein, the term "Exploitation Period" means the period after the termination of the term hereof and ending on the date that is three (3) months after the release or servicing to radio or other media of the last single record or "focus track" in connection with the final Commitment Album required to be delivered by Artist to Company during the term; provided, that, in no event shall such period extend beyond eighteen (18) months after the termination of the term.

When we say "Exploitation Period," it means six months after the release and marketing of the last Single from the last Album you were required to "deliver" during this term.

But it will never be more than 18 months after the end of the contract.

REALITY: Assume the worst. If the label can hold you, they will. Count on there being a period of 18 months during which time you're still bound to all the terms of this contract. This clause exists for one reason: so that you don't immediately go and record the same songs for another label.

The Artificial Term-Extension Scam

Artists' representatives have become hip to the fact that their clients are being "held without bail," so to speak, for lengths of time that most industries would consider unconscionable. That's why labels usually give in on most of what I outlined above. But the sneaky lawyers have an insidious counterstrategy: they claim that accounting gets screwed up due to all these periods ending and beginning so many times. To balance the scales, they have begun to add this to the end of most "Terms" clauses:

```
Notwithstanding anything to the contrary contained herein,
[loophole creator] the months of October, November and
December shall not be included when computing the ending
date of any Period.
```

What it doesn't say is whether they will round this time up or down to the closest end of a month. It just says that a "period" won't end in October, November or December.

So for example, if a "Period" is scheduled to end on October 10, will the label just round it back to September 30, or will they round it forward and say it ended on January 1?

You can be sure that unless you specify, the label will always round it up in their favor to the longest amount of time possible.

This just about negates all the good efforts that you achieved, if you asked for and got most of what I just suggested in "Negotiate" above. Look and see. Compare the timetable below to the previous one. You'll see that because of this new addition, just about every "period" begins on January 1.

Jan 2011	Jan 2012	Jan 2013	Jan 2014	Jan 2015	Jan 2016	Jan 2017	Jan 2018	Jan 2019	Jan 2020
1st Option Period (a.k.a. "Initial Period")			2nd Option Period		3rd Option Period		4th Option Period		

Jan 2020	Jan 2021	Jan 2022	Jan 2023	Jan 2024	Jan 2025	Jan 2026	Jan 2027	Jan 2026	Jan 2027
5th Option Period			6th Option Period		7th Option Period			Exploitation Period (Sunset Period)	

When added up, this has a domino effect on the total length of the Term and artificially extends it by an extra year to the first quarter of 2027. And this is assuming that you signed in January. Look how this same negotiation would affect you if you signed in June:

Jan 2011	Jan 2012	Jan 2013	Jan 2014	Jan 2015	Jan 2016	Jan 2017	Jan 2018	Jan 2019	Jan 2020
1st Option Period (a.k.a. "Initial Period")				2nd Option Period		3rd Option Period		4th Option Period	

Jan 2021	Jan 2022	Jan 2023	Jan 2024	Jan 2025	Jan 2026	Jan 2027	Jan 2028	Jan 2029	Jan 2030
5th Option Period		6th Option Period		7th Option Period		Exploitation Period (Sunset Period)			

Just by signing six months later, your contract would end about two years later, in April 2029.

Obviously, this is insane.

NEGOTIATE

Since the label will probably not remove this stupidity from the deal, you might have to refer them to this page in the book to help them see the light. After that you should ask for a clause that states that regardless of when the Option Periods begin or end, the accounting periods will be based on when they *would have* ended, regardless of this no-October-November-December bullshit.

Employee or Independent Contractor?

In most states, the difference between an employee and an independent contractor is more than just what type of form you fill out (W4 or 1099). Just because you wish your employer didn't withhold taxes and you ask to be paid on a 1099 does not mean that the IRS will agree that you're an independent contractor instead of a full-time employee. There are specific things that constitute "employment." Why is this relevant to "selling" millions of records? Well, because if you're an employee, a company generally provides standard benefits as a matter of course, such as unemployment benefits, health insurance, worker's compensation, and pension or 401(k) retirement accounts. These might be things that you're not thinking about right now, but believe me, they're important. Especially if you are thinking about starting a family or already have a child.

In most companies in the US, an employee gets all of the above, and if they are with the company for more than two years, they get stock in the company as a bonus. Between stock, pension/401(k), health insurance, and unemployment, altogether we are talking about tens of thousands of dollars that an employee gets that an independent contractor does not. So are you an "employee" of the record company? Are you interested?

What is an "employee?" This is the usual standard for determination in most states:

(i)   Are you in control of the quality of the product?

(ii) Are you using your own materials?

(iii) Can you leave the job any time you want?

(iv) Is the work performed on your premises?

If the answer to all of the above is "no," then you are an "employee" in the eyes of most states, and are entitled to benefits. If you've been following along in all these chapters, you'd know that the answer to each of the above in a major-label contract is "no." So are you ready to collect? Sure, but there's a problem. The record company says you are *not* an employee. Even though you fit the legal standards above to a T, you are not entitled to any benefits simply because the contract says so. Check it out. This comes under the subheading YOUR RELATIONSHIP TO LABEL. (A bit of irony.)

You are an **independent contractor hereunder,** and nothing herein contained shall in any way constitute you as the agent or employee of Pacific. You do not intend Artist, Producer or any other Person to be a third party beneficiary of this agreement.

You are the master of your own domain. You're an independent contractor as far as we're concerned. We take no responsibility for you whatsoever and nothing in this contract will in any way make you an employee of Pacific or a representative of Pacific. Nor is the Producer or anyone else in your family or friends allowed to make that claim or benefit from this agreement.

REALITY: This may seem irrelevant, but it's not. Your status is very important if you want to try to sue the label for breach of contract. As an *employee,* the standard for an injunction is far different and more slanted in your favor, because the law has requirements as to what an employer can do with an employee. A female recording artist would be hard-pressed to sue the A&R person or producer for sexual harassment, for example, because she's classified not as an employee but as a "contractor," and technically she should be able to walk away from the job. She can't. In 360 Deals, this is somewhat moot. Since the 360 Deal by definition is a "partnership," there should be no vagueness about the artist's status. And yet depending on the interpretation of law, the artist might still be. I am convinced that someday an innovative attorney will find the angle to sue a label on these grounds. At that time the legal interpretation of whether an artist is truly an employee will go under the microscope.

NEGOTIATE

Artists are treated as employees whether the contract says they are or not. The only question is how much of the benefits pie can you get the label to cough up in contract negotiations? My advice here is limited. I've heard of situations in which valued artists were given stock in the company. I know of only two instances in which an artist was given a pension fund and health benefits, dental, and counseling (much needed in those cases). But the common way that labels reward valued artists is to give them their own label. Then they can go get other artists to sign this same contract and make money off of them. In this way *One-Deep, Two-Deep,* and *Three-Deep*[4] labels are created.

Regarding any of the things in this paragraph, you can ask, but don't hold your breath. But definitely ask.

[4] One-Deep and Two-Deep labels: My own home-spun term for what many people call "independent labels." For a complete definition, see the *Confessions* chapter "Understanding Distribution."

Breach of Contract

Had enough? Want out? Here's a suggestion: What if you just don't perform? Or what if you make annoying, demanding phone calls to the president of the label until they cut you loose? It ain't gonna work. Here's why. This little ditty comes from the subheading often called DEFAULT REMEDIES:

Except with respect to the breach of a **negative covenant** or other provision hereof which is not curable, no failure by you to perform your obligations hereunder shall be deemed a	Unless **you do something really bad that we don't like** and which we can't figure out a way to remedy [*such as burning down the recording studio*], even if you fail to perform, make your record, or show up when and where we

breach hereof unless you have not cured such failure within thirty (30) days (except sixty (60) days with respect to your failure to deliver Master Recordings hereunder within the time specified herein above) after the date of Pacific's written notice to you of such failure.

say to, none of this will entitle you to say that you're leaving us or that this contract is over. The only way out is if you totally diss us and don't give us props within thirty days (60 days if you are late "delivering" your Album, after we send you a little reminder, saying, "You're late, fool!").

REALITY: So you can't quit without doing something that will likely hurt you more than it hurts them. Many people over the years have tried all kinds of things to get out of paying back Advances and getting a fresh new deal. I love to talk about some of the great scams in lectures and on my website. Here, I'll just give you the granddaddy of them all in the sidebar "Billion-Dollar Bait." Any similarity to the late Michael Jackson is entirely intentional.

BILLION-DOLLAR BAIT

Some of you may recall a certain pop star in the mid-'80s, whom we'll call Sydney. Sydney made a deal worth almost one *billion* dollars with his major label. This was to cover TV and movie development, as well as records. The one billion was to be paid out over eight years in $125,000,000 in annual Advances, with benchmarks for each, just like a normal record deal, only much bigger. A deal this size, however, required some serious collateral. To justify it, Sydney put his entire empire on the block, which included large catalogs of other artists' hit records, including one particular classic rock artist's publishing from the 1960s, plus his own hits and his ample real estate portfolio.

As soon as the ink on The Thick was dry, Sydney became reclusive, took sick, and retreated into a cloistered life. Five years later, the label had paid out about $625,000,000, but Sydney hadn't produced anything except a 10-minute music video.

His accountants and lawyers saw the writing on the wall. His label was going to call in the collateral. If that happened, Sydney would be wiped out and his entire empire would come crashing down. His only hope was to get the label to drop him, thus making the debt "forgiven".

Step one was a campaign started by his team, possibly without his knowledge, that involved Sydney in nasty pedophile allegations. Oddly enough, the media didn't bite, and neither did the label. The PR machine escalated it, forcing an arraignment on the charge of "rape." The District Attorney himself was going to oversee this case. But, despite a thorough investigation, there was no direct evidence to be found, only rumors and secret "closed file" depositions. The charges were dropped, and sealed "settlements" were issued to the "victim." (Years later the "victim" recanted.)

But the label stood by Syd. They would not let go, and even insisted that Sid "deliver" an album immediately or lose everything. So Sydney "delivered" a bad album with racist and anti-Semitic lyrics. And the label distributed it, claiming that they had no idea that there was anything offensive on it. Syd's record "slipped through the cracks."[5]

Sales were poor, but still the label did not buckle. And why should they? They had Sydney's entire empire in their sights.

What to do? Poor Sydney was trapped. He needed to figure out a way to shelter his assets with someone he trusted, so that no one could get to them. So Syd found a woman to bear him a son.

Ain't love grand?

Sydney was still on the label when he died in 2009 of a medication-induced heart attack. At the time he was preparing his first comeback tour since he signed the big deal. The label has paid him close to $700 million, and will be engaged in a bitter estate dispute with Syd's family for years. Despite the huge sales of Syd's music shortly after his death, the label money remains unrecouped.

[5] A record "slipping through the cracks" is, of course, impossible.

Buying Back Your Masters Once You've Had Enough

Quitting is impossible, as we see in the sidebar, since lack of performance on your part does not get you out of the deal, nor does creating negative controversy.

But every contract has a series of clauses that allow the artist to buy their way out of the deal. Maybe when you were recording your first album the A&R person was fired (or left the company). The new one who took his place could give a rat's ass about you. He didn't sign you, so if you do well it doesn't reflect on his good judgment, and if you fail, everyone will wonder why he didn't pull the plug. He may also have an artist he wants to sign that sounds a lot like you. You're now competing with others on your label who may be better connected. Or, perhaps your label merged with another one and has been told by the new upper management team to trim back the recording funds. If they had good ethics they would just release you, but labels are not known for releasing people if they can keep them without spending any extra money. Their M.O. is to hold on to you like real estate and take a "wait and see" posture. Maybe the wind will blow in a different direction in a month or two, and you'll want to come back. Maybe you'll commit suicide, causing the Master Records you did for them to suddenly be worth trillions. In this way, the label keeps you on hold while the wheels of politics and time spin. But you want to settle up and get the great recordings (finished or partially finished) that are collecting dust in the label's vault out. The following comes under the subheading REMEDIES (I wonder what they're really a remedy for?):

If Pacific **refuses without cause** to allow you to fulfill your Recording Commitment for any Contract Period and if, not later than sixty (60) days after that refusal takes place, you notify Pacific of your desire to fulfill such Recording Commitment, then Pacific shall permit you to fulfill said Recording Commitment by notice to you to such effect within sixty (60) days after Pacific's receipt of your notice. Should Pacific fail to give such notice, you shall have the option to terminate the term of this Agreement by notice given to Pacific within thirty (30) days after the expiration of the latter sixty-day period; on receipt by Pacific of such notice, the term of this Agreement shall terminate and all parties will be deemed to have fulfilled all of their obligations hereunder except those obligations which survive the end of the term (e.g., warranties, re-recording restrictions and obligations to

If **for no particular reason** we prevent you from finishing any record [*such as withholding recording money, or bottlenecking contracts in the legal department, etc.*], then it's your job to let us know [*because we're kinda busy and could have forgotten about you*]. You have 60 days to tell us that you still want to make records with us. Then we'll let you know within 60 days after that if we still want you.

If we don't send you some notice that we still want you, then consider yourself officially out of this recording deal. But first you must send us a letter, reminding us that we fired your sorry ass, within 30 days after the 60-day period. When we get this notice [*which is now about five months after we started not returning your calls, in case you lost count*] the parts of this contract that deal with your recording services will end [*while the other parts will continue forever, such as the warranties, re-recording restrictions, and obligations to pay "royalties"*].

pay royalties), at which time Pacific shall pay to you, in full settlement of its obligations to you (other than those royalty obligations) an Advance in the amount equal to:

(a) The aggregate of the minimum Recording Funds agreed to herein for each Commitment Album, then remaining unrecorded, for the Contract Period during which such termination occurs,
less:

(b) The average amount of the Recording Costs for the last two (2) Commitment Albums recorded hereunder (or, if only one Commitment Album has been recorded, the amount of the Recording Costs for that Album), multiplied by the number of such unrecorded Albums referred to in subparagraph (a).

If Master Recordings sufficient to constitute at least the first Commitment Album to be recorded under this Agreement have not been completed, then the amount of the Advance payable to you under the preceding sentence will be the

But, as a parting gift for playing the "Major Label Recording Game," we'll give you an advance equal to…

(a) The total Floor (or Minimum) amount for the budget of the Album you were going to record (or were in the process of recording when we fired you) [*usually $250,000 for the first Album. See the tables below.*]
But from that amount we're gonna subtract some stuff first. You didn't think this was gonna be simple, did you? We're gonna subtract:

(b) The average cost of the final budget for the last two Albums you recorded for us (or, if only one Album has been recorded, the amount of the Recording Costs for that Album). We'll then multiply that number by the number of Albums you were about to record when we fired you.

If, however, you haven't finished your first album, then we'll give you an advance equal to the minimum union scale fee [*about $100 per hour*] that you would have been paid for your studio work on this Album only.

amount equal to the Artist's minimum union scale compensation for the unfulfilled portion of the Recording Commitment for that Contract Period. If you fail to give Pacific either notice within the period specified therefore, Pacific shall be under no obligation to you for failing to permit you to fulfill such Recording Commitment.

If you fail to give us the first 60-day notice and the second 30-day notice, then we aren't going to give you squat.

REALITY: There's two issues here. One, as we learned, is that the label can create circumstances that make it impossible for you to complete your record. They've just carved themselves a nice loophole for not paying you. They even make it your responsibility to let them know they're not paying you, and if you don't, you lose the right to complain about it.

The second issue is this parting "gift" of cash that they are willing to give you, because they're such nice guys. If it's the scenario described in the second half of "b" above, then it's going to be very little, maybe $5,000 at most. But, what about the other, more complicated scenario, in which you've made Albums for them? Let's do the math. If they fire you, they are promising an amount of money (often called an "exit fee" or a "parachute"). The basic equation (based on the above) will be something like this:

$$\boxed{\text{Cost of the album you are presently recording}} - \boxed{\frac{\text{The cost of your last album} + \text{the cost of the album before that}}{\text{the number of albums recorded in both "periods"}}} \times \boxed{\text{The number of unrecorded albums scheduled for the "period" when they fired you}} = \boxed{\text{The amount they will pay you to get lost}}$$

Let's say you get fired on your third album and that the label followed their own guidelines for recording funds. (So you don't have to keep flipping back and forth and for simplicity, we're going to presume that the Advance and the recording fund are the same. Below is the table of recording funds from the "Advances" chapter.) Here's how it looks:

RECORDING FUNDS

Current LP	Floor Amount	Ceiling Amount
First LP	$250,000	$500,000
Second LP	$250,000	$500,000
Third LP	$300,000	$600,000
Fourth L	$325,000	$650,000
Fifth LP	$350,000	$700,000
Sixth LP	$375,000	$750,000
Seventh LP	$400,000	$800,000

Egghead Box

$$\$300,000 - \frac{\$500,000}{2} \times 1 = \mathbf{\$50,000}$$

Congrats—they owe you $50,000 just for playing the game. When they have to pay it to you is rarely specified in The Thick, and all of it is based on an assumption that you only owed them one album for the Contract Period. This is not a good assumption, since a Contract Period is not really a "period" as we know the word; it's a nebulous amount of time that is connected to certain events. In this case, the events are the recording of Albums. There is a real concern here for you. Though, in most cases, if you get "fired" at any time during the "Term," you can expect a bit of exit cash, or just walking papers, there are many times when this formula can really screw you. Check out the following sidebars for some true exit stories about how much cash the *artist owed the label* after the deal was done.

POST MEN APOSTLES GET THE AX

Remember the group called the Post Men Apostles from the "Royalties" chapter? They had a flop with their first release. In fact, were it not for Jerry, the A&R person who signed the Apostles, the label would never have looked twice at them. Now that Jerry has been asked to step down and go to rehab for several months, the new A&R person filling his desk doesn't see the need to keep this band on the roster.

They got the news right in the middle of recording basic tracks for their second Album.

This was a tough break, but the Post Men knew that they would land softly. Their contract had an exit clause, and they were expecting around $50,000 to "go away." But, alas, they got nothing. Here's why:

The Initial Period consisted of two Albums. The first one flopped and the second one was never finished. Let's do the math for the Apostles to show you what happens if you get fired while recording Album number two when it's part of the Initial Period:

$$\$250,000 - \frac{\$500,000}{2} \times 1 = \textbf{\$0.00}$$

They got zip, nada—no cash, no carry, not even a home version of the game. And here's the really nasty part—Pacific owns all the Master Recordings, not the Post Men.

DANGER, WILL ROBINSON!!!

Country artist Will Robinson was in his fourth Contract Period. Will doesn't earn much on record sales to begin with because he's a good ol' boy based in the Northeast, where country still isn't considered by many people to be "real music." Consequently, Will receives little airplay and spends most of his time touring. He's fond of saying that the truck stops of America are his main stage.

But as time wears on, his tours are getting longer and longer. Now signed to Harmony Grits Records (a well-funded Two-Deep label distributed by a Big Four), Will's fourth Option Period started to run longer than a year, due to Will's heavy touring schedule. Now, as per the contract, Will owes Harmony Grits two Albums for that one "Period."[6]

[6] See "Advances," page 17.

To make up for lost time, he decides to record Albums five and six one after the next in the same "Period." Although nothing goes over budget, Will's wife, who had run off with his dog and truck some years ago, returns to begin their marriage over again. This robs Will of all the "hard life experience" on which he's always based his songs. The label worries that he's lost his edge. They "fire" Will in the middle of Album five because they don't like the sound of the masters, and the duet with his wife sounds just plain awful. How much do they owe him?

$$\$350,000 - \frac{(\underline{\$325,000 + \$300,000})}{2} = \$37,500 \times 2 = \textbf{\$75,000}$$

Harmony Grits owes Will $75,000 for his bad timing, and for having a wife that can't make up her mind. That's a lot of cornmeal!

MASTER PEE SPRINGS A LEAK

When Rapper Master Pee's third Album did stupid, dope, phat sales of over 5,000,000 units, the Master decided to put all his friends on his payroll. He had three personal assistants, the brother of the mother of his second love-child became his head of security, and every homie from his 'hood became part of his entourage. This was expensive, but Master Pee had earned it, so the label didn't mind.

But when his fourth Album didn't do so well, their attitude changed. And on the fifth Album, for which the Master flew in the London Philharmonic Orchestra for a session because he didn't want to use any more samples, his label, Wonder Records, sent their bean counters into the cave to figure out how much it would cost to get rid of him. They were pleasantly surprised.

Pee's overage for the fourth and fifth Albums was $50,000 and $75,000, respectively. So Wonder Records, seeing that this was getting out of control, "fired" Pee while he was recording his fifth album, *Pee in the Snow*.

By contract, even though Wonder approved the budget overage at the time, they were entitled to demand that Pee shell out $225,000 before leaving the label.

$$\begin{array}{ccc} \text{(4th album)} & \text{(2nd Album)} & \text{(3rd Album)} \\ \$325,000 - & (\underline{\$250,000 + \$300,000}) & = \textbf{-\$225,000} \end{array}$$

It seems like the more you work for the label, the higher your chances of owing them money. Shouldn't loyalty and commitment be rewarded?

NEGOTIATE

Obviously this clause is in desperate need of reform, especially when you take into consideration the Double-Dip being created. So start by adding a clause that specifically states that any money you still owe the label will be disposed of as "forgiven debt." Although this will be tough to get in writing, the good news is that labels rarely enforce this clause, unless the artist has a large reserve from previous masters that sold well.

Your next rung on this ladder is to try to get a limit on the money that you can owe them, so that it never exceeds, say, 10 grand. This is also tough to get. If it fails, then make sure that this money hasn't already been taken out of "royalties" or "reserves," so that you don't end up paying for it twice.

The formula they're using is quite dumb, as proven by the examples above. Try to get them to change it, so that any money you still owe on previous records is excluded. If they "fire" you on Album five, you should have to pay them back for Album five only, and nothing else. But if all this is too much to remember, here's a new mantra for you:

Never, ever, ever agree to more than one Album in a single "Period."

Leaving Members

Okay, so you can't leave the label, and the label won't let you go. (Sounds like an Italian marriage.) Is there a loophole that maybe they forgot about? What if you quit the group? What if you have "creative differences"? I mean, they can't make you do business with people you hate, can they? Let's see. These three clauses (a, b, and c) come from the subheading often called GROUP RIGHTS.[7] Like most subheadings, this one is confusing; it actually refers more to the label's rights than the group's.

[7] Look for these under "Miscellaneous."

(a) (i) If, during the Term, any Member ("Leaving Member") separates from, and/or ceases to perform with, the remaining Members ("Remaining Members"), then you shall promptly give written notice of such occurrence, and, whether or not

(a) (i) If, during the total amount of time of this contract any member gets snappy, or starts thinking he's more important than the rest of the group and bails on a session, and then refuses to jam with the rest of the group, we'll call him a "Leaving Member." If that Leaving Member bails, you have to immediately tell us

you give Pacific such notice, Pacific, in its sole discretion, by written notice to you, may elect:

(A) to terminate the Term effective upon the service of said notice; or

(B) to require the Remaining Members to either (at their election) (I) furnish promptly a substitute for the Leaving Member, or (II) perform as a reconstituted act, without replacement of the Leaving Member.

(ii) If Pacific makes the election specified in the subparagraph (B) above, then, at any time thereafter and prior to delivery of the Product LP next scheduled to be delivered hereunder above subsequent to Pacific being informed about the Leaving Member, **Pacific may elect, by giving you written notice, to terminate the Term effective on the date of such notice.**

(b) Pacific shall have an **irrevocable option** to acquire exclusively the individual services of each Leaving Member as a recording artist, and such

in writing. But in case you are so pissed that you forget to write a simple letter (I mean, really, is that asking too much?), we can still, in our sole discretion, do the following:

(A) end the contract for the whole group, as soon as you tell us; or

(B) require the remaining group members to either (I) find a replacement quickly [*even though the label will have to approve this "promptly"—how likely is that?*] or (II) keep on performing as a group but don't replace the one who split.

(ii) If we decide for you to go for option B above—the one in which you stay together and just deal with it—then we can:

Decide to bag the whole group, right on the spot.
[*And even after that, we're not quite done with you ...*]

(b) We still have the **permanent right** to bind the guy who left the band to yet another indefinite Term of fun, this time as a solo recording artist at the same "royalty" rates already in here. We just

option shall be exercisable by Pacific by sending written notice to such Leaving Member within thirty (30) days after notice to Pacific under subparagraph(i) above or (c) below (as the case may be). If Pacific should exercise said option with respect to any Leaving Member, then, Pacific shall have the right to elect to do any or all of the following (and during the period of Pacific's rights of election as hereinafter set forth, the right to such Leaving Member's recording services shall be exclusive to Pacific in accordance with the terms of this agreement):

have to send him a letter within 30 days after we learned of his little tantrum with the other members in the group.

If we decide we want him, then we get the right to do any or *all* of the following:

REALITY: This is just plain nuts. I understand the label's desire to hold on to a piece of something they created, but this is seriously overreaching. Groups break up all the time. Here the label gets an added benefit for this tragedy—four new deals. The "b" part needs to be tossed completely. It makes no sense that a "Leaving Member" should be paid the same rates as the other members. Chances are the reason a member is leaving is because he writes most of the material, or is the lead singer, or some such commodity that is not as easily replaceable. He should therefore be allowed to renegotiate his deal for market rates.

UNIVERSAL TRADES GARBAGE AND LOVE

Philosopher John Stuart Mill said, "Trade is a social act." But this motto took on a possessive twist in the wake of two lawsuits against mega-label Universal Music Group (UMG); one was by alternative trip-grunge band Garbage, and the other by hard rocker Courtney Love.

Love claimed that she was signed to a One-Deep imprint and got traded like a ball player right in the middle of her contract to another label in the Universal family that didn't have the first clue as

[8] Alpert and Moss, the "A" and "M" in A&M Records.

[9] A "key man" clause, or "yenta clause," as I sometimes call it, is when the relationship between the two parties making a deal will exist only so long as the person who brought the parties together remains involved. It's routine between actors and large agencies, but in the music biz it's not as common.

to how to market her. She sued for a severance on the grounds that the deal exceeded California's seven-year limit on a service contract. Most recording contracts last well over seven years, so much would be at stake if Love kicked ass.

That same year, the wildly successful group Garbage filed suit against UMG claiming that they used "strong-arm tactics" about honoring their contract.

In 1994 producers Butch Vig, Doug Erikson, and Steve Markson formed Garbage with singer Shirley Manson. Manson was performing as Angelfish on Radioactive Records, another UMG imprint. She had sold barely 10,000 units on that deal, so when Vig and Co. asked her to sing for them, it was a match. They formed Garbage and signed to Almo Sounds, founded by veteran record men Herb Alpert and Jerry Moss.[8] Moss was "keyed" into the deal[9]: as long as Moss remained with Almo, so would Garbage.

By December 2000, this was no longer the case. UMG absorbed all of Almo's assets and dismantled the label. UMG claimed that Moss was retained as a "consultant." But a consultant to what? Almo was defunct. Garbage, thinking they had a ticket out of the deal, wanted to walk with him.

However, sneaky lawyers at UMG pulled a rabbit out of the hat to get Garbage to stink up the place a bit longer. They claimed that Radioactive never released Manson from her Angelfish deal (even though they remained silent while she sold millions of records in Garbage). Under the terms of that 1992 deal, Manson could be made to perform for any UMG label for up to seven more Albums, even though the old deal was with a different band, on a different label, with different material, and over seven years ago.

UMG was hoping that, faced with the threat of losing Manson, Vig and the boys would succumb and stick around as Garbage. Instead they all banded together, and in January 2001, sued the industry giant.

Feel the Love. Smell the Garbage. And remember—trade is a social act.

NEGOTIATE

It will be hard, but it's worth the fight to get rid of this. Especially if the deal is one that originated as a producer's production deal, and the artists are being paid via the producer's company. A reasonable compromise would be an option in which the label can only do this after the fourth album during a window that remains open for 60 days. If you can't get rid of this, here's what you're in for:

(i) to require such Leaving Member to perform for the making of "demonstration recordings" pursuant to budgets approved by Pacific in writing and Pacific shall have all rights in such "demonstration recordings" as if such "demonstration recordings" were Master Recordings recorded hereunder; provided, Pacific shall not market or promote such "demonstration recordings" as ["name of Artist"];

(i) to require you to make demos *exclusively* for us and within our approved budget. These can be produced as elaborately as records with "master quality" [*whatever that means*] as long as we promise we won't release them under the old group name;

(ii) to require such Leaving Member to perform for the making of Master Recordings constituting two (2) to four (4) Sides (the amount of such Sides to be determined by Pacific) pursuant to budgets approved by Pacific in writing and Pacific shall have all rights in such Sides as if such Sides were Master Recordings recorded hereunder; and/or

(ii) oh yeah—and we can make you record anywhere from two to four tunes with the full intent of releasing them;

and/or

(iii) to deem such Leaving Member a party to an exclusive term recording agreement on the terms and provisions of this agreement, except as follows:

(iii) to assume that you are now going to do a "Term" as a solo artist with the same trapdoors, Double-Dips, and loopholes that you're already comfortable with under the old deal, but now, we're gonna make a few modifications, such as:

(A) a term (with options for extension by Pacific) consisting of the remaining balance of the Term (as it may be extended by Pacific's exercise of the options granted

(A) the amount of time will only be for the remaining balance of the "Term" [*even though that can go on for God knows how long*] (and all of the rights we have to extend it as

[10] Refer to "Master Quality," page 109, for what the "Minimum Recording Requirement" clause is.

[11] Refer to "Master Quality," page 109, for what the "Minimum Recording Requirement" clause is.

Pacific in "the Minimum Recording Requirement"[10] hereof but in no event shall the term consist of less than an initial period plus two (2) such options);

(B) a minimum recording obligation of one (1) LP for the initial period and per option; and

stated in "the Minimum Recording Requirement"[11]). But we have a heart, so the amount of time will only be a minimum of three "periods" [*in English, about a three- to five-year minimum*];

(B) at least one Album recorded and "delivered" within (approximately) the first 10 months and another Album for each other "period"; and …

LOOPHOLE ALERT!!!

EXPLANATION: This requires you to record two albums within one Contract Period. As you can see from the sidebars in the previous section, this is a dangerous position to be in, especially considering the circumstances that put you there; i.e., the group is breaking up and destroying label confidence. Most of these deals end badly, and if you don't fix this loophole you will be in position for a bad "get lost" calculation if the label drops you, which they probably will.

NEGOTIATE

Change this so that the maximum recording obligation is not more than making the demos, or until such time that the label decides they are keeping you for a "new deal."

(C) a royalty rate corresponding to the rates herein granted above[12] for the penultimate LP previously delivered by Artist hereunder ("Penultimate LP"), with so-called "ancillary rates" being reduced therefrom in the same proportion as the ancillary rates in subparagraph "Royalties,"[13] and with all royalties otherwise being calculated and determined in the same manner as set forth herein; and

(C) a "royalty" that is equal to the ones in here.[15] [*No need to reinvent the wheel. If we want you as a solo artist, you've clearly distinguished yourself and deserve more respect.*] Your "royalties" will **start at the level we were at on the old deal when you "delivered" your second-to-last album.** We'll also keep the same rates for foreign sales and third-party licensing (such as to our "fake" indie labels and "record clubs") called "ancillary rates" in this contract, the same as already stated.[16] Why try to improve upon perfection? Every "royalty" on your new deal will be calculated just like the old deal, with all the same loopholes, trapdoors, and Double-Dips, even though you are now probably a star;

(D) (I) an Advance (inclusive of Recording Costs) equal to the "Floor Amount" as set forth in subparagraph "Advances"[14] above for the Penultimate LP for the First LP to be recorded by such Leaving Member and

(II) an Advance (inclusive of Recording Costs) for subsequent LPs to be recorded by such Leaving Member calculated in the same manner as advances for Product LPs subsequent to the Penultimate LP are calculated hereunder.

(D) (I) an Advance equal to the minimum amount that you were supposed to get on your old deal for the second-to-last Album you "delivered" (as set forth in subparagraph "Advances"[17]), and

(II) An Advance for all future Albums on the "new deal" with the leaving member of the band that is equal to the previous deal. Except that we don't start at Album one; rather, we go back two Albums from where the "old deal" ended.

[12] Refer to "Royalties" for "royalty" rates, page 64.

[13] Refer to "Royalty Configurations," page 48.

[14] Floor and Ceiling amounts for recording funds are listed on page 23.

[15] Refer to "Royalties" for "royalty" rates, page 64.

[16] Refer to "Royalty Configurations," page 48.

[17] Floor and Ceiling amounts for recording funds are listed on page 23.

EXPLANATION: The label will argue that this is "reasonable" because, even though you've made hits with your old group, there's no guarantee that you'll continue to do so as a solo artist. Oh yeah? So that's why they want to keep you—because you're such a big risk? This logic doesn't add up. Mathematically and theoretically, the risk is always the same, whether you are in this group, another group, or you're a solo artist. One could just as easily argue the opposite. For example, now that you are out of the group, you can realize your full potential. Besides, if the group was the product of a "production deal,"[18] then the same producer will likely still be producing all four new acts, making the chances of success the same as they were under the "old deal."

[18] Production deal: See *Confessions* chapter "The Baby Deal."

Nice try, though.

In the event that Pacific makes the election referred to in subparagraph (b)(i) or (ii) above, Pacific shall have the right to elect, within thirty (30) days after delivery to Pacific of the applicable "demonstration recordings" or Sides (as the case may be), to make any other elections referred to in this subparagraph (b) which Pacific has not theretofore made. Twenty-Five percent (25%) of all advances and charges against royalties hereunder may be recouped by Pacific from royalties accruing under any agreement with a Leaving Member and all advances and charges against royalties under any agreement with a Leaving Member (including, without limitation, any sums paid

If we insist that you make more demos or singles under the "new deal" we can, within 30 days after your "delivery" of the new stuff to us [*and after we've had a chance to see if you're still worthy of a deal on our label*], demand that you do a few more things that we didn't already ask for, such as:

Pay us back 25% of the debt from the previous deal. If you're a bit light at the moment, we'll charge it to your account…

(This includes the cost of:

or incurred by Pacific in making the "demonstration recordings" referred to in subparagraph (b)(i) above or the Sides referred to in subparagraph (b)(ii) above) may be recouped by Pacific from royalties accruing hereunder.

the demos we just made you do

or the singles we just made you do.)

… from "royalties" that you rack up from this deal.

DOUBLE-DIP DETECTOR

EXPLANATION: This one is really nasty. To put it simply, you're already paying back the label through the revenue stream created by the old record deal.[19] They're paying themselves twice. Plus, there's another problem here: Under the new deal, you will be responsible for 1/4 of the debt from the "old deal." But what if there are five members in the group? Each pays back 1/4 of the debt? That means that the record company is recouping 125% of the debt. Nice.

[19] To completely appreciate the evil here, you must first understand the nature of "cross-collateralization" (see page 114).

NEGOTIATE

Get rid of this. If you can't convince the label by appealing to their basic humanity, then settle for a closing of the old account with no collateralizing of the new "royalties" into the recording fund of the "old deal." Keep the "new" Advances pure, and never allow the songs written for the "new deal" to be used to recoup debt from the "old deal." Look for this trap in the contract. It's often hiding in the subheading called MECHANICAL ROYALTIES.

When the Act Breaks Up

All the above has to do with what happens if one member leaves the band. But what happens if the band completely breaks up? What if everyone is going in separate directions, like Bell Biv Devoe, New Edition, The Beatles, or N.W.A.? They got a clause for that as well.

(c) If, during the Term, Artist shall disband completely, then:

(i) you shall promptly give Pacific written notice of such occurrence;

(ii) **each member shall be deemed a Leaving Member;** and

(iii) the provisions of subparagraph (b) above shall apply to each such Leaving Member.

Notwithstanding the occurrence whereby any Person becomes a Leaving Member as described in subparagraph (i) or (c) above, both you and such Leaving Member shall continue to be bound by the provisions hereof, including without limitation subparagraphs (b) above.

(c) If, during the "Term" [*the infinite length of time that this contract can engage you for*], you guys break up completely, then:

(i) you shall immediately let us know in writing and;

each one of you will be considered a "Leaving Member." (This way we can get three or four new Artists.)

(iii) all the restrictions just mentioned above apply to every member of the band individually.

Even if no one actually leaves the group and it doesn't disband, we can still create "new deals" for each of you individually—we can make you do demos and consider you to be solo artists, and there's little you can do about this without spending a lot of money on attorney's fees.

Summarize

Let's summarize all the above before we pick it apart.

I. At any time during the infinite "Term" you get pissy with your group and want out, a series of things are set in motion. The label can:

   a. Fire you on the spot.

   b. Make the rest of the group do your parts on the record or perform with a new name. (A name that the label will probably own.)

c. Fire the whole group on the spot, while still insisting that you record one more album for them (sometimes called by lawyers an "exit album" or more frequently by artists as a "piss-off album").

II. The label can fire you with less than a month's notice and immediately:

a. Insist that you perform on demos of new material.

b. Record two to four singles, which the label agrees not to release under the old group name.

c. Automatically throw you into another exclusive contract for another "Term." They will, however, make a few "improvements" on the old deal. Such as:

A. The amount of the "Term" will be the remaining time of the old "Term" plus three Option Periods, which, if you recall from the previous chapter, could last from five to seven years.

B. Commit you to record at least one Album per "period," including the "period" that you quit (which is a **loophole trap,** as it requires you to record two albums in one "Period").

C. Keep all the "royalties" the same as the old deal.

D. Move back to the minimum amount paid for the album you did for the label last year.

E. Make this the level at which your "sliding scale" starts for all future advances.

If all this isn't enough, they can also "collateralize" 25% of the debt from the old deal into the new deal, including the cost of the material they just said was obligatory. (A huge Double-Dip.) So they have, once again, forced you into debt. Is there a lawyer out there who can explain to me how that's legal?

III. Finally, whether you leave the group or it breaks up, the label can do all of the above to any individual in the group.

I don't know about you, but I could use a Tums.

REALITY: These clauses are no joke. The label means every word of them. This is how they build a stable of talent. It's the reason why some producers try to create singing groups rather than single artists. Several solo acts can emerge from one group, and the producer and the label will be tied to each one individually and collectively. Remember this if you are being asked to sign into a group. It's not *like* a marriage, it *is* a marriage. And as anyone who's been down this road can tell you, divorce is expensive. The moral of this story:

Make sure that the people in your group are people you can work with
for a long time, because you will be tied to them,
in one way or another, forever.

Non-Compete:
Not Working for Anyone Else

Now that the label has locked up your copyrights, image, identity, professional name, cyber rights, past history, and any future ideas that you have, they want to make sure that no one else can get at them. *Non-compete* clauses ensure that you will not sneak through the gaps in this agreement to perform for others. Way in the back of the contract, under a subheading that goes by the name NEGATIVE COVENANTS, you will find this little nasty:

(a) (i) During the Term, Artist shall not render any performance or service for any Person other than Pacific in connection with the manufacture and/or exploitation of Master Recordings or Records.

(a) (i) During the total amount of time you are under this contract, you're not allowed to perform, or do anything for anyone other than Pacific, in regard to the recording and selling of your music.[20]

(ii) **Notwithstanding anything to the contrary** contained in subparagraph (a)(i) above, Artist shall be permitted to perform as a non-featured "sideperson" at recording sessions for other record labels than Pacific, provided that:

(ii) **With one exception**: you can perform on other people's records, even those on different labels, but not as a soloist or a lead singer. As long as:

[20] See page 280 in "Terms and Exclusivity" to see how long that really is.

(A) neither the Records embodying such performances nor the exploitation of said Records shall feature Artist's likeness;

A) your picture is not on the record or its packaging;

(B) The Member of Artist rendering such performances shall receive credit only as a sideperson, solely on the liner or in the liner notes of such Record(s). Such credit shall contain only the name of the individual Member rendering said performances or services and in no event shall such credit refer to Artist's group name, i.e., "Pacific" without Pacific's prior written consent;

(B) your credit in the record's liner notes says you are a "sideperson," and only lists your name, not the name of your band, unless we give written approval;

(C) such credit shall not be larger than the credit accorded to other non-featured sidepersons;

(C) your credit isn't any bigger than any other sideperson listed in the liner notes;

(D) a courtesy credit shall be included in such instances to the effect that the respective Member of Artist is appearing courtesy of Pacific; and

(D) the liner notes say that you are an artist on our label, and mention that we are great sports for allowing you to appear on the product of one of our competitors; and

(E) such performances do not interfere with the timely completion of Artist's services hereunder.

(E) this little "favor" you're doing [*obviously for a friend*] doesn't set you back from your real career, which is completing the record you're making for *us*.

(b) You shall not use, or authorize or permit any Person other than Pacific to use, Artist's names (including any professional names), facsimile signature, voices, likenesses or biographies in connection with the manufacture and/or exploitation of Master Recordings or Records.

(b) You will not let anyone (other than us) use your name, signature, voice, likeness, or bio to sell their records.

REALITY: This seems fairly reasonable, but what if this is not your first record deal? What if you have master recordings on some small indie? Or what if you're currently selling a self-made and self-distributed CD on your own and don't want to give Pacific rights to it because it's your bread and butter? Tough luck.

NEGOTIATE

In order to not be in breach, carve an exception to previously recorded records in the above clauses. Most majors will let you keep your home-spun tracks as long as you agree to put them behind you to work on creating and promoting the new record.

So they let you keep your past. What about your future? Is there life after this deal? Let's see.

(c) (i) For five (5) years following the completion of recording of any material recorded and released hereunder or two (2) years following the expiration of the Term, whichever shall expire later (the "Restriction Period"), **Artist shall not**, for the purpose of making and/or exploiting Master Recordings, Records, radio or television commercials or soundtracks, **perform such material for any Person other than Pacific.**

(c) (i) **You can't record or play your songs for anyone other than us** (unless it's at a party, or some non-commercial event) for five years after we release your last record. If we don't release the last record you "delivered," then you can't record or play your songs for anyone other than us for two years and 10 months after that. This period of time we call a "Restriction Period."

(ii) For a period of two (2) years after the date of delivery of any Master Recording hereunder, neither you nor Producer shall produce or co-produce (or cause the production or co-production of) a Master Recording embodying, in whole or in part, the material embodied in any such Master Recording recorded and released for any Person, firm or corporation other than Pacific.

(d) If, during the Term, Artist renders any performance for a Person other than Pacific which is recorded for use other than in connection with Records hereunder, or if prior to the end of the Restriction Period, Artist renders such a performance of material recorded hereunder, then, in either such case, such performance will be rendered only pursuant to a written agreement specifying that such performance will not be utilized, directly or indirectly, in connection with Records in contravention with the time periods set forth in subparagraphs (c)(i) and (ii) above. Artist shall promptly submit to Pacific, upon Pacific's request, a copy of any such agreement.

(ii) For two years after you "deliver" anything, neither you nor the Producer will record other versions of those phat jams for anyone else. [*That includes using samples from one record on another.*] And you can't give cred or props to anyone else to do it either.

(d) The only way you can lay down some new tunes during the time you are contractually bound to us, or re-record any of the material that you created during this time for anyone other than us, is if we give you permission. You must agree that the new recordings are not created in an attempt to escape the far-reaching clutches of this contract.

You will tell us about all such requests to record new material if we ask you about them.

(e) Neither you nor Producer nor any Person deriving any rights from you and/or Artist and/or Producer shall at any time do, or authorize any Person to do, anything inconsistent with, or which might diminish or impair, any of Pacific's rights hereunder.

Nobody's allowed to try to come between us and break your commitment. This includes you, your producer, and anyone else in the world you get to work on your behalf.

REALITY: No, there isn't any life after this deal. Ninety-nine percent of the time this deal will essentially be your entire career. They've got you for seven albums and then two years after. I'd say that just about buttons up your musical artist career.

Submitting to Drug Testing

Who would have thought that to sign a record deal you are required to "stay clean."

While insisting in several places in the contract that you are not an employee (see page 288), the label sure does seem to treat you like one in this paragraph, which you will often find in the MISCELLANEOUS subheading of your contract:

Pacific will have the right, throughout the term of this Agreement, to obtain or increase insurance on the life of the Artist, at Pacific's sole cost and expense, in such amounts as Pacific determines, in Pacific's name and for its sole benefit or otherwise, in its discretion. The Artist will cooperate in such physical examinations without expense to you or the Artist, supply such information, sign such documents, and otherwise cooperate fully with Pacific, as Pacific may request in

We will have the right, during the next eight to 10 years, to take out an insurance policy on you, in case you kick off, so we can collect some ducats [*about a million bucks' worth*].

So, to ensure that you're not about to OD before we get into bed with you, you will submit to a physical examination, supply personal information about all your habits, sign all kinds of papers that say you're okay, and otherwise cooperate in every imaginable way with doctors who will examine you connection with any such insurance. You warrant and represent that, to your best knowledge, the Artist is in good health and does not suffer from any medical condition which might interfere with the timely performance of the Artist's obligations under this Agreement. You will not be deemed in breach of this Agreement by reason of Pacific's inability to obtain any such insurance, unless it results from failure by you or the Artist to comply with your obligations under this paragraph.

for the insurance [*so that if you buy the farm, we can collect with no problem*]. You assure us that you're okay, and that, to the best of your knowledge, you're not suffering from any serious diseases or other conditions that might interfere with your work for us. If we can't get the insurance [*because you couldn't stay sober long enough to get a clean urine sample*], don't worry. As long as you cooperate, and go see doctors and take tests when we want you to, we won't be mad and you can basically shoot up all you want.

REALITY: This entire clause is hypocritical. If labels really cared about your health, they could try issuing a health plan for you. Even the mailroom boy gets health benefits on a label, but an artist? Rarely.

If you think they're kidding, think again. The last part of this clause, about it not being a breach of contract if the label can't get the insurance (the only reason they would be *unable* is because you are too much of a risk), was added in the '70s, when it became clear that if an inability to get insurance was deemed a breach, then almost every artist on every major label would be off the roster! Yes, this is a severe invasion of privacy, but think about it: If you were going to invest about $1.5 million in a band, wouldn't you want some assurances that they weren't terminally ill? How many of the people you hang out with would you invest $1.5 million in without an insurance policy?

One caveat that stands out here is that I have never known of a label that didn't make a bundle off of record sales when one of their major artists died. Labels want to make it appear as if they need you around, but the truth is, after you record a few hits for them, you're far more valuable to them if you're pushing up the daisies.

A Life Outside of Music?

But there's something extra you get, just for playing with us today: you can't work at any other job unless it's related to being an entertainer. Now, you might think that you would never want to flip burgers or deliver pizza again, so this clause is a cinch. But what if you left school in the middle of an engineering degree and you want to get back to it after this major-label ride is over? Not so fast, partner.

The Artist will, during the term of this Agreement, actively pursue a career as an entertainer in the live engagement field.

All you ever want to do for the next eight to 10 years is be an entertainer, live an entertainer's life, perform everywhere and anywhere to screaming fans, and work toward making both you and the label as much money as you possibly can.

REALITY: So you're an entertainer. But you can't drink, smoke, or do just about anything else we expect of entertainers. When you include the length of the contract and then the period afterward (the "Sunset Period" or "Restriction Period"), you will be in bed with this company for seven to 10 years from the day you sign. After that you may just want to try something else with your life. But this will be harder than you think, if you have been prohibited from laying any groundwork in the interim.

The reality is that this is basically a "Don't Ask, Don't Tell" clause. Every artist with half a brain plans for the afterlife of his deal. He just does it in private. He does it in private not only because it could violate some of the clauses above, but because he doesn't want the label coming along and claiming they are entitled to a piece of any new gigs.

NEGOTIATE

I've saved the bulk of "Negotiate" for the end of this section, because there's little sense in fighting over these clauses. You can't really get them removed. Labels will rarely drop a successful artist if she played on someone else's record without permission. As long as you're selling records, they don't really care *what* you do. (Witness Michael Jackson.) However, there are a few things that you should have put in the contract that will limit their ability to do some disagreeable things. I have seen all of these below successfully negotiated in major-label deals in an artist's favor, even for artists that are on their first deal.

Tasteless Films

Make sure there is a clause that prohibits the label from licensing your songs or performances to films that have NC-17 or X ratings, or to the advertising of any similar film. This is not about being a prude. I admit it, I have the Pamela and Tommy home movie on DVD with commentary and Spanish language track. But association with these films will damage the value of your master and your copyright; others may not want to license it after if it's been used to sell smut.

Special Mixes or Cuts

I'd advise trying to insert a clause that disallows any edit or mix of the song that grossly misrepresents your style and theme. This way no one can strip the vocal off your record and do a cheesy dance mix, unless you approve of it in writing.

Non-Compete

The label just spent five pages telling you that you can't work for one of their competitors, so how about turning the tables? They might have another artist with a similar sound as you. Would you want them to release both records at the same time? A clause specifying that they cannot release similar artists within less than five months of your release will stop this. Make sure this includes any "Greatest Hits" records of any artist who is on his way out while you're on your way in. If both records are released at the same time, the other artist's record will probably win the market share. So make sure your label is giving you a fair shot. Many times a label will justify dropping an artist if his initial sales are not good, but they usually neglect to look at what the artist was competing with when the record came out.

And while we're on the Greatest Hits subject, there is a sister subject—the *compilation album,* or *soundtrack album.* This is where your singles are placed alongside those of other artists on the same release. Insert a sentence that prohibits the label from putting more than two of your songs on compilations with other artists, unless they are willing to pay you a disproportionate "royalty" for doing this.

Cutouts

Cutouts are the records that the label sells for scrap (see "Royalties," page 77). As I have said in *Confessions* and in other places here in this book, cutouts take money out of the pocket of the artist. There is no way I know of to prevent a label from "selling" some records as cutouts, but a clause that prohibits them from doing it with your record for a period of time after your initial release comes out (like 15 to 24 months) is fair.

Outtakes

Remember, the label owns everything that comes out of your head, your mouth, and your ass. So what about the outtakes? What about all those bad versions of songs and demos that you would rather forget about? What you may call trash, the label may call *The Lost Basement Tapes* after you're a superstar. So insert a clause that ensures that none of these "outtakes" will see the light of day.

> Conclusions

As far as the prime years of your career are concerned, every recording contract on a Big Four (or one of their "fake" indies) is a *lifetime* contract. Most last about five years, whether a record ever hits the street or not. This is ironic when you consider that a successful record should mean a longer contract. Statistically, it doesn't mean that at all. Deals seem to last longer on labels as long as the artist continues to "show promise." Once a hit is realized, even though everyone is happy, there is a hidden attitude that the artist has "peaked." For the majority of deals signed, records are held on the shelf more often than they are released, and all you can do about it is buy out your own masters.

Therefore, here is the mother of all axioms for this book:

Make sure that you sign with a label that really likes you
and that they are signing you
for the right reasons.

That's all.

>Final Word: Toward Creating Sensible Contracts

"Whoever fights monsters should see to it that in the process he does not become a monster. And when you look long into an abyss, the abyss also looks into you."
—**Friedrich Nietzsche,** *Beyond Good and Evil*

"There is more stupidity than hydrogen in the universe, and it has a longer shelf life."
—**Frank Zappa**

For all their education, an unfortunate fact about music lawyers is that they have but one main component to their professional survival: they must inspire greed.

Without greed, there can be no negotiations, nor a sense of entitlement, for we could not be persuaded that a better deal is around the corner. Without entitlement, there can be no pride. Without pride, no self-expression. And without self-expression, there would be no art.

The irony of the above is that through the button-pushing of our lowest common denominators, positive and meaningful things are created. Many emotions can inspire art. But it is greed that tempts us to turn our art into an enterprise, and it's greed that will make us compromise.

Being aware of this double-edged sword, artists should not allow themselves to be maneuvered into deals that they don't want, or persuaded to think a better one is their right, simply so their lawyers can rack up a few more billable hours. No. We must not blame the attorney if our legal bills are too high. We must blame ourselves. We must accept responsibility for our greed and accept that it does not necessarily oppose creativity, but rather is an element of it. As such, our greed needs to be kept in check.

The problem arises when attorneys don't understand their client's primary objective for entering into a contract. They often think the purpose is to establish who gets what, when, and how many.

But here's an illuminating fact: Most major-label negotiations cost, in combined attorneys' fees, about $20,000. In this contract the artist wants nothing more than to ensure that the label will release and promote his or her record. The label wants nothing more than for the artist to continuously produce quality master records that they can easily sell. The Thick attempts to guarantee that both these objectives are met. And the odd part is that after all this time and money, neither side can force the other to do what they are contracted for; the label always reserves the right to *not* release a recording, and nothing on God's green earth can force an artist to produce *good music* for a company he or she hates.

So, at the end of the day, who is sleeping better for the existence of this document?

One guess.

The truth is that no artist, producer, or label ever cares about a piece of paper that claims something. Invariably, all contracts are renegotiated or ignored outright in the daily practice of business. What, then, is the purpose of a contract?

It has two: 1) to establish the delivery of services; and 2) to keep the parties *out of conflict*. By acting as a guideline, a *good* contract should embody terms that are "reasonable" to *both* parties. Unfortunately, too often a "well-crafted" Thick shows its teeth only after both parties are knee-deep into its terms. This causes tension and leads to lawsuits. If, however, people are comfortable with each other, they tend to labor toward workable solutions.

The simplicity of this logic is, unfortunately, undervalued by most attorneys. Lack of accord is the backbone of their usefulness, and the contract is their primary agent. It's designed not so much to serve the needs of both parties as it is to maintain the status quo of a cartel and create prophylactic clauses that you can, down the line, hang an expensive lawsuit on.

How did this system evolve? Sometime during the early 1980s, certain events positioned lawyers as the vice-presidents of major recording labels. Suddenly, what used to be a tool of the business became the controller of it. Twenty years ago, lawyers were all contained within the legal affairs department of a label. Now one in every five people who works at a major label is likely to have a law degree. Astounding.

Since lawyers are now in the driver's seat, the language of the music business has became the language of lawyers; i.e., Legalese. Over the past 30 years, the creative elements that used to control the industry—managers, producers, and artists—now find themselves needing an attorney in an entirely new way, to serve as an agent or middleman between the label and the artist, even to perform the simplest function.

With both sides now armed with attorneys, negotiations for contracts, which used to take a few weeks, dragged on into months, even years. Lawyers got "smarter," artists got "smarter," and soon everyone wanted more and more in the contract to give him- or herself peace of mind. All this in a contract that neither side could enforce.

Like a virus, this spread throughout the entire business. Major-label contracts swelled from 13 pages (the average in 1965) to 51 pages (the average in 1995), and now with 360 Deals, many have swelled to over 150 pages. Did the conditions of the business of selling a record become that much more complex in 30 years? Maybe, but the music business in the past was controlled by only a small number of companies. They set the rules. They made the standards, and if a lawyer wanted to survive, he or she had to play their game.

Fortunately, things change. The Internet, digital recording, and affordable technology have forever altered the tapestry of American business. With the consolidation of the major labels, there are fewer and fewer big clients for the music attorney. Now if lawyers want to survive, they need to have several sizes of clients, many of which will be boutique independents, as well as artists and producers looking to make "mini record deals."

Lawyers will also have to relearn how to service more educated clients if they want to carve a niche in the new frontier. This service will have to involve creative contracts that are not merely designed to pigeonhole the artist or label into a series of commitments, but that are also fair in their terms and engineered to abort litigation. There are few attorneys interested in creating such documents. But this, too, will change.

Change

"Change, Doctor, is the essential ingredient in life."
—Mr. Spock, *Star Trek*, 1967

The purpose of this book was not to rag about what's wrong with the world, but to inspire change for the future. It's often thought that shame is the ultimate motivator. Threats of lawsuits and jail only seem to inspire further corruption. But hopefully, exposure into the light of what we know in our hearts to be fair and just will produce results. When we are put in the position of being judged by the very people that we've used as stepping stones, when we empower such people to have a say in our future, change is inevitable, lest we die of embarrassment. It *is* possible to die of embarrassment. Many pop stars have proven this.

I hope I've succeeded in making a good case for change, and I hope that labels take a look at the way they do business and see that it is a model that can no longer yield effective results, for them or the artist.

As I write these words, companies with new ideas for distribution are fighting vast financial powers. But what they represent is greater than their opponent's resources, for they represent the future, and the future can't be stopped. But it can have enemies. Who are they? They are anyone who opposes change. And as long as they can keep things from changing, these enemies of the future will continue to make money without adapting to new ideas and new concepts.

Progress is historically unkind to such people. Progress is the future. You are the future. You are progress.

Lead, follow, or get out of the way.

Peace.
Moses Avalon

●＞I. The Quick-Step E-Z Guide
to Decoding Your Recording Contract

1: Decoding

This book gives you powerful tools for decoding the LabelSpeak of any recording contract. Here is a distilled, step-by-step process.

Step 1: Definitions

1. Read the Definitions section and become clear on the real meanings of the words "sales," "Net Sales," "Net Profits," "Gross Sales," and "Normal Retail Sales" or "Normal Retail Channels."

2. Create a cheat sheet for the above.

3. Scan for any stray definitions in other clauses in the contract. Look for quotation marks around words or common words that are capitalized.

4. Add these to the cheat sheet.

Step 2: Loopholes and Double-Dips

5. Scan the contract for all uses of the three primary loophole creators:

   i.   "Notwithstanding anything herein contained to the contrary…"

   ii. "Without limiting the generality of the foregoing…"

iii. "Except as otherwise used (or set forth) herein ..."

6. Write down each exception they create on your cheat sheet.

7. Using the phrases above, scan for the word "Aggregate," and write down every place where an amount of money is being defined.

8. Apply all the above to the following phrases: "new technology," new medium," "Audiophile records," and "New Configuration."

9. Find the words "Offset Right." (If you can't find those exact words, then find the words they are using that mean the same thing.) Then write down everywhere the "Offset Right" is applied.

Step 3: Misrepresentations (Lies)

10. Carefully read the section called NEGATIVE COVENANTS. And MISCELLANEOUS. Decode all clauses and make note of what you *can't* do under this agreement.

Step 4: Mis-directors

11. Scan the contract for every time that a reference is made to other parts of the contract. Look for paragraph numbers as a first sign.

12. Read those paragraphs first and summarize them in a *very brief "shorthand" description* (three to four words) on your cheat sheet.

13. Scan to those places where reference is made and where the paragraph number is located, and cross out and write the "shorthand" description over the paragraph number.

Step 5: Finally

14. Read the contract from start to finish. Compare it to your cheat sheet when necessary. Write down all exceptions to rules that it establishes.

2: Do the Math

Those in the know call this figuring out the "penny rate." This means calculating in pennies how much each "sale" is worth.

1. Make a photocopy of the "Flow of Deal Points" in the Master Chart on pages 352–353.

2. Scan The Thick for everywhere money points are given and write them in the appropriate box on the Chart.

3. Watch out for "lesser than/greater than" clauses. In most cases, flip lesser to greater (and vice versa) and see which way the math works better for you.

4. Figure out exactly what your royalty or split should be, and also what it would be if "greater than" replaced "lesser than" in the clause you are dissecting. Do the same with "whichever is higher" and "whichever is lower." If you need some help, go to www.MosesAvalon.com, and click on the MARC (Moses Avalon Royalty Calculator).

>II. A Real Deal Memo

John Hardhart
Senior Vice President
Business & Legal Affairs
Pacific Records
1000 Avenue of the Stars
Century City, CA 90078

Stan Leatherface
Grubman, Indursky & Shindler
152 W. 57th Street
New York, NY 10019

March 1, 2010

Dear Stan:

The following shall set forth the terms pursuant to which Pacific Records would enter into an exclusive recording agreement with the artists p/k/a "_____" (individually and collectively, "Artist"). The following is subject to the execution of a formal agreement:

1. TERM: An initial period consisting of one (1) album, with seven (7) options for one (1) album each.

2. TERRITORY: The Universe.

3. ADVANCES/RECORDING FUNDS:

a. Recording Fund in respect of the first LP (inclusive of all recording costs, individual producer advances, etc.) of Two Hundred and Fifty Thousand Dollars ($250,000). In addition, Pacific Records would pay Artist an Advance of One Hundred Thousand Dollars ($100,000) in respect of the first LP of the recording commitment (the "LP1 Advance") as follows: (A) Fifty Thousand Dollars ($50,000) promptly following the full execution of the agreement between Artist and Pacific Records; and (B) Fifty Thousand Dollars ($50,000) promptly following Delivery of LP1. The LP1 Advance would include, without limitation, Artist's living expenses, as well as reimbursement to the Artist of the cost of (i) recording equipment, and (ii) a van for use by the Artist in promotional touring.

b. In connection with each of the Second through Ninth LPs, Pacific Records would pay a Recording Fund to be calculated on the basis of Pacific Record's standard sales formula, subject to the following minimums and maximums:

LP	MINIMUM	MAXIMUM
First LP	$250,000	$500,000
Second LP	$250,000	$500,000
Third LP	$300,000	$600,000
Fourth LP	$325,000	$650,000
Fifth LP	$350,000	$700,000
Sixth LP	$375,000	$750,000
Seventh LP	$400,000	$800,000

4. ROYALTIES/PROFIT SPLIT:
Standard "Old School" Deal

a. In respect to Top Line sales through normal trade channels ("NTC Sales") in the United States ("USNTC Sales") of LPs, Pacific Records would pay a royalty at the applicable rate indicated below:

LP	0–500M	500–1MM	1MM+
LP 1 & 2	14%	14.5%	15%
LP 3 & 4	14.5	15	15.5
LP 5 & 6	15	15.5	16
LP 7 & 8	15.5	16	16.5
LP 9	16	16.5	17

Newer "360 Deals"

We shall credit Artist's account with 40% (escalating to 50% for each album prospectively after sales of 1,000,000 units as reported by SoundScan) of net profits[1] with respect to the sale and exploitation of Artist's masters in the United States, including gross receipts received in the United States from licensees outside of the United States.

b. USNTC Sales of Singles and EPs: Ten percent (10%)

c. NTC Sales of records outside the United States:

    i. Canada—80% of the applicable basic US rate

    ii. United Kingdom—70% of the applicable basic US rate

    iii. European Union, Japan, Australia, New Zealand—60% of the applicable basic US rate

    iv. ROW—50% of the applicable basic US rate

d. CD RATE: 90%

5. MECHANICAL ROYALTIES: 75% of minimum statutory rate (the "Mechanical Rate"), subject to a ceiling of ten (10) times the Mechanical Rate for an album, two (2) times the Mechanical Rate for Singles, and four (4) times the Mechanical Rate for an EP.

6. TOUR SUPPORT: Pacific Records would make available up to $75,000 in deficit tour support for LP1, subject to Pacific Records' customary provisions.

[1] Absent from many of the deal memos is the way "net profits" are calculated. In most cases it means a deduction of manufacturing costs and mechanical royalties—the same ones labels often promise to keep sacrosanct (instead of the usual 75% and without cross-collateralization). This promise, if given, is covertly taken back by including it in "net profits."

7. CREATIVE DECISIONS: All creative decisions in connection with the recording process (i.e., the choice of producer, compositions, recording studio, etc.) will be determined by Pacific Records.

8. ENTERTAINMENT SERVICES: As used herein, "Entertainment Services" shall mean Artist's exclusive services for all aspects of the entertainment industry, including, without limitation, as a sponsor/endorser. Splits of revenue and or commissions shall be payable to us on the same gross revenue basis as Artist's then-current management company commission and payable for the same events as Artist's then-current management company commission. Splits and particulars will be as follows:

   i. Touring: During the so-called album cycle, split shall be 90/10 in Artist's favor.

   ii. Merchandise: As a special "Merch/Fan Club Advance" of $75,000 payable promptly following full execution of the long form agreement. We will pay to Artists against this Advance (with adjustments made for sales outside the US and Canada) between 22% and 28% of retail receipts (depending on the tier level of the outlet: "Mid–tier," e.g., J.C. Penney; "Specialty Stores," e.g., Hot Topic, Musicland; Mass Market Stores, e.g., Target and Wal-Mart in accordance with our customary percentages), escalating to 30% after the Special Advance is recouped.

   iii. Fan Clubs: We shall have the exclusive right to the "Official" Artist Fan Club (the "Fan Club"). We shall host and maintain a Fan Club website and message boards and provisions for order fulfillment with respect to goods and services made available on the Fan Club Site. Artist and label shall split on a 50/50 basis net profits (after deduction of direct out-of-pocket costs and a 5% administrative fee) in connection with all income hereto, subject to recoupment of the special $75,000 Merch/Fan Club Advance.

   iv. Licensing: For approved licensing opportunities, 85/15 in Artist's favor, of net profits.

Please note that this proposal is subject to the approval of Pacific Records' management, and I must hereby reserve Pacific Records' rights to change, modify, or rescind the above based on management's review and approval.

Very truly yours,
John Hardhart
PACIFIC RECORDS
Senior Vice President
Business & Legal Affairs

cc: President, V.P. of A&R

●III. Legonics 101

A translation of common legal phrases and their meanings when used in recording contracts.

Some Easy Ones

When it says:

It really means:

`"Audiophile Recording(s)," "LPs,"`
`or "Phonorecords"`

An antiquated term for any record, CD, DVD, or tape.

`"pursuant to the receipt of a`
`financial instrument"`

"when money is actually received." As opposed to when the contract *says* you will be paid. There is a distinct difference.

`"commercially satisfactory master"`

An album that the record company feels they can easily sell.

`"in perpetuity throughout the known`
`universe." Also "Territory: the`
`Universe."`

Anyplace you can think of and till the end of time itself. This bit of sci-fi is designed to cover all possible territory in which any money might be made. It almost always pertains to the transfer of rights and is taken to mean that the rights granted are granted forever, just in case someday we find a way to sell the record on the planet Jupiter.[1]

[1] I have heard of an artist who tried to cave out Martian rights to his Masters. The label didn't go for it.

"…refuses without cause…"

"…do without giving any particular reason…" Used often in relation to the resale of master recordings to the public.

"irrevocable option of label"

"a right that once granted to the label they have forever." Usually related to releasing Masters to the public, and if they ever have to do so.

Advanced Legonics: Loophole Creators

"Notwithstanding anything herein contained to the contrary..."

"If anything else in the contract contradicts the next half of this sentence, then this sentence is the prevailing rule." This is the biggest red flag. Often it is used to construct a trapdoor or "loophole" by creating an exception to what is fundamentally promised in the agreement. The exception created will often be a brutal and costly one.

"Except as otherwise hereinafter set forth..." also "Except as expressly noted otherwise…"

"Except when the contract says otherwise further on down the page or later in the agreement."

Upon seeing this phrase one should carefully scan the entire contract to find exceptions to what is about to be promised in the second half of the same sentence. Example: "Except as otherwise herein set forth, artist will be paid on 100% of sales." It's certain that somewhere else buried within the tome of the contract there is a phrase that will contradict this. Often it will begin with one of the phrases mentioned in this section.

Note that where the phrase above this ("Notwithstanding anything…") creates a loophole by making specific exceptions to general concepts, this does the opposite; it creates a loophole by making generalities out of things that appear specific.

"Notwithstanding the foregoing..."

"What follows is an exception to what was already established."

This is a first cousin to the two phrases right above it. You will often find that these three seemingly innocent words are being used to carve a loophole in certain obligations that the record company would prefer to dodge. Following it may also be the things they want the artist to do that will be over and above the "normal" duties listed in the agreement.

"Without limiting the generality of the foregoing, the Artist (producer, writer, etc.) hereby…"

The words following this phrase should be taken to have the broadest possible interpretation. This phrase is often used when discussing the transfer of copyrights and is a common strategy of a sneaky lawyer for overreaching. Instead of listing every possible situation or granting of rights (and risk leaving something out), the attorney will insert a phrase like this one, which basically means "plus anything else I can't think of right now." It can also mean, "interpret this next phrase in the way it can hurt you the most."

Advanced Legonics II: Confidence Instillers

"...shall be completed in a timely fashion"

Whenever the word "timely" appears in a contract, it's time for caution. Contracts that use this phrase are attempting to keep certain time frames nebulous and subjective, often for the benefit of the party offering the contract. Example: "The recording of the album shall be completed in a timely fashion." Who decides what "timely" is? Answer: the one who has the checkbook. A fair agreement will usually spell out time frames *precisely*.

"Company shall consult with Artist on..."

A meaningless phrase designed to instill false confidence in the artist that the record company is duty-bound to ask the artist's permission on a particular subject. A provision containing this phrase usually refers to cover art or selection of the single. In reality, if the company even asks the artist, "Hey, what do you think?", they have "consulted." Artist's lawyers and managers use this one to bamboozle their clients into thinking they did a great job negotiating on their behalf. It's a joke.

"Approval from Artist will not unreasonably be withheld."

Living in the same neighborhood as the phrase above will be this little trickster. It sounds as if the artist has been given power over something, but in fact it's the opposite. This phrase actually prevents the artist from holding out too strongly on any issue that needs to be determined after the contract is written (like cover art, tour support, and marketing decisions). Example: "Artist's approval of cover art not to be unreasonably withheld." Although this seems to protect both parties, in essence it only protects the record company, because they have more leverage in deciding what is and is not "reasonable."

"prior to the expiration of the applicable period"

"before time has run out" on whatever issue this phrase is connected to. This would be relatively harmless except that figuring out when the "applicable period" begins and ends in most recording contracts can be confusing. Scan carefully for any sentences using this phrase and see if the "applicable period" is really what you think it is. Lawyers have sneaky ways of extending a two-year Period so that it turns into a three- or four-year Period.

"The invalidity or unenforceability of any provision hereof shall not affect the validity or enforceability of any other provision hereof."

"If one item in the contract is later deemed invalid or illegal, the rest of the contract will still be in effect." A blanket license that gives the label the prerogative to throw all kinds of junk into the contract that they know would normally be unenforceable. This elevates the potential for enforceability. If a judge later determines that one clause is completely enslaving (or "overreaching"), then the artist will still be bound to produce and perform for the company.

"Company shall give reasonable notice of…"

Usually pertains to the label's legal requirement to send an artist relevant information about the status of their recording agreement. It often refers to royalty statements. In reality, the record company won't give a rat's ass whether they notified the artist or not. If the artist didn't get the notice, the label will assume it must have been lost in the mail—the mail being "reasonable notice" in the eyes of the record company. Good contracts will insist on "registered mail" as reasonable notice.

"Company warrants and represents…"

"The label swears on their honor as a record company." A flaccid attempt to instill confidence in the artist that the label will or will not do something wherever this phrase is applied.

▶Glossary of LabelSpeak

Legend

lblspk	=	LabelSpeak
ind slng	=	Industry slang
eng	=	English
lglese	=	Legalese
ava	=	Avalonism

Note: The default definition is always LabelSpeak, unless noted otherwise.

10× Statutory — (*ind slng*) Ten times the Statutory Rate. Designed as shorthand to indicate the total amount of the Mechanical License that the labels pay to publishers for the rights to duplicate their copyrighted material on phonorecords. Example: If the Statutory Rate is 7 cents, then 10× Statutory would be 70 cents. However, usually incorporated into the expression is also the "three-quarter rate" not mentioned but implied. Example: If the Statutory Rate is 9.1 cents, 10× Statutory would then be equal to 68 cents. See *bullshit statutory rate, statutory rate, Statutory Rate,* and *three-quarter rate*

A&R person — 1) (*ind slng*) Short for "Artists and Repertory." The person at the label who decides to sign the artist and shepherd him or her through the major-label experience. 2) (*ava*) A person the artist tolerates in order to get what he wants from the label.

accepted level of theft — (*ava*) An amount (or threshold) of money that all parties covertly agree is padded into a budget, expressly for the purposes of overpaying a subcontractor so that they may kick back a portion to the main contractor. See *kickback*

Accounting Period — A unit of time whereby all "royalties" and "mechanicals" are accounted for and paid to artist or Furnisher. Generally every six months. Periods are usually January to June and July to December. See *floating accounting period*

Advance — 1) (*lblspk*) A prepayment of "royalties." 2) (*ava*) A special type of loan that the artist or Furnisher pays back out of the money the label collects from all revenue streams the music recorded under The Thick earns. "Although the definition of Advance often excludes recoupment from things like Mechanical Royalties, other clauses in The Thick (unless specifically negotiated otherwise) allow all income to be recoupable." See *cross-collateralization, Offset Right,* and *recoupable*

AF of M, AFM — American Federation of Musicians. A union.

AFTRA — American Federation of Television and Radio Actors. A union. Artists appearing in music videos are required to join. They also represent Artists when they sing in a studio environment.

aggregate — A total sum of money. Example: "The aggregate cost" means "the total amount of money spent."

Album — When capitalized means specifically between 8 to 12 individual songs that the artist recorded just for the label and no one else. If the same song appears twice on a single Album, even if it's another mix or version, it's not counted as a separate song. See *Commitment Album, LP,* or *Product LP*

Album Artwork — Means all artwork, photography, or other graphics and related materials for the packaging of the applicable Album.

anticipated returns and credits — 1) (*lblspk*) The estimations of sales, usually based on reports from SoundScan, for the express purpose of a Reserve. 2) (*ava*) The label's estimates based on a meeting with a fortune teller called a "financial analyst" who uses a crystal ball called "a marketing report" to determine how many records shipped may return to the label. See *Reserves* and *SoundScan*

applicable recording fund — 1) (*lblspk*) The exact amount of money earmarked for the budget of the Album. It is separate from any producer's fee and/or artist's Special Advance or signing bonuses. 2) (*ava*) A sneaky lawyer way of saying "recoupable" without bringing attention to the fact that the money being earmarked for recording is still an Advance. See *Advance* and *recoupable and reimbursable costs*

artificial term extension — (*ava*) A sneaky lawyer ruse that extends the length of a term or Option Period or Accounting Period. The most common ones are creating a scenario whereby no Option Period will end on a certain group of months. See also *floating accounting periods, Option Period*, and *"Period"*

artist — 1) (*lblspk*) The person or group responsible to the label for acting as a centerpiece of a body of recorded material and the accompanying road show that will promote said material. 2) (*ava*) The person whose picture is on the cover of the record packaging.

"artist's approval," "artist's consent," and **"mutually determined"** — 1) (*ava*) "Fake comforters" placed in contracts to instill a feeling in the artist that the label will work with him or her on the issue at hand. 2) (*ava*) Meaningless words in practice, since what will be "mutually determined" is controlled by whoever has the most leverage. See *reasonable*

ASCAP — See *Performing Rights Organization*

Audiophile Records — See *New Medium Records*

audit, auditing — 1) (*lblspk*) An independent accounting of "royalties" by artist or Furnisher. 2) (*ava*) an attempt on the part of the artist or Furnisher to catch the label in a lie or "error." 3) (*lglese*) When auditing a label, an artist generally can: only see the books once a year; only go back three years (unless fraud is discovered); only audit the royalty statements of any one "period"; only audit the company once; must give them 30 days' notice; only examine "royalty" statements, and nothing else, such as manufacturing records; audits cannot take more than 30 days provided the label makes the books "available" for inspection. If there are any disputes between artist and label, the label generally won't allow an audit until said dispute is settled. The CPA cannot show his or her finding to anyone except the label and artist's attorney. Artist pays for the entire audit, even if it turns out that the label was in serious error. All the above is negotiable.

Big Four, the — (*ind slng*) Refers individually and collectively to the four largest distributors of recorded music in the music business: UMG (Universal Music Group), Sony Music Entertainment, WMG (Warner Music Group), and EMI (Electric and Musical Industries).

Big Three — (*ind slng*) Same as the Big Four (see above) except without EMI. Since EMI has been downsized in 2007, some experts no longer include it in the cartel of major distributors.

BMG — Acronym for the German media giant Bertelsmann Music Group, now part of Sony. See also *Big Four*

BMI — See *Performing Rights Organization*

breakage — A deduction applied to records shipped that goes back to the days when records were made of vinyl and some of them broke during shipping. Labels would apply a 10% deduction for the "breakage." They did this whether 10% of the records actually broke or not. It was a questionable practice (even before most records were CDs and made of virtually unbreakable material), because records are and have been always sold as a consignment item. Nowadays the word "breakage" will only appear in the most amateur contracts. Majors don't use the term any more. Instead they just bury the same concept in the definition of the words "records sold." See *Free Goods* and *"sold"*

Budget Record — 1) A Record (old or new) marked down to 67% or less of the sticker price of any similar type of record in the same region. 2) (*ava*) A LabelSpeak way of saying records sold at a discount when they're still new and the list price is high. 3) (*ava*) An arbitrary number, chosen by the label to create a threshold (usually 67% or less of the SRLP) below which all "sales" will result in a reduction in the artist's Royalty by about 50%. The number is deliberately manipulated to allow a disproportionate amount of records "sold" to be categorized as "Budget."

bullshit statutory rate (the) — (*ava*) Used to draw attention to the fact that labels want those reading The Thick to assume that a "Statutory Rate" created by the contract has the same legal significance as the "statutory rate" established by law. In reality, there are many differences. These differences and the fact that a deliberate attempt is made to covertly substitute one for the other earns it the title of "bullshit statutory rate." See also *controlled composition, Copyright Arbitration Royalty Panels, "sales," statutory rate,* and *Statutory Rate*

Ceiling Amount — The maximum amount of money Advanced to an artist in any given Contract/Option Period. Often this amount is inclusive of a Recording Fund, and, if done in the Initial Period, a signing bonus. Synonym: *Maximum Amount.*

Commitment Album — Any collection of no less than 10 songs that the label approves of, to be recorded by artist.

composition — 1) (*lglese*) A collaboration or arrangement of lyrics to a musical melody. Or, a musical melody without lyrics. 2) (*ava*) Basically, a song. However, different versions of the same song on the same Record in most contracts will be considered collectively "one composition."

compulsory license — 1) (*lglese*) A mandatory license that a copyright owner of a published composition must issue to anyone interested in recording an original version of that composition. There is a minimum amount called a statutory rate. 2) (*ava*) Once a song is published, anyone can cover it without permission as long as they pay the minimum statutory rate to the song's copyright holder. By law that copyright holder is "compelled" to give them this license; thus the term "compulsory license." See *Copyright Arbitration Royalty Panels* and *statutory rate*

Configuration and **"configuration"** — 1) A type of record (Top Line, Budget, New Medium) in concert with other factors such as (but not limited to) a medium of record such as CD, cassette, download, stream, or LP. 2) (*ava*) When in quotes, it's designed to draw attention to the fact that the contract is referring not only to a Configuration that is a type of record (like a CD, LP, download, etc.), but also a series of deductions that are incorporated into the category of that "configuration." 3) The equation that calculates the exact style of payment to be paid on a particular "sale." The anatomy of a "configuration" consists of the medium of the record, the sale price/venue, and various deductions. See *the Meat Grinder, royalties, Royalty Base,* and *"types" of records*

Container Charge or **Packaging Deduction** — A percentage of the sticker price charged to the artist for the packaging of the record. Usually: cassette tapes: 20%, music videos: 20%, CDs and New Medium Records (i.e., Internet stuff, MP3s, MiniDiscs, etc.): 25%, 12-inch vinyl: 12.5% –15%, depending on the elaborateness of the packaging.

Contract Period, Option Period, Period — 1) (*lblspk*) A unit of time that contains within it the recording and "delivery" of an Album and its promotion after release. Typical recording contracts ask for between five and seven Option Periods. Each usually lasts from a year to 14 months. There are places in The Thick where "Initial Period" is used interchangeably with "Option Period." 2) (*ava*) "…not a specific length of time, but rather a unit of time that starts when you sign the contract and ends in conjunction with certain events. The key event being the 'delivery' of an Album." 3) (*ava*) "…these amounts of time may be lengthened or shortened at label's discretion." 4) (*ava*) "…starts right after the previous Period ends. Unless they drop you, it will go for eight months after the domestic release of the artist's Album. If they don't release the Album the Option Period generally ends 12 months after the 'delivery' of the Album. Nine to 16 months is a normal length of an Option Period." See *Initial Period*

Controlled Composition — A song written, co-written, or "controlled" by the artist or Furnisher; i.e., a song the artist or Furnisher has the right to collect money from.

copyright — 1) (*lglese*) The right to make a copy of an original work, granted exclusively to the author of said original work the instant it is fixated in any medium. 2) (*ava*) A temporary monopoly on a creative work.

Copyright Arbitration Royalty Panels (CARPs) — The Copyright Royalty Tribunal Reform Act of 1993, Public Law 103-198, eliminated the Copyright Royalty Tribunal and replaced it with a system of ad hoc Copyright Arbitration Royalty Panels (CARPs). The panels are administrated by the Library of Congress and the Copyright Office to adjust the copyright compulsory license royalty rates (including the mechanical rates for the making and distributing of phonorecords) and to distribute the royalties collected by the Licensing Division to the appropriate copyright owners.

Covered Videos, Videogram — (*lblspk*) A fancy name for a Music Video.

CPA — 1) (*eng*) Certified Public Accountant. 2) (*ava*) Also stands for Cleaning, Pressing, and Alterations, or Constant Pain in the Ass, depending on who hires the CPA.

cross–collateralization — 1) (*eng*) Mingling (or transferring) of funds from account "A" into account "B" for the express purpose of paying back a debt from account "B." 2) (*lblspk*) Using monies earned from one revenue stream to pay back debts created from areas not related to that revenue stream. Example: Using "royalties" to pay back "mechanical overages." Or using "royalties" from Album 2 to pay back Advances from Album 1. See *Offset Right*

currency exchange scam — (*ava*) Any manipulated situation designed to create the perception that a foreign subdistributor is not in complete cooperation with its parent company, implying that Royalties from foreign "sales" should be reduced and/or take longer to collect due to currency exchange fluctuations or excise tax regulations.

cutouts — 1) (*lblspk*) Records that the label has "cut out" of the catalog and now intends to sell at or below cost to scrap dealers and rack jobbers. 2) (*ava*) Titles that did not "sell" well and that the label announces are "cut out" of their catalog. This invites all the companies with this title in their warehouse, and people who have received free promo copies, to return them to the label for a refund. The label then sells the returned units for $1 to $3 per unit to scrap dealers, record clubs, and rack jobbers. Hundreds of thousands of records are returned and "rotated" this way every year. Not only are artists not paid on the sale of the unit, but the "returned" unit is charged to their account and deducted from their "royalties." See *"fake" indie shells, Rack Jobbers, Record Clubs,* and *Stock Rotation*

DAT — Digital Audio Tape.

Deadline Date — Usually eight months from the start of each Option Period. It is the final date that the artist or Furnisher can "deliver" the Minimum Recording Obligations without penalty. See *"deliver"* and *Minimum Recording Obligations*

Deficiency Payment — An amount of money (often called a Special Advance) paid to an artist by the label that should have been paid by a Furnisher (usually a Record Producer), but was defaulted upon. Often these are "Special Advances" that are annual payments to the artist for their work.

Delivered or **"delivered"** — 1) (*lblspk*) A recording made under contract that has been presented to the label and accepted as "commercially satisfactory." 2) (*ava*) When in quotes, it's meant to draw attention to the fact that when a label is speaking of an artist "delivering" a master recording, that does not just mean the tapes themselves or the artist's "feeling" that they are done—"delivered" includes immigration papers, sample clearances, personnel lists, and mostly approval and acceptance by the label of the Master Recordings. See *"commercially satisfactory master"* and *Master Recording*

Delivery Schedule — 1) (*lblspk*) A timetable of "delivery" requirements. Generally, six months from the date of signing to comply with *all* requirements for "delivery" of the first Album; nine months after that to "deliver" the second Album; all additional Albums are to be "delivered" no later than four months after the beginning of each Option Period. 2) (*ava*) The schedule for "delivery" can have a drastic effect on the amount of the next Advance, as artists are routinely penalized for "late delivery." It also leaves little time for the artist to compose new materials, as revealed in the clauses regarding the "Minimum Recording Obligations," which are crucial in order for the artist to qualify for their next Advance. See *"delivered"* and *Option Period*

Distribute and **Distributor** — 1) (*eng*) To part with *permanently*. It does *not* mean "to sell," although that's what it's intended to imply. Giving away records for free is also distributing them. 2) (*lblspk*) When capitalized, refers to any record label or company in the business of distributing records. In many Thicks, the word "Distributor" is interchangeable with "Company" (or "label").

Double Scale — Twice the minimum payment required by most musicians' unions. See *scale*

Double-Dip — 1) (*lglese*) Any covert or "clever" contradiction causing a second payment, or second deduction in monies, to be paid. 2) (*ava*) A special kind of loophole. Labels charge artists for certain things. They do it by making deductions to the money they owe the artist from the sale of records. This is unavoidable, but in many cases the contract will sneak in the same or a similar payment (or deduction) *twice*; thus the expression "Double-Dip." As you might guess, there are sometimes Triple-Dips as well.

EMI, EMD — Formerly called CEMA; now incorporates the EMI labels, which include Capitol and Virgin Records and the SBK catalog. See *Big Four* and *Big Three*

Exploitation Period, also **Restriction Period** or **Sunset Period** — 1) (*lblspk*) In most contracts, an extra "period" where artist is still bound to the material conditions and non-compete clauses of The Thick. 2) (*lblspk*) Starts when the last Option Period ends, or six months after the release and marketing of the last Single from the last Album artist was required to "deliver" during the Term. 3) (*ava*) A way of clinging to an artist's popularity for just a bit longer.

"fake" indie shells — (*ava*) Smaller companies linked to, owned, or controlled, in whole or in part, by a Big Four, expressly manifested to create a corporate veil, or to create an A&R pipeline to more street-oriented artists. See *Three-Deep labels*

first use — (Controlled Composition) A warranty made by the artist or Furnisher to the label that this is the first time the material (songs) is being licensed since its creation.

fixed rate — Refers to the fact that in major-label contracts the Statutory Rate does not escalate in time like its distant cousin the "statutory rate," but is fixed from the time the contract is signed by the artist.

floating accounting period — (*ava*) A device used by the label to shift the schedule by which the label is supposed to issue accounting statements and "royalty" checks. Called "floating" because the way the clauses are worded in The Thick gives the label an enormous amount of latitude as to when the real Accounting Period begins and ends. See *Accounting Period*

Floor Amount — (*lblspk*) The minimum amount of money Advanced to an artist in any given Contract/Option Period. Often this amount is inclusive of a Recording Fund, and, if done in the Initial Period, a signing bonus. Synonym: *Minimum Amount*.

Free Goods — (*lblspk*) A fixed percentage of units that are deducted from records shipped to account for the number of units given away as promotional gifts or sales incentives. No royalties of any kind are paid on "Free Goods." 2) (*ava*) Free Goods may imply records "given away for free," but, they are, in fact, records that are royalty-free to the label. In reality records are almost never given away for free. Boxes of records are often discounted, like, "Buy three boxes, get a fourth one 'free.'" In reality, the cost of the free box is absorbed and the label gets paid, but it does not pay the Artist. They should really be called "Royalty-Free Goods." See *breakage*, *Net Sales, Records Sold,* and *"sales"*

Furnisher — Anyone agreeing to "deliver" Master Recordings (as defined in The Thick) to a label. Furnishers can be and often are the artist or producer, but can also be a production company or Two-Deep or Three-Deep label. See *Two-Deep label* and *Three-Deep label*

garage sale — See *Special Sales Programs*

get lost fee — (*ind slng*) Amount of money a party will pay to have another party forfeit the rights to perform future services. See *go away formula* for how this applies to an artist leaving the label while in the middle of an Option Period.

go away formula — (*ind slng*) A calculation to determine the amount of buyout money paid to an artist by a label as a kill fee for termination of the Term. See *Term*

Harry Fox Agency, Inc. — An agency that routinely audits record companies to ensure that the correct mechanical license money owed to publishers is paid.

They charge a 5% commission for any money they find that a publisher was supposed to get and didn't. They also issue mechanical licenses for cover songs if you want one on your Album.

imprint — See *Two-Deep label*

Indemnification, indemnify — 1) (*lglese*) To reimburse, usually due to a legal dispute. "Artist will indemnify Label." To hold harmless and reimburse a party for expenses incurred due to legal action. 2) (*lblspk*) If the label gets sued, the artist has to pay for everything, including lawyers' fees and damages, the recordings you make, the songs you've written, what you call yourself in public, and any performances you do in movies, TV, videos, ads for the record, books you write, or ideas that you have. 3) (*ava*) "…means that if the label has to lay out cash to defend itself against a lawsuit in which your record is involved, you pony up."

independent contractor — 1) (*lblspk*) A Furnisher not employed by the label. 2) (*ava*) A contracted party who, despite the fact that all the minimum requirements for "employment" as defined under the law are met, is not granted basic employee status, recognition, or benefits.

Independent Promoter — A salesperson who, through his or her "relationship" with radio program directors, can get singles in rotation on radio. See *rotation*

initial commercial release — See *Release*

Initial Period — The first Option Period. Sometimes equivalent in duration to two Option Periods. See *Option Period*

kickback — A covert payment made by a subcontractor/vendor to the main contractor in exchange for employment or services (usually services listed on the recording budget). Examples: An engineer to a producer. A Furnisher to an A&R person. See *accepted level of theft*

LabelSpeak — (*ava*) The language of recording contracts and record company jargon.

Leaving Member — 1) (*lblspk*) Any member of a signed group wishing to withdraw from or refusing to perform with said group. 2) (*ava*) Any member who develops an attitude can be called a "Leaving Member" under the terms of the contract. If that happens, the label can: fire or suspend the whole group as soon as they learn of any dispute; require the remaining members to either find a replacement immediately, or keep on performing as a group minus the Leaving Member; bind the Leaving Member to another record deal as a solo recording artist at the same "royalty" rates to which he or she initially agreed; record new masters with the full intent of releasing them; and/or do a Term as a solo artist with the conditions of the old deal, while being responsible for paying back 25% of the debt from the previous deal; break up the group and declare each member of the group a "Leaving Member." All the above are negotiable. 3) (*ava*) Since 99 groups out of 100 break up within four years, the Leaving Member clause becomes little more than the label's way of building a stable of talent while simultaneously amortizing the debt from development of the original act onto the individual members. A Double-Dip.

Letter of Direction — 1) (*lglese*) A letter or legal instrument instructing the Company to pay a vendor of the Furnisher or artist directly. 2) (*ava*) "…As far as producers go, many prefer to be paid *directly* by the label. In order for this to happen, the label must agree to pay the producer's share of the artist's royalties for them. This agreement is created via a Letter of Direction."

Licensees — Does not mean what is on the back of your car. It means granting of rights to your recordings to anyone with whom the label is doing business.

liner notes — Credits listed on a record.

loophole — 1) (*lglese*) Any covert or "clever" contraction created during negotiations. 2) (*ava*) A contradiction made in the contract that will cost you money due to its ambiguity or trickery. 3) (*ava*) Anytime they promise you one thing and it turns out to be something else.

LP — Short for "Long-Playing Record." **master quality** — (*ind slng*) 1) Any Master Recording that the label states is "commercially satisfactory." Usually this will only include recordings that sound expensive, whose performance meets the label's standard of quality and sounds at least as good as the demo, and that proves the artist hasn't changed his/her style since being signed. 2) (ava) Not a description of the recording quality.

Master Recording — (*lblspk*) 1) Any recording on any medium (except video), even ones that haven't been invented yet, that the label considers "useful" in the sale of records and promotion of the artist. 2) (*ava*) This can arguably include any recording that the artist made in this lifetime or any other, since the label will likely consider all such recordings "useful." 3) The definition of "Master Recording" includes any outtakes. And anything "delivered" on which the label will pay a "royalty." See *Record*

Master Tone — A licensed loop (usually not more than 30 seconds) of a sound recording that is used as the call alert for a cellular phone. See *ring tone*

Master Use — (*lblspk*) A grant of rights to a particular Master Recording. Usually done by a label granting rights to a motion picture company or TV production company for use of recorded music in a movie or TV show.

Maximum Amount — See *Ceiling Amount*

Meat Grinder, the — (*ava*) Term of art for the Royalty Configuration Matrix, where "sales" are calculated and "royalties" are assessed. See *Royalty Configuration Matrix*

Mechanical Royalties — (*lblspk*) The "royalty" paid to the publishing company for the use of a composition in their catalog when it is reproduced on any record "sold." See *mechanicals*

mechanicals or **"mechanicals"** — 1) (*lblspk*) The total amount of money a label will pay for the Mechanical License for all compositions on any particular record or LP. 2) (*ava*) When in quotes refers to definition #1, inclusive of all deductions and loopholes.

merchandising plan — 1) When the label bundles records with T-shirts, posters, and even records by other Artists that they are trying to sell as a "lot" to an entire chain of record stores, like Best Buy or Wal-Mart. 2) Same as definition #1, when done as promotional packages to radio stations, MTV, etc.

Mid-Priced Record — 1) (*lblspk*) A Record (new or old) selling for between 67% and 85% of the list price (SRLP) for most new releases selling in that region. 2) Any record that is selling for a 15% discount from the sticker price (roughly $13.98 for CDs). Records called "Mid-Priced" are paid at the Royalty for "Mid-Priced"

records (usually three-fourths of the Royalty promised in the deal memo). 3) (*ava*) An arbitrary number, chosen by the label to create a threshold (usually between 67% and 85% of the list price or SRLP) below which all "sales" will result in a reduction in the artist's Royalty usually by 25%. The number is deliberately manipulated to allow a disproportionate amount of records "sold" to be categorized as "Mid-Priced."

Minimum Amount — See *Floor Amount*

Name — Any name that the artist is known by to the public.

Negative Covenants — (*lglese*) Things you shouldn't do while under contract that are in direct conflict with the terms in The Thick.

Net Sales or **Net Profits**— A percentage of gross revenue where a split is applied, part of which is the record company share and part the artist's share. Usually a series of deductions are applied such as a 6% service fee, all manufacturing costs, Advances and other fees and licenses (including in many cases mechanical licenses). The balance remaining after these are deducted is considered the "net".

New Configurations — 1) (*lblspk*) Any type of record that, due to its unusual qualities, does not have a specific category in the Royalty Configuration Matrix ("The Meat Grinder"). Such records are traditionally paid at a rate that is 3/4 of the Base Royalty. 2) (*ava*) A "type" of record designed to create an additional deduction for "New Medium Records." See *Meat Grinder, New Configurations scam,* and *New Medium Records*

New Configurations scam — (*ava*) Any clause in a contract using the term "New Configurations" to create a loophole so that the label does not have to pay a full Royalty on a "type" of record. See *loophole, New Configurations,* and *"type" of record*

New Medium Records — 1) (*lblspk*) Any type of record that isn't a cassette tape or vinyl disc (including CDs, unless specifically negotiated out of this "type"). 2) Records (other than videos) in any software medium (including, without limitation, "digital audio tape," digital compact cassette," "MiniDisc," and transmission directly into the home). 3) (*ava*) A method allowing the label to pay an artist less. Records in this category are typically paid at 75% of the normal Royalty. The concept behind the reduction comes from the idea that research and development costs for new products should be passed on to the artist or Furnisher. CDs were considered "new" by major labels up until 2001, when labels began voluntarily removing the CD configuration out of the New Medium category. Because of its vague language, "software mediums" will most likely include Internet downloads, MP3s, DVDs, and more. See *Three-quarter rate*. Synonyms: *Audiophile Records*, *New Technology Records*

New Technology Records — See *New Medium Records*

Offset Right — 1) (*lblspk*) The right by the label to demand that artist pay back any money expended by label from any revenue stream created by The Thick. 2) (*ava*) A sneaky lawyer way of saying "Cross-Collateralization." See *revenue stream*

One-Deep label — 1) (*ava*) Homespun term of art for what many call "major labels." It's derived from a series of tiers beginning with a Big Four distributor to labels wholly owned by them extending to sub-labels controlled by them. The sub-label is once removed from the Big Four Distributor and is, therefore, "One-Deep." Example: WEA/Warner/Sire (One-Deep). See *Two-Deep label*, *Three-Deep label*. See also *Confessions* chapter "One-Deep and Two-Deep Labels."

One-Stop — (*ind slng*) A middleman subdistributor that distributes records from record companies to smaller "Mom & Pop" stores. They are called One-Stops because they also offer complete turnkey merchandise packages to stores to buy everything they need at "one stop"; i.e., blank tape, T-shirts, posters, caps, etc.

P&D deal — 1) (*lblspk*) "Pressing and Distribution." Includes records that a Big Four distributes for other small labels in exchange for a percentage of profits. 2) (*ava*) Synonymous with Two-Deep and Three-Deep label deals because the small label is two or three levels removed from the main Distributor. See *Confessions*, "What Is a Real Independent Label," and the "Who Owns What: The Family Tree" charts in the chapter "The Big Picture." See also *One-Deep label* and *Two-Deep label*

Packaging Deduction — See *Container Charge*

Performance — (*lblspk*) Singing, speaking, conducting or playing an instrument, alone or with others.

Performing Rights Organization (PRO) — A company that collects the money due publishing companies and songwriters from public performances, licenses, and airplay. BMI, ASCAP, and SESAC are the three PROs that operate in America.

"period" — (*ava*) Put in quotes and lowercased to draw attention to the fact that a Contract Period or Initial Period is not really a period at all, but rather an amount of time that can be extended or shortened at the will of the label. See also *Contract Period* and *Initial Period*

Personnel List — 1) A complete list identifying all featured vocal performers, background vocal performers, and instrumental performers on each song and what they played on every track of an Album. Often used as the basis for the liner notes. 2) A requirement of the label to be completed and included by the artist or Furnisher at the time the Album is "delivered" and without which the Album cannot be considered "delivered."

pipeline income — Refers to money from "sales" which, due to a variety of factors, have not yet matured into a realized payment to artist. Examples: Overseas "sales" that take an extra pay period to reach the US, income from licensing Master Recordings to TV and motion pictures or commercials, etc.

platinum record — Any record that is certified by the RIAA as Platinum. Usually 1,000,000 units sold, but can vary in number, depending on the country and the mood of the RIAA.

play event — A single play of a sound file by a consumer, usually more than 90 seconds and one that triggers a calculation, usually for a royalty. Play events are used mostly by subscription services.

producer — The person hired by the artist to oversee the recording of the Album. Typically label approval is required, not to be "unreasonably withheld."

Product LP — A finished Album, ready for commercial distribution. (LP means "Long-Playing Record.") Therefore, CDs, tapes, and downloaded Albums, when done as a complete unit, are all Product LPs.

production budget — 1) The music video budget paid for by the label. Structured as an Advance. 2) Not the budget for the production of the Album in most contracts.

promote — 1) (*eng*) To make the public aware of your existence. 2) (*ava*) There is no qualification as to how well the label will promote an artist, or to what extremes this promotion will be attempted. "We will promote…" unless specified, could mean, "We will make at least one other person aware of you."

public domain — (*lglese*) Intellectual property works that no longer have a copyright due to copyright expiration, lack of copyright renewal on the part of the author of said work, or lack of any initial copyright.

published — 1) (*eng*) To make publicly known by producing or releasing the work of an author (or artist) to the public. 2) (*lblspk*) A composition manifested on a Master Recording. See *Master Recording*

publishing deal — A deal a songwriter makes with a publishing company to collect all money earned by copyrights under the songwriter's control. Typically the publishing company takes 50% of the Publisher's share (which is equivalent to 25% of the total amount earned by the composition). See *composition*

Rack Jobber — (*ind slng*) A middleman subdistributor that buys mostly overstock or returned records at bargain-basement prices and resells them in discount venues or for scrap. They get their name from the now-obsolete rotating racks that were placed in the stores that carry their records. See *returns, cutouts*

"reasonable," "reasonably," "unreasonable," "unreasonably" — (*ava*) Put in quotes to draw attention to the fact that anytime there's a reference in The Thick to decisions that are to be mutually decided upon by both the artist and the label, the label always has the upper hand. Example: "…such consent not to be unreasonably withheld."

Record Clubs — Companies that distribute records at substantial discounts, usually through "Special Sales Programs" and mail-order campaigns. See *"fake" indie shells*

Record, record — 1) (*eng*) Any fixation or memorializing of data. 2) (*lblspk*) When capitalized, any technology that allows sound to be experienced. This would include CDs, tapes, and LPs, but also includes MP3s and other Internet-related mediums. 3) (*lblspk*) Anything that can be duplicated and sold that embodies the work of an artist contracted to the label. Example: 12-inch vinyl, CDs, DVDs, cassette tapes, MiniDiscs,

Internet postings, MP3s, and any technologies not yet developed—these are *all* "records." Sometimes called a "phonorecord" or "Phonograph Records" by industry folk born before 1955. 4) (*ava*) Any goddamn thing the label can think of that has your music on it.

Recording Costs — Any money the label spends to produce a "commercially acceptable master." This could include payment for all the people who work on the recording and their personal expenses, rehearsal time and space, costs for getting permission to use any samples that are in your songs, attorneys' fees, and mastering costs.

Recording Fund — An amount of money referred to in The Thick that is earmarked by the label specifically and exclusively for the production and completion of an Album.

records "shipped" — 1) Total units shipped from the warehouse to stores and sub-distributors minus units given as part of any "merchandising plan." 2) (*ava*) This will very likely result in a 20% reduction in the actual number of "shipped" units. See also *breakage, Free Goods, merchandising plan,* and *"sales"*

Records Sold, Record Sales — 1) Means *all* the records shipped by the label for which the label is paid, not counting any that were returned to the label, or any that were exchanged by the label. 2) Employs within it a discount of between 15% and 23% of actual sales.

recoupable — To be reimbursed, usually out of all revenue streams accessible to the label. "Money that is Advanced to artist is recouped out of royalties."

recoupable and reimbursable costs — Any cost the label incurs that the artist or Furnisher is required to pay back though the collection of "royalties" or mechanicals. Another sneaky lawyer way of saying "Advance."

release — 1) (*lblspk*) "Initial commercial release." The moment in time when a distributor places an announcement in trade papers that a particular product LP is now available, or will be in the near future, for consignment purchase. 2) (*ava*) It's not when the record is expected to be in stores. Many records are "released" that never get to stores because nobody orders them.

reserves — 1) (*lblspk*) Because records are sold as a consignment item, a percentage of units (usually 35% of the number of records "shipped") is deducted from "royalties." The balance is usually paid out sometime between six months and two years after the Period during which "royalties" are earned. As used in The Thick, "reasonable reserves." 2) (*ava*) A Byzantine philosophy that can barely survive logic now that modern commerce can compute with certainty how many units have sold within 30–60 days. 3) (*ava*) A special account in which an artist's money is held for up to two years in case records ship back. Typically it's 35% of records "shipped," but can be as high as 40% of records "sold" in some contracts. It's applied to all "sales," including over the Internet, where the confirmation of a "sale" is instantaneous and nonreturnable. This is what the label calls "reasonable." See *reasonable*

returns — Any records that ship back to the Distributor unpaid for. See *Distributor*

revenue streams — 1) (*eng*) Any direct line of monetary income. Examples: Advances and "royalties" from "sales" of records. 2) Any continuous source of monetary income.

Ring Tone — A licensed song's melody that is used as the call alert for a cellular device. See *Master Tone*

rotation — Refers to placement—either via radio, MTV, or the Internet—in which a particular Master Recording is played several times a day.

Royalty, Royalties, royalty, royalties, "royalty," "royalties," and **Royalty Rates, royalty rates** — 1) (*lblspk*) Royalties and Royalty Rates are more or less synonymous. They are all a percentage of a sale price that is *promised* as a payment to the artist or Furnisher in the deal memo and appears in The Thick under the subheading "Royalties." It is not necessarily the actual percentage that the artist or Furnisher will be paid. 2) (*ava*) When used in quotes means the *actual* percentage of a "sale" price that the artist or Furnisher receives. It includes, as part of its matrix, all deductions, Double-Dips, and loopholes; i.e., the percentage of SRLP promised in the deal memo, minus a series of deductions indicated by the Meat Grinder. "…artists are never paid Royalties (as promised in the deal memo). They are paid Royalty Rates as they are affected by the factors in the Meat Grinder." Example:

(SRLP – deductions) × (Royalty Rate – deductions) = a "royalty." See *the Meat Grinder* and *SRLP*

Royalty Base — 1) (*lblspk*) The amount of money that the royalty rate will be calculated upon. Usually, the sticker price of the record minus taxes and the Container Charge. 2) (*ava*) Actual per-unit dollar figure that the artist royalty will be calculated upon. It consists of several factors that can be found in the Meat Grinder.

Royalty Configuration Matrix — (*ava*) A table demonstrating a combination of "types" of records, Packaging Deductions, licensing deductions, and "royalties" that, when calculated together, equal the net amount that an artist will be paid on the sale of records. Synonymous with the Meat Grinder. See *the Meat Grinder*

royalty participant — Anyone who can or should get a royalty from selling the product.

Royalty Statement, "royalty" statement — 1) (*lblspk*) A letter sent once every six months from the label to the artist or Furnisher accurately documenting the accounting of Royalties. 2) (*ava*) (*mythology*) A piece of paper that clearly and accurately documents an accounting of "royalties." 3) (*ava*) A piece of paper that an artist will not understand without the assistance of a professional accountant to determine whether or not his or her "royalties" are computed accurately. On smaller deals the artist's manager or lawyer will have to send "reminders" to the label in order to actually see one. 4) (*ava*) A ticket to an audit.

"sales," "sell," "selling," "sold" — (*ava*) All forms and tenses. Used in quotes to draw attention to the LabelSpeak meaning: that Records Sold does not refer to 100% of the units that the label receives money for, but rather the actual number of units that will count toward calculating "royalties." It incorporates a built-in "discount" for each configuration of record. Examples: When referring to CDs, it means 20% less than actually sold; when referring to 12-inch vinyl, it means 15% less than actually sold; when referring to singles, it means 23.08% less than actually sold; when referring to cassettes, it means 15% less than actually sold; when referring to the Internet, it means 20% less than actually sold. See *Free Goods* and *Records Sold*

sold through Normal Trade Channels (NTC) — Records sold through stores and catalogs only. It does not normally mean things like downloads or "data streamed via transmission" sales or budget sales, only sales through stores and catalogs. Synonyms: "sold through Normal Trade Channels," "Normal Retail Sales" (NRS), and "USNRC Net Sales."

sample clearances — 1) (*ind slng*) Permission slips that allow an artist to use bits of other artists' recordings in their original recording. 2) (*lblspk*) Artist must provide: A complete list of any and all samples mixed into each track; proof that they have received permission for the ongoing use of the sample from the copyright owners of the Master Recording that was sampled and from the copyright owner of the song that was sampled (which may or may not be the same party); any and all credit information for the liner notes of your record.

scale, union scale — The minimum payment required by most musicians' unions. About $200 per hour.

scrap — (*lblspk*) Records sold at or below manufacturing cost to a scrap dealer. The disc will be melted down and recycled into new records.

sell through — (*ind slng*) When merchandise makes the entire journey from warehouse to store to consumer and is not returned to the manufacturer for a refund.

SESAC — See *Performing Rights Organization*

Severability — (*lglese*) A fancy word for separating a party from the company to which they are contracted.

side — One recorded song. See *Singles*

sideperson — Any musician or performer who is not the lead singer (or lead soloist if the artist is an instrumental soloist). An exception is made if the band as a corporate entity consists of more than one person. Then all those who perform on the record who are not part of the corporate entity are considered "sidepersons."

Singles — In today's A&R parlance, this means one song that will be used to promote the record. The one song that the label will push to radio and, in most cases, the one that will be made into a video for MTV and other music video programs. It hails from the time of the 45 (a vinyl 7-inch record that had only one song on each side). A record company would introduce a new artist by releasing a 45, and if this did well, a second single would follow, and then an LP that contained both singles and several other new songs put together on one disc called an Album. See *Album*

Sliding Scale Royalty, The — 1) (*lblspk*) A royalty that escalates at precise sales markers. Designed as a bonus or incentive to the artist or Furnisher to promote the sales of records. Example: 14% of SRLP for the first 500,000 units sold, 14.5% for the next 500,000 units sold, 15% for the following 500,000 units sold, etc. 2) (*ava*) A pathologically optimistic offer by the label designed to persuade the artist or Furnisher that s/he has a fighting chance of seeing healthier "royalties" or a big payday if certain "sales" projections are met. Rarely achieved due to the loopholes that disqualify most sales as "sales that can be applied to the Sliding Scale."

sneaky lawyer — 1) (*ava*) (*mammal*) Any attorney who willfully engages in any deception by occlusion of the truth, omission of the truth, distortion of the truth, or distraction from the truth. 2) A lawyer.

Sony — A major record distributor owned by Sony Corporation. Formerly CBS Records. See *Big Four*

SoundScan — An accounting system that scans the bar code on the back of the unit at the point of purchase. In use since 1991.

Special Advance — See *Deficiency Payments*

Special Packaging Cost — 1) (*lblspk*) Costs for packaging that are implemented at the special request of the artist or Furnisher. Such costs that exceed the normal budget allocated for packaging by the label; i.e., special cover art, inserts, etc. 2) (*ava*) Just about anything that is not a boring two-fold jacket with the artist's picture will be called "Special" by the label. All such additional costs are charged to the artist's account and are recoupable from "royalties."

Special Sales Program — 1) (*lblspk*) Records sold in conjunction with a special marketing plan involving special stores or TV or radio advertising campaigns. 2) (*lblspk*) Any program in which artists are bundled together with other artists or with merchandise as part of a promotional campaign. No records "sold" under such circumstances are applied to the SSC or the Sliding Scale Royalty. 3) (*ava*) Due to its vague and nebulous definition in The Thick, it basically means anything the label wants it to mean as long as it involves any sales program that is "special." This lack of commitment allows labels to cut an artist's or Furnisher's payment because it states in most contracts that records "sold" as part of a "Special Sales Program" will receive only a half or two-thirds Royalty. 4) (*ava*) "Garage sales," as I call them, in which they give away boxes of many different artists but charge all artists in the Special Sales Program the same deduction. A *huge* Double-Dip, as the artist is subsidizing another artist's promotion. 5) (*ava*) "Special Sales Programs are not actually very *special*, since every artist gets them, and do not generally involve *sales*, since records are usually given away 'free' during these drives." See *Free Goods, Sliding Scale Royalty, SSC*

SRLP — An acronym for Suggested Retail List Price. Basically, this is the sticker price of the record. It's rarely the same as what the record sells for.

SSC — An acronym for Schedule of Standard Costs. A fancy term for the total amount of debt the artist owes the label.

statutory rate — (*lglese*) 1) The minimum amount of a compulsory license. Presently 9.1 cents per song per copy distributed. 2) A biannually escalating rate established by Congress for the minimum amount of a compulsory license. Established by the Copyright Office of the United States in 1976 at 5 cents per song, this goes up a fraction of a penny every couple of years (adjusted for inflation). It's currently about 9.1 cents per song per copy distributed. 3) (*ava*) The minimum amount allowed *by law* for a license that a label pays a songwriter (or publisher) for the rights to duplicate that song on their record. See *bullshit statutory rate, compulsory license, Controlled Composition, Copyright Arbitration Royalty Panels,* and *Statutory Rate*

Statutory Rate — 1) (*lblspk*) An amount of money universally agreed to by leaders of the recording industry that songwriters and publishers receive for compulsory licenses. This amount is usually fixed at the time an Album is manufactured. 2) (*ava*) In The Thick, be aware that "Statutory Rate" (when capitalized) does not mean the same as the statutory rate required by law, but rather the rate that a committee of record industry executives agrees to pay. Currently it's 9.1 cents per song. 3) (*ava*) An amount of money, which is usually the same amount as the current "statutory rate," fixed at the time The Thick is signed, on which an artist will

be paid for "first use" of their songs on records "sold." See *bullshit statutory rate*

Stock Rotation — 1) Term of art for retail business. Merchandise that is resold to other like merchandisers, usually via special "stock rotation" brokers. 2) (*lblspk*) The act of taking records that return and reselling them to scrap dealers and Rack Jobbers. 3) (*ava*) An insane method of accounting created by the consignment system by which records are sold. It puts the artist in a deficit position and creates greater incentives for sub-distributors (like one-stops and Rack Jobbers) to return merchandise to the label rather than sell it through to retail stores. See *sell through* and *returns*

Super-Duper Cross-Collateralization — (*ava*) When a label or group of labels are grouped into a single debt to a One-Deep or parent major label. When this occurs no one is paid royalties (even if they have recouped) until the entire debt from all Artists on the label (or all labels in the group, if it is a group label deal) is recouped.

Subscription Service — Any service wherein a subscriber pays a renewable fee in exchange for access to an online downloadable music catalog. When the subscriber stops paying the fee, the library they have amassed and all future access evaporates. Example: Yahoo Music. See *tethered downloads*

Term — 1) (*ava*) The length of time artist will be in business with the label. 2) (*ava*) The Term equals the sum total of the Initial Period, all Option Periods, and a last bit called a Restriction Period (sometimes called a Exploitation Period and which functions like a Sunset Clause). See *Exploitation Period, Initial Period,* and *Option Period*

Territory — (*lglese*) 1) The physical geography covered by any particular contract. Usually listed as "the World" or "the Universe." 2) Refers to the grant of rights and how limited or unlimited the area of exploitation is.

Tethered downloads — A temporary download that has embedded within its metadata a code that pipelines DRM information back to its distributor. Such information is used to calculate royalties based on the number of plays from a subscriber. See also *play event*

Thick (The) — (*lglese*) The complete recording contract.

Three-Deep label — (*ava*) Homespun term of art for what many call "independent labels" or "vanity labels" or production companies that think of themselves as labels due to a connection to a distributor via a Two-Deep label or a P&D deal. The term is derived from the series of tiers beginning with a Big Four distributor and going to labels wholly owned by them and extending to sub-labels and then to labels partly controlled by them (imprints), and finally to their vendors and/or Furnishers, who act in an independent A&R/production capacity. These production companies or vanity labels often call themselves "indies," but are nonetheless working within the system of Big Four Distributors, except they are thrice removed from the main distributor, or "Three-Deep." See *"fake" indie shells, One-Deep label*, and *Two-Deep label*

three-quarter rate (the) — 1) (Mechanicals) When used in conjunction with a clause referring to mechanicals, it means three-quarters of the Statutory Rate being paid to the songwriter/publisher of the material to be reproduced on a record. 2) (Royalties) When used in conjunction with a clause referring to Royalties or "royalties," it usually means a 2/3 reduction in the promised Royalty percentage. Example: "For records in the compact disc configuration, artist shall receive three-quarters of the applicable Royalty Rate." See *Royalties*

Top Line Record — A new release, stamped with a list price that is the same as most other new releases sold in that region. Example: If new releases from big artists sell in a region for $15, then "Top Line" is $15. If they sell for $17, then it's $17. It's important to keep in mind that it's not a fixed number. It changes based on region. In major cities, the price is usually $17.98 for CDs and $10.98 for tapes, depending on the artist and the region. Only a minority of records are actually "sold" at this price.

tour support — 1) (*lblspk*) An amount paid by the label to the artist for a reimbursement of artist's expenses while on the road promoting the Album. Typically, new artists receive about $75,000 for the first Commitment Album if the tour happens during the Initial Contract Period. The aggregate overage is paid only if the label approves of the tour and each item on the itinerary, and the tour is completed in accordance with the itinerary. Unless specifically negotiated otherwise, all tour support is recoupable and considered an Advance. 2) (*ava*) This usually pays for about four weeks' worth of expenses. Most Album tours last about six weeks.

Two-Deep label — (*ava*) Homespun term of art for what many call "imprints." It's derived from a series of tiers beginning with a Big Four distributor and going to labels wholly owned by them and descending to sub-labels controlled by them (major labels) and then Furnishing labels partially controlled by them with a small stable of signed artists. The imprint is twice removed from the Big Four Distributor; therefore, "Two-Deep."

"type" of record — (*ava*) Refers to the form of records configured in the Meat Grinder. Specifically: Top Line, Mid-Priced, Budget, New Medium, New Configuration, Foreign, Online.

UNI or UMG — UNI is short for Universal; UMG is an acronym for Universal Music Group, once owned by Seagram (makers of vodka), and recently purchased by the French-owned Vivendi Media Corporation. See *Big Four*

unique and extraordinary — When referring to the artist, indicates that the label will exercise every legal right to protect their relationship. The label will be entitled to seek injunctive relief to enforce the provisions of The Thick.

Universal/Vivendi — See *UNI*

vanity label — See *Three-Deep labels*

WEA — Acronym for Warner/Elektra/Atlantic, now Warner Music Group (WMG), a major record distributor that was recently spun off from Time Warner into its own separate company. See *Big Four*

wholesale vs. retail accounting — It will specifically say in The Thick that the label can change the method of computing "royalties" from a retail basis to a wholesale basis. When they do this, they typically double the percentage of the Royalty Rate to compensate, basing this increase on the assumption that wholesale is exactly half of retail, and therefore one retail point would equal two wholesale points. This is not a solid assumption. See *Royalties*

Road Map of Royalty Deal Points

Start: ⟶

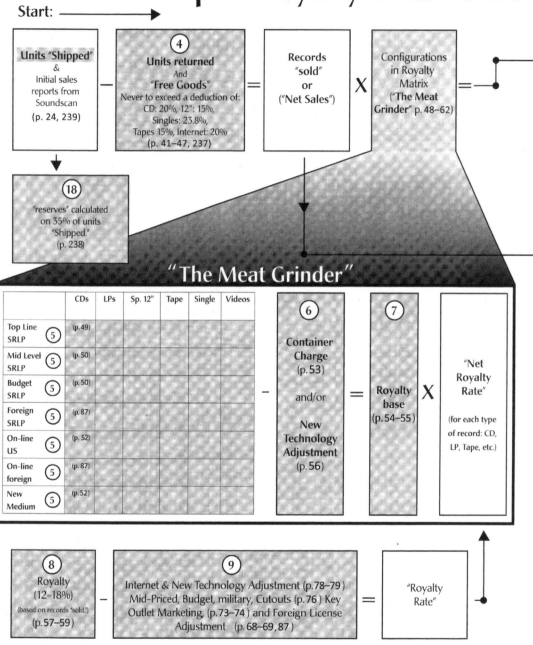

	CDs	LPs	Sp. 12"	Tape	Single	Videos
Top Line SRLP ⑤	(p. 49)					
Mid Level SRLP ⑤	(p. 50)					
Budget SRLP ⑤	(p. 50)					
Foreign SRLP ⑤	(p. 87)					
On-line US ⑤	(p. 52)					
On-line foreign ⑤	(p. 87)					
New Medium ⑤	(p. 52)					

Units "Shipped" & Initial sales reports from Soundscan (p. 24, 239)

④ **Units returned** And **"Free Goods"** Never to exceed a deduction of: CD: 20%, 12": 15%, Singles: 23.8%, Tapes 15%, Internet: 20% (p. 41–47, 237)

= **Records "sold" or ("Net Sales")**

X **Configurations in Royalty Matrix ("The Meat Grinder" p. 48–62)**

⑱ "reserves" calculated on 35% of units "Shipped." (p. 238)

"The Meat Grinder"

⑥ **Container Charge** (p. 53) and/or **New Technology Adjustment** (p. 56)

⑦ = **Royalty base** (p. 54–55)

X **"Net Royalty Rate"** (for each type of record: CD, LP, Tape, etc.)

⑧ **Royalty (12–18%)** (based on records "sold.") (p. 57–59)

⑨ − **Internet & New Technology Adjustment** (p. 78–79) Mid-Priced, Budget, military, Cutouts (p. 76) Key Outlet Marketing, (p. 73–74) and Foreign License Adjustment (p. 68–69, 87)

= **"Royalty Rate"**

The money earned at any given Contract Period of most major-label recording contracts is calculated on the flow of this chart. Shaded areas are points for negotiation. There are 62.

Through Your Recording Contract

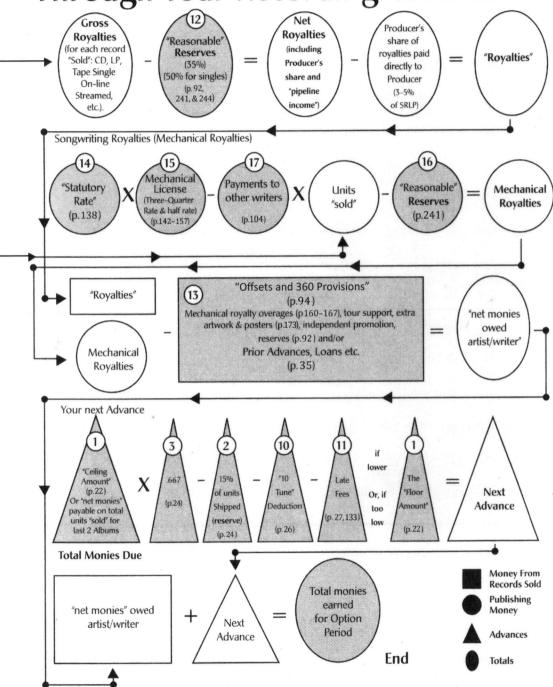

ACKNOWLEDGMENTS

The sad part about this page is that the people who need to be thanked the most cannot have their names printed here for fear of reprisals. They are the numerous lawyers, accountants, managers, and artists who looked at this manuscript and contributed to its content with their personal experience. For every strategy that you absorb from this book, you owe just as much credit to them as you would attribute to me.

There are a few that can be named:

In the legal area there is Richard Wolfe of Miami and Timothy S. Kelley of Chicago: Richard for his bare-knuckled-brass-balled legal strategies that showed me angles I'd missed and Tim for sharing his extensive knowledge of the law beyond his region and providing a glimpse into some of the worst contracts I'd ever seen.

In Atlanta, Darryl Cohen, for support and encouragement.

Julee L. Milham in Orlando, for her eye-opening leftist view of statutory rates. Because of you, I had to rewrite the chapter on Controlled Compositions.

I'm also indebted to Mat Greenberg in New York, whose ethics and expertise have always been an inspiration.

As well as other great attorneys who've been inspirational to me over the years, Andy Tavle, Michael Morris, Dina LaPolt, John Simpson, and Neville Johnson, who has become a great friend.

On the publishing side, there is this book's original editor, Paul Zolo, who has interviewed more Grammy Award–winning artists than I have holey socks in my hamper. He tightened the screws and kept this complex document organized. And the book's second edition editor, Rusty Cutchin, who showed me how to use an FTP. At Hal Leonard there is also Diane Levinson in marketing and the Group Publisher, whose faith in my work seems to exceed my own, John Cerullo.

Personally, I must thank my business manager and partner for crunching numbers and keeping accounts in the black; Dean, for changing his opinion of me; Lauren, for not going blonde and keeping me posted; the "spear," for his courage and investigative prowess; Jim Progress and the University of Miami, for their dedication to music-business education; John Braheny, for his keen research; and mostly Ms. Pat Cameron, who created the initial link between myself and Hal Leonard years ago and without whom there may never have been a Moses Avalon.

And finally, I wish to acknowledge and thank all the artists who stand up for their rights and the people who help them. You are the ultimate inspiration. Blessings to each and every one.

Moses Avalon
www.MosesAvalon.com